16 make-at-home celebration cakes from a world-famous sugar artist

CARLOS LISCHETTI

ANIMATION
IN SUGAR

TAKE 2

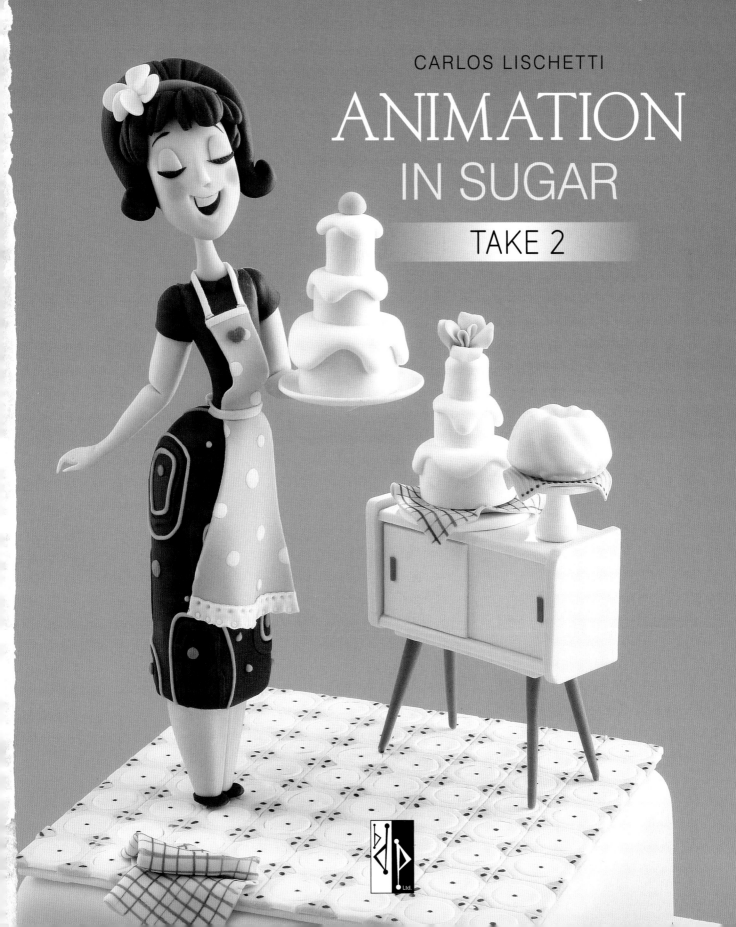

Elio grew up in Rosario, Argentina. He has been drawn to art since childhood and decided to pursue a career in traditional animation shortly after leaving high school. He took the opportunity to study animation at the acclaimed Vancouver Film School for a year, after which he was offered work on various feature films for different studios around the world, including Dreamworks and Disney.

For several years Elio has combined his work as an animator with creating characters alongside his twin brother, Carlos. This unique collaboration starts with an initial sketch from Elio which Carlos transforms into a sugar figurine; Elio then photographs the finished work to share with a global audience of followers. The combination of both Elio and Carlos' exceptional talents lead to their first published book, *Animation in Sugar* in 2012 (B. Dutton Publishing). Its success and popularity with avid sugar modellers all over the world led them to combine their skills once again to create more sugar characters to be published in this, their second book.

Elio and Carlos both share a vision to bridge the gap between art and people. Their fun, clear and inspirational approach has captured the imagination of hundreds of thousands of followers all over the world.

INTRODUCTION

After writing my first book, *Animation in Sugar*, I was still full of ideas for exploring modelled figurines and decorated cakes for different occasions. I wanted to put together a second book of new ideas and modelling techniques as well as presenting some of my favourite characters which had become popular with students and people who had started to follow me online.

As a tutor I am always looking for ways to show students how to follow an easy, step-by-step process to make a finished piece in sugar. This makes everything achievable, regardless of a person's skill level, and it gives my students the confidence to be creative. I always focus on ways to present ideas that people can simply take as a starting point to develop their own projects and, most importantly, to trigger their imagination.

My brother, Elio, is always an essential part of this process. He is the one who sketches the initial idea on paper before I turn it into a three-dimensional sugar piece. Everything you see presented in this book is the result of our joint efforts, including all of Elio's beautiful photography.

As you look through the pages you will find a variety of projects to suit many different occasions – some of them will be familiar to those who follow me and there are some brand new ones to complete the collection. Professional sugarcrafters will find plenty of ideas for celebration cakes while beginners will find everything they need to have a go at making any of the projects in the book. You will also find basic guidelines for decorating biscuits with flooded icing, perfect for gifts, party bags or a treat at any time. The goal for me is to reach a broad audience of home cake makers, experienced cake decorators and complete beginners who are taking their first steps in cake decorating, to present this art form and give you the necessary tools to banish any fears you have of decorating a cake. I'd like to bring people closer to this fantastic way of being creative – nothing gives me greater satisfaction than knowing I have inspired someone to explore the wonderful world of sugarcraft.

I am proud to present my second book to you and hope it encourages and inspires you to explore your own artistic skills through baking and decorating.

Carlos

DEDICATION

To my parents for giving me the freedom to choose what I wanted to become in my professional life.
To my niece Emilia, who has brought happiness into our family.
And to my granny Amable, who is always on the ball and can never sit still.

First published in March 2015 by B. Dutton Publishing Limited, The Grange, Hones Business Park, Farnham, Surrey, GU9 8BB, UK.

Copyright: Carlos Lischetti 2015

ISBN-13: 978-1-905113-51-4

Publisher: Beverley Dutton

Group Editor: Jennifer Kelly

Art Director/Designer: Sarah Ryan

Book publishing

Copy Editor: Frankie New

Senior Graphic Designer and Photography Stylist: Louise Pepé

Magazine publishing

Editor: Jenny Royle

Copy Editor: Adele Duthie

Senior Graphic Designer: Zena Deakin

PR and Advertising Manager: Natalie Bull

Printed and bound in Slovenia by arrangement with Associated Agencies, Oxford

Acknowledgements

First of all, after the warm reception for my first book, *Animation in Sugar*, I feel that I need to thank all of you who have been following my work over the last couple of years. I am overwhelmed and words are not enough to express my gratitude. I hope this, my second book, brings new ideas and techniques to keep you enjoying sugarcraft as much as I do.

I am glad once again to work with all the team at B. Dutton Publishing – from Sarah on the layouts to Jenny (my editor) and Frankie for their constant help, patience and support and for making it all look just perfect. Many thanks to Beverley and Robert for their constant enthusiasm in every project we embark upon together and for giving me the chance to be part of the Squires Kitchen team. It is always a pleasure to work in such a professional environment.

To my twin brother, Elio, for his never-ending perfectionism that constantly pushes me to my boundaries and for all the hard, detailed work he puts into his photography to make my figurines, cookies and cakes look beautiful. His high standard drives me mad as usual but is part of the exploring process.

To my sister Mercedes and Mauro, for bringing Emilia into our lives.

To Adrian, who is always willing to help me through the good and bad times and for his constant support and great enthusiasm!

To Maxi, for his priceless help when I am rushing to finish projects, especially when I have a deadline to meet!

To all my friends, colleagues and relatives who are always there to support in many ways.

To my mum, with all my love.

CONTENTS

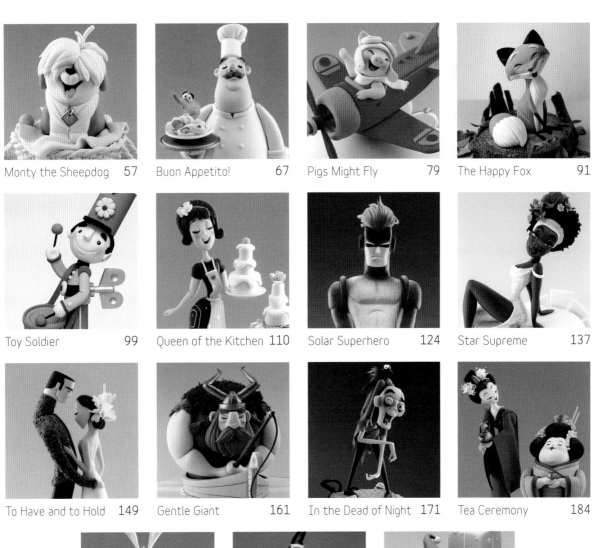

ESSENTIAL EDIBLES AND EQUIPMENT

Equipment

You will need the same basic items for most of the projects in this book, so it is worth investing in any items that you don't already have. Any specific requirements for either edibles or equipment are listed at the beginning of each cake so make sure you have everything you need before you start a project. All of the items are readily available from sugarcraft suppliers, see page 256.

Cake smoothers (1)

Clear alcohol, e.g. gin or vodka (2)

Cocktail sticks (3)

Cornflour/corn starch/maize starch in a muslin bag (4)

Cutting wheel (5)

Dresden tool (6)

Edible food colours (SK) (7)

Floral wires (8)

Icing/confectioners' sugar (for dusting)

Kitchen paper

Non-slip mat (9)

Non-stick board (10)

Non-toxic glue stick

Paintbrushes for painting, dusting and gluing (SK) (11)

Palette knives, straight and cranked

Plain-bladed knife (12)

Plastic cake dowels

Pliers (13)

Polystyrene base and pieces (to use as support during drying)

Round cutter set (14)

Ruler

Serrated carving knife

SK Black/Brown Professional Food Colour Pen

SK Cutting Tool (15)

SK Edible Glue (sugar glue)

Small and large rolling pins (16)

Small, medium and large ball tools (17)

Small parchment paper piping bags (18) (see page 8)

Small scissors (19)

Toothbrush, new (20) (for paint effects, see page 54)

White vegetable fat/shortening (21)

Wooden skewers (22)

How to make a cornflour dusting bag

A dusting bag is always useful for dusting the work surface evenly when you are going to roll out pastillage, flower paste or modelling paste, and can be used to dust your hands to keep them dry when you are modelling. However, when rolling out marzipan or sugarpaste to cover a cake, always use icing sugar rather than cornflour (see page 34).

Edibles

1tbsp cornflour/corn starch/maize starch

Equipment

A piece of muslin

Elastic band

1   Cut a piece of muslin into two squares and layer one on top of the other. Place a full tablespoon of cornflour in the centre.

2   Bring the four corners together to create a bag and secure with an elastic band.

How to make a paper piping bag

Paper piping bags are always useful when only a small amount of royal icing is needed. They are good for piping small amounts of royal icing into eye sockets, sticking pieces of dry pastillage together and piping details such as hair.

Edibles

Royal icing (see page 29)

Equipment

Parchment paper

Scissors

Piping nozzle (optional)

1 Take a triangle of parchment paper and fold it in half to mark the central point on the long side.

2 Bring one side of the triangle round to form a cone shape, ensuring that the point is in the centre of the long side.

3 Holding the first side in place with one hand, bring the other side around to complete the cone.

4 Hold the ends in place, ensuring that the points of the triangle are all at the back of the cone.

5 Fold the points over twice so that the bag holds its shape. If you are using a piping nozzle, snip off the tip of the bag and drop the nozzle into the bag, then half-fill the bag with royal icing. Once the icing is in the bag, squeeze it to the end then fold the top over again to seal the bag ready for piping.

RECIPES

Butter sponge cake

There are many recipes for butter sponge cakes that I personally like; you can try the one suggested here or use your own favourite. This is a classic Victoria sponge recipe that I often use as it gives a spongy consistency and a firm crumb for coating the cake with marzipan or sugarpaste (see page 34). This basic recipe for a vanilla-flavoured cake can be changed to chocolate, lemon, orange or walnut by adding extra flavours (see notes on variations overleaf).

Ingredients

300g (10½oz) softened butter

2tsp natural vanilla essence

300g (10½oz) icing or caster sugar (I prefer to use icing sugar as it gives a finer crumb when baked)

300g (10½oz) eggs (equivalent to 4 medium free-range eggs)

300g (10½oz) self-raising flour or 300g (10½oz) plain/all-purpose flour with 2 level tsp baking powder, sifted

Equipment

3 x 20cm (8") shallow round cake tins or rings

Baking parchment

Stand mixer with paddle attachment

Rubber spatula

Sieve

Wire rack

Cling film

1   Grease and line the bottom of each tin with baking parchment. Preheat the oven to 170–180°C/350°F/gas mark 4.

2   Cream the butter, vanilla essence and sugar in an electric mixer with the paddle attachment until light and fluffy. Scrape the bowl to make sure there are no lumps of butter stuck to the bottom.

3   Add one egg at a time, mixing well after each addition. (Don't worry if the mix curdles at first, this is normal as the butter can't emulsify properly with the addition of the extra water in the eggs.)

4   Stir in the sifted flour in two batches, mixing at a slow speed.

5   Scrape the sides and bottom of the bowl with a rubber spatula to make sure that all the ingredients are completely mixed and that there are no traces of flour left.

6   Split the mix into three tins and spread out evenly. Place the tins in the middle of the oven and bake for approximately 20 minutes. The cake is ready when it is light brown on top; if you insert a skewer it should come out clean. Another test is to gently press your fingers on the centre of the cake

and, if it is done, it should bounce back. If it's still wobbly put it back in the oven for a few minutes until it is completely baked.

7 Once the cakes are baked, turn them out onto a wire rack and allow to cool.

8 Once the cake is cold, wrap it in cling film to prevent it from drying out.

The following chart can be used as a reference when baking cakes of different sizes using the butter sponge recipe.

Tin size (round or square)	Amount of mix for 3 layers	Multiple of recipe
3 x 10cm (4")	400g (14oz)	1/3
3 x 15cm (6")	800g (1lb 12oz)	2/3
3 x 20.5cm (8")	1.2kg (2lb 10¼oz)	1
3 x 23cm (9")	1.6kg (3lb 8½oz)	1 1/3

TUTOR TIP

The eggs should be at room temperature.

The butter should be soft but not melted. If you live in a warm country, keep the butter in the fridge until it is needed.

Always cream the butter with the vanilla essence or the citrus zest to achieve maximum flavour.

Flavourings

Chocolate: replace 70g (2½oz) of flour with 50g (1¾oz) of a good quality cocoa powder.

Lemon or orange: add the zest of one lemon or one orange when you cream the butter and sugar.

Walnut: add 120g (4¼oz) of chopped walnuts to the flour and fold into the mix.

TUTOR TIP

I prefer to split and bake the mix in two or three tins rather than using one as it produces an even shape and a lighter crumb. If you overfill a cake tin, the cake crumb becomes tighter and heavier than it should be. Bake as many layers of cake as necessary to reach the height required for the cake.

Cake mix quantities

This chart shows the quantities of the sponge recipe used for the cakes in this book. The amount of cake mix given is enough to make a cake that can be split into three before baking. The amount of mix you use in the tins will depend on the height your layer needs to be, but remember not to overfill the tins with the mix or the cake will turn out heavy and doughy.

PROJECT	CAKE SHAPES/SIZES	AMOUNT OF MIX	MULTIPLE OF RECIPE (Chocolate cake or vanilla butter sponge)
Monty the Sheepdog	2 x 15cm (6") round	600g (1lb 5¼oz)	$^1/_2$
Buon Appetito!	3 x 15cm (6") round	800g (1lb 12oz)	$^2/_3$
Pigs Might Fly	15cm x 8cm (6" x 3⅛") dome	Light sponge sheets, see page 38	
Queen of the Kitchen	3 x 16.5cm (6½") square	800g (1lb 12oz)	$^2/_3$
Solar Superhero	18cm x 10cm (7" x 4") dome	See page 38 and note below	
Star Supreme	5 x 15cm (6") round	1.2kg (2lb 10¼oz)	1
To Have and to Hold	3 x 20.5cm (8") round	1.2kg (2lb 10¼oz)	1
Gentle Giant	5 x 15cm (6") round	1.2kg (2lb 10¼oz)	1
In the Dead of Night	3 x 15cm (6") square	800g (1lb 12oz)	$^2/_3$
Tea Ceremony	3 x 23cm (9") round	1.6kg (3lb 8½oz)	$1^1/_3$
The Illusionist	3 x 12.5cm (5") round	400g (14oz)	$^1/_3$
Santa's Little Helpers	2 x 15cm (6") square tins	600g (1lb 5¼oz)	$^1/_2$

*For the Solar Superhero project I recommend lining the 18cm (7") dome shape with a light sponge sheet as explained on page 38, then build the cake with layers of butter sponge cake. This will give more support to the figurine when inserted into the cake.

Light sponge

I use this recipe when using the sponge sheet technique to line the mould when assembling a cake (see page 37). I would always recommend making one small batch of the light sponge recipe at a time. The maximum number of eggs that I use for one batch is eight (double the recipe below), as that fits perfectly into any regular size electric mixer bowl and will still give your sponge a light and airy texture.

Ingredients

4 large eggs, yolks and whites separated (medium free-range eggs)

120g (4¼oz) caster sugar

120g (4¼oz) plain/all-purpose flour, sifted

1tsp vanilla essence

Equipment

40cm x 30cm (16" x 12") baking tray, lined with baking parchment

Whisk

Spatula

Sieve

Palette knife

Flavouring

Chocolate: replace 30g (1oz) of flour with 30g (1oz) of cocoa powder, then sift together and follow the recipe as for the vanilla sponge.

Baking sponge sheets

When baking light sponge sheets in a 30cm x 40cm (12" x 16") tray, the height of the sponge will depend on the amount of batter poured into it. You can determine the thickness of the sponge by changing the amount of eggs used in the recipe: the more eggs, the deeper the sponge sheet will be.

Eggs (large)	Caster sugar	Plain flour	Baking time
3	90g (3oz)	90g (3oz)	6 minutes
4	120g (4¼oz)	120g (4¼oz)	6–8 minutes
5	150g (5¼oz)	150g (5¼oz)	10–12 minutes
6	180g (6¼oz)	180g (6¼oz)	12–15 minutes

Note: The average weight of a large, free-range egg is 60g (2oz).

Baking sponge layers

Split the light sponge mix between two tins to produce an even shape and a lighter crumb. Bake as many layers of cake as necessary for the height required.

The chart below tells you how much cake batter you need for different tin sizes.

Amount of eggs (large) in recipe	Cake tins
3	2 x 10cm (4")
4	2 x 15cm (6")
5	2 x 18cm (7")
6	2 x 20.5cm (8")
7	2 x 23cm (9")

1 Preheat the oven to 220°C/425°F/ gas mark 7.

2 Whisk the yolks with 60g (2oz) of sugar and the vanilla essence at medium to high speed until thick and pale. Set aside.

3 In a separate bowl, whisk the whites at medium to high speed until light and fluffy. Incorporate the rest of the sugar into the whites while whisking at medium speed, until soft peaks are formed.

4 Fold half of the soft-peak meringue into the yolks. Once they are combined, add the rest.

5 Sift and fold the flour into the mix two or three times using a spatula.

6 Spread the batter evenly on the tray using a palette knife.

7 Bake for six to eight minutes until the surface is light brown and the sponge springs back to the touch. Remove from the oven, transfer to a wire rack and leave to cool. Wrap the sponge with cling film to prevent it from drying out.

8 Store the sponge in the fridge or freezer until needed.

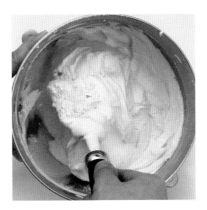

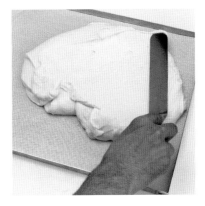

Chocolate sponge cake

This delicious chocolate sponge cake recipe can be baked in cake tins or in a tray, depending on the cake you want to create. It is best to bake the sponge in a tray if you want to cut out different-sized layers of cake, e.g. for the domed cake in the Solar Superhero project (see page 125).

Ingredients

210g (7½oz) lightly salted butter

150g (5¼oz) muscovado sugar

90g (3oz) SK Belgian Dark Couverture Chocolate 70%

150ml (5¼fl oz) whole milk

120g (4½oz) egg yolks

1½tsp vanilla essence

30g (1oz) caster sugar

270g (9½oz) strong plain flour

15g (½oz) baking powder

30g (1oz) dark cocoa powder

210g (7½oz) egg whites

Equipment

30cm x 40cm (11½" x 15½") tray, lined with baking parchment (or see chart below)

Heavy-based saucepan

Spatula

Digital thermometer

Whisk

Sieve

Palette knife

Large bowl

Stand mixer fitted with whisk attachment

Variation: Replace half the amount of milk with natural yoghurt for a moister crumb.

1 Preheat the oven to 180°C/350°C/ gas mark 4.

2 Place the butter, muscovado sugar, dark chocolate and milk in a pan over a low heat. Stir with a spatula until all the ingredients have completely melted and a creamy consistency is reached. Do not bring the mix to the boil at any time.

3 Remove the pan from the heat. Pour the chocolate mixture into a large bowl and let the temperature drop to approximately 50°C–60°C.

4 Add the yolks and vanilla essence to the chocolate mixture. Whisk to combine all the ingredients.

5 Sift the flour with the cocoa powder and baking powder two or three times into a separate bowl, then add to the chocolate mixture and whisk until incorporated.

6 Whisk the egg whites at a medium speed in an electric stand mixer until light and fluffy. Add the caster sugar to the egg whites while whisking at medium speed, until soft peaks are formed.

7 Fold half of the soft-peak meringue into the chocolate mixture to loosen it slightly, then fold in the rest.

8 Spread the batter evenly over the tray with a palette knife.

9 Bake for 15–20 minutes until the cake springs back to the touch or a skewer inserted into the cake comes out clean. Remove from the oven and leave to cool on the tray.

10 Wrap the cake in cling film to prevent it from drying out.

Round or square chocolate cakes

Divide the mixture between two or three tins rather than one (see page 10) and make sure not to overfill the tins. Bake as many layers of cake as necessary for the height required.

The chart below is a guide to how much cake batter you need for different tin sizes.

Cake tins (round or square)	Amount of mixture	Multiple of recipe
3 x 10cm (4")	400g (14oz)	⅓
3 x 15cm (6")	800g (1lb 12oz)	⅔
3 x 20.5cm (8")	1.2kg (2lb 10¼oz)	1
3 x 23cm (9")	1.6kg (3lb 8½oz)	1⅓

Note: The baking time will vary depending on the amount of mixture used.

Brownies

Ingredients

170g (5¾oz) SK Dark Belgian
Couverture Chocolate

80g (2¾oz) unsalted butter

2 eggs

150g (5¼oz) caster sugar

75g (2½oz) plain flour

1tsp baking powder

Pinch of salt

100g (3½oz) walnuts, roughly chopped

Equipment

Large bowls

Saucepan

Stand mixer with whisk attachment

Rubber spatula

Sieve

25cm (10") square tray, lined with
baking parchment

Palette knife

TUTOR TIPS

Try not to over-bake the brownie as
it will lose moisture and become
crumbly.

I recommend chilling the brownie
layer in the fridge after it has
been baked to make the crumb
firmer and avoid it crumbling while
assembling the cake.

1 Preheat the oven to 180°C/350°F/
gas mark 4.

2 Place the dark chocolate and
butter in a large bowl. Place the
bowl over a pan of simmering water,
ensuring the bowl does not come into
contact with the water, and stir with a
spatula until the mixture has completely
melted. Remove the bowl from the pan
and set aside.

3 In a separate bowl, whisk the
eggs and caster sugar together
at a medium to high speed until thick
and pale. Fold into the chocolate
mixture with a spatula.

4 Sift the flour, baking powder and
salt into the mix and fold them in
with a spatula. Incorporate the walnuts
into the batter.

5 Pour the brownie mixture into the
baking tray and spread the batter
evenly with a palette knife.

6 Bake for 15–18 minutes until the
surface forms a crust and springs
back to the touch. Remove from the
oven and leave to cool on the tray.

7 Once cold, cut to the size
required. Wrap the brownie in
cling film to prevent it from drying out.

Using brownie in a layered sponge cake

For a delicious twist, I recommend using a layer of brownie at the base of a sponge
cake. However, you should only use brownie for the bottom layer because of its dense
consistency.

For best results, make a full batch of brownie batter following the recipe above then
pour enough mixture for one layer into your chosen cake tin. This way you can control
the size and thickness of the brownie layer. Any leftover mix can either be used to
make a base layer for more cakes (see below) or baked in a tray and served as
accompanying party treats.

As a rough guide, you can make base layers of brownie in the following sizes (either
round or square) using the quantity of brownie mix in the recipe above:

4 x 10cm (4") layers

2 x 15cm (6") and 1 x 10cm (4") layers

1 x 25.5cm (10") layer

Alternatively, once the tray-bake brownie has cooled you can cut out a round or square
layer using a template for the size required.

Sablé biscuits

It's always good to have a reliable traditional biscuit recipe to hand. These sablé biscuits are delicious when eaten on their own but their consistency also makes them ideal for decorating with run-out icing (see page 30).

Ingredients

200g (7oz) butter

100g (3½oz) icing sugar

1tsp vanilla extract (or seeds of 1 vanilla pod)

Pinch of salt

2 egg yolks

250g (8¾oz) plain/all-purpose flour

Equipment

Stand mixer with paddle attachment

Plastic scraper or spatula

Cling film

Rolling pin

5mm (¼") marzipan spacers (optional)

Biscuit cutters

Baking tray

Baking parchment

1 Cream together the butter, icing sugar, vanilla extract (or seeds from the vanilla pod) and a pinch of salt in a mixer fitted with a paddle attachment at a medium speed. Add the egg yolks and mix until all the ingredients are well blended.

TUTOR TIP

If using a vanilla pod, open the pod lengthways with a knife and scrape the seeds out using the tip of the knife.

2 Add the plain flour to the batter and mix at low speed until all the flour has been incorporated. Take care not to overwork the dough.

3 Scrape the dough out of the bowl using a plastic scraper or spatula then wrap it in cling film, leaving the dough in a flat, square shape. Place in the fridge to firm for at least one hour, or leave overnight.

4 Before cutting out the biscuits, knead the dough with the palms of your hands to make it pliable. Lightly dust a work surface with plain flour then roll the dough out to 5mm (¼") thick. To achieve an even thickness, place the spacers either side of the dough and roll it out between them.

5 Cut out the biscuits with your chosen cutter then set them out on a tray lined with baking parchment. Place the tray in the fridge to chill the biscuits before baking.

6 Bake at 170°C/340°F/gas mark 3 until the biscuits are slightly brown around the edges. Baking time will depend on the size of the biscuits, but as a guide, 6cm (2³/₈") round biscuits will take approximately 15–20 minutes.

Flavourings

Chocolate: replace 50g (1¾oz) of flour with 50g (1¾oz) of unsweetened cocoa powder.

Crisped rice cereal mix

Crisped rice cereal mix is very useful when you want to create large yet lightweight shapes. I've used this mix for the rounded body of the chef in the Buon Appetito! project (see page 67) so that he can still be large without sinking into the cake.

Ingredients

50g (1¾oz) unsalted butter

200g (7oz) marshmallows

180g (6¼oz) crisped rice cereal

1   Melt the butter in a saucepan on a low heat.

2   Add the marshmallows and continue to cook over a low heat, stirring constantly until the marshmallows have melted and the mixture is well blended. Remove from the heat.

3   Add the crisped rice cereal and stir with a spatula until it is fully coated with the marshmallow mixture.

4   Lightly grease a work surface with butter, then pour the mix onto the work surface. Grease your hands with a little butter, then take the required amount of mix between the palms of your hands. Mould the mix into the desired shape while it is still warm. Alternatively, press the mix into a mould that has been lightly greased with butter. Remove and leave to set.

5   Allow the cereal mix to cool before covering with sugarpaste.

FILLINGS

Swiss meringue buttercream

I use this recipe as a filling and for crumb-coating sponge cakes: the Swiss meringue gives a smooth texture and lightness. This is a straight-forward recipe that can be easily flavoured to suit your taste.

Ingredients

100g (3½oz) egg whites (approximately 3 medium egg whites)

150g (5¼oz) caster sugar

300g (10½oz) unsalted butter, softened

A few drops of vanilla essence (or any other flavour suggested opposite)

Equipment

Large bowl

Saucepan

Thermometer

Stand mixer with whisk attachment

Spatula

1 Place the egg whites and sugar into a large bowl and place over a pan of simmering water.

2 Whisk until the sugar dissolves and reaches 60°C–65°C in temperature. Remove from the heat and pour into the bowl of the mixer.

3 Whisk on a high speed until the meringue is lukewarm and stiff peaks have formed.

4 Gradually add the softened butter into the meringue. Continue whisking at medium to high speed until the butter has been fully incorporated.

5 Add your chosen flavour and use straight away for filling or crumb-coating.

Storage

Store Swiss meringue buttercream in an airtight container in the fridge for up to a week. Take the buttercream out a few hours before you need to use it and whisk to achieve a creamy consistency.

Flavourings

Vanilla: open two vanilla pods lengthways and scrape out the seeds with the tip of a knife. Mix the seeds into 500g (1lb 1¾oz) of buttercream. Add 10ml (2tsp) of natural vanilla essence to enhance the flavour.

Coffee: dilute 60g (2oz) of instant coffee granules in 15ml (1tbsp) of hot, boiled water and add to 500g (1lb 1¾oz) of buttercream. Alternatively, add 60ml (2fl oz) of strong espresso coffee, instead of instant coffee granules. A dash of brandy complements the coffee flavour perfectly.

Lemon: mix in 150g (5¼oz) of lemon curd (see page 25) into 500g (1lb 1¾oz) of buttercream. Add candied lemon peel to enhance the flavour.

Strawberry (or any homemade jam): add 100g–150g (3½oz–5¼oz) of good-quality strawberry jam (homemade if possible) to 500g (1lb 1¾oz) of buttercream.

Brandy: add 50ml (1¾fl oz) of brandy to 500g (1lb 1¾oz) of buttercream.

Caramel: add 100g (3½oz) of dulce de leche (caramel toffee) to 500g (1lb 1¾oz) of buttercream. A dash of brandy complements the caramel flavour perfectly.

Dark chocolate: bring 150g (5oz) of melted dark chocolate (minimum 50% cocoa solids) to 27°C in temperature, then add to 500g (1lb 1¾oz) of buttercream.

Sugar syrup

Sugar syrup can be brushed over a baked sponge cake with a pastry brush to keep it moist and also to add flavour. It is difficult to say exactly how much syrup needs to be added as every sponge can vary in texture, so when brushing the syrup over the sponge, take into account its thickness and the moistness of the crumb.

Ingredients

250g (8¾oz) caster sugar

250ml (8¾fl oz) water

25ml (1fl oz) lemon juice (optional)

Equipment

Saucepan

Whisk

Jar or heatproof airtight container

TUTOR TIP

Remember to brush over enough syrup to keep a balanced moisture throughout the cake. Do not add too much sugar syrup as the cake will be too sweet and too soft to hold its shape. Remember that the sponge cake will also take some of the moisture from the filling after a few days in the fridge.

1 Combine all the ingredients in a saucepan and place it over a medium heat. Stir occasionally to make sure that the sugar crystals have dissolved.

2 Let the syrup boil for a minute then remove from the heat.

3 Pour into a clean jar or airtight container and put the lid on while it is still hot to stop the water evaporating. Allow to cool to room temperature before use.

4 Store the jar or airtight container in the fridge for up to a month.

Flavourings

Brandy: add 100ml (3½fl oz) of brandy as you remove the pan from the heat.

Orange: boil the ingredients with some fresh orange peel (avoid the white pith as it makes the syrup bitter). Add 50ml (1¾fl oz) of orange liqueur (Cointreau) when you remove it from the heat and pour the syrup through a sieve into the jar.

Lemon: add lemon zest (avoiding the white pith) to the ingredients and a dash of limoncello once you have removed it from the heat. Pour the syrup through a sieve into the jar.

Vanilla: boil the syrup with two vanilla pods, seeds scraped out. Add a few drops of natural Madagascan vanilla essence to the syrup once it has boiled and remove the pod before using.

Chocolate: add one level tablespoon of cocoa powder and 50ml (1¾fl oz) of brandy to the recipe and bring to boil. Use this chocolate syrup only for chocolate sponges.

Dark chocolate ganache

This is one of my favourite fillings because of its creamy texture and consistency. This recipe can be used as a filling and for crumb-coating cakes.

Ingredients

500ml (17fl oz) double cream

50ml (1¾fl oz) honey

500g (1lb 1¾oz) SK Dark Belgian Couverture Chocolate

Equipment

Saucepan

Large bowl

Whisk

Spatula

1 Pour the cream and honey into a pan over a medium heat and bring to the boil.

2 Place the couverture chocolate into a large bowl. Remove the pan from the heat and pour the cream and honey mixture onto the chocolate. Whisk from the centre to the sides of the bowl until the ganache has a shiny and smooth texture.

3 Cool the ganache down in the fridge, giving it a stir with a spatula from time to time, until it has a creamy and workable consistency.

4 Store the ganache in the fridge in an airtight container to prevent any unwanted fridge odours affecting the flavour of the ganache.

Flavouring

Brandy: when the ganache is ready, stir in 100ml (3½fl oz) of brandy or another liqueur of your choice (optional).

TUTOR TIPS

To give the ganache a firmer consistency for coating a cake, use 750g–850g (1lb 10½oz–1lb 13½oz) of chocolate to 500g (1lb 1¾oz) of cream.

If preferred, you can replace the honey with glucose. Either of the two will give the ganache a creamy texture.

In hot weather conditions (over 25°C/77°F), it is advisable to cool the ganache down in the fridge, stirring with a spatula from time to time.

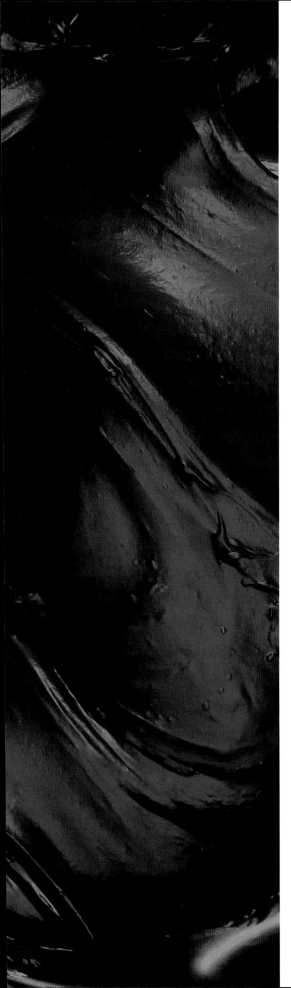

Raspberry ganache

I love this filling as the raspberry purée gives a tangy flavour and extra creaminess. For a delicious combination, layer a chocolate sponge with thin layers of raspberry ganache and homemade raspberry jam. Soak the sponge with sugar syrup flavoured with raspberry liqueur for extra moisture and flavour.

Ingredients

300g (10½oz) raspberry purée

200ml (7fl oz) double cream

50ml (1¾fl oz) honey

50ml (1¾fl oz) raspberry liqueur

500g (1lb 1¾oz) SK Dark Belgian Couverture Chocolate (50% cocoa solids)

Equipment

Saucepan

Large bowl

Whisk

Spatula

1   Pour the cream, honey, raspberry liqueur and raspberry purée into a pan and bring to the boil.

2   Place the couverture chocolate into a large bowl. Remove the pan from the heat and pour the mixture onto the chocolate. Whisk from the centre to the sides of the bowl until the ganache has a shiny and smooth texture.

3   Cool the ganache down in the fridge, giving it a stir with a spatula from time to time, until it has a creamy and workable consistency.

Passion fruit ganache

I love this filling layered between a lemon or almond sponge soaked with peach-flavoured syrup.

Ingredients

300g (10½oz) passion fruit purée

100ml (3½fl oz) double cream

30ml (1fl oz) honey

650g (1lb 7oz) SK Milk Belgian Couverture Chocolate

100g (3½oz) butter

Equipment

Saucepan

Whisk

Large bowl

Cling film

1   Place the passion fruit purée, honey and cream in a pan and bring to the boil.

2   Place the milk chocolate into a large bowl. Remove the pan from the heat and pour the passion fruit mixture onto the chocolate. Whisk to combine and add the butter last. Cover with cling film and leave in the fridge to set overnight.

TUTOR TIP

It is advisable to cover the ganache with cling film before storing in the fridge. This will prevent any unwanted fridge odours from affecting the flavour of the ganache.

Lemon curd

This lemon curd recipe makes a great cake filling when used on its own or layered alternately with fruit jam, or you can mix it with buttercream to create a delicious lemon-flavoured filling (see page 20).

Ingredients

5 medium egg yolks

120g (4¼oz) caster sugar

Zest of 1 medium lemon

80ml (2¾fl oz) fresh lemon juice

150g (5¼oz) unsalted butter, cubed

Equipment

Large bowl

Saucepan

Rubber spatula

Whisk

Digital thermometer

1 Combine the egg yolks, sugar, lemon zest and juice together in a bowl. Place the bowl over a pan of simmering water. Stir the mixture with a spatula until it thickens to a creamy consistency and the temperature reaches 80°C–85°C.

2 Remove the bowl from the pan and allow the temperature of the mixture to drop to 60°C.

3 Gradually add the cubes of butter and whisk until the butter is fully incorporated.

4 Cover the surface of the curd with cling film and allow to cool. Spoon the curd into sterilised jars and store in the fridge for up to two weeks.

TUTOR TIPS

Lemon curd will remain stable up to room temperature, so can be used as a filling for cakes that have to be displayed. However, if the ambient temperature is over 27°C, it is advisable to refrigerate the cake until it is served. In this case, avoid coating the cake with sugarpaste as it will sweat when removed from the fridge. If you are using lemon curd as a filling, it is preferable to cover the cake with Italian meringue, buttercream or ganache.

If you are making this recipe in a warmer climate, you may need to add 2g (¹/₁₆oz) of gelatine to the mixture to help it set. Simply soak one leaf of gelatine in cold water for five minutes, then squeeze out the excess water and add it to the curd once you remove it from the heat.

ICINGS AND SUGAR PASTES

Sugarpaste

I usually use ready-made sugarpaste as it saves time and has a consistent and workable consistency, however it is always useful to have a sugarpaste recipe to hand if you like to make your own. Remember that the consistency will change depending on the climate so you may need to adjust the recipe slightly.

Ingredients

120ml (4¼fl oz) water

20g (¾oz) unflavoured gelatine powder

40g (1½oz) white vegetable fat

200g (7oz) glucose syrup

30g (1oz) SK Glycerine*

10ml (2tsp) clear vanilla essence

2kg (4lb 6½oz) icing/confectioners' sugar

5ml (1 level tsp) SK CMC Gum

Equipment

Heatproof bowl

Rubber spatula

Whisk

Bain marie

Microwave

Sieve

Sealable food-grade polythene bag

*Avoid using glycerine in extremely humid weather conditions.

1 Pour the water into a heatproof bowl. Sprinkle the gelatine over the water and leave it to soak for about five minutes. Place the bowl over a pan of simmering water, making sure the bowl isn't touching the water. Stir until the gelatine is completely dissolved and has become transparent.

2 Melt the white vegetable fat in a bain marie (double boiler) or a microwave. While the bowl of gelatine is still over the bain marie, add the melted vegetable fat, glucose, glycerine (if needed) and vanilla essence to the gelatine. Whisk thoroughly until all the ingredients are combined. Remove the bowl from the heat.

3 Sift 500g (1lb 1¾oz) of icing sugar with the CMC and pour this into the gelatine mix. Stir well until all the ingredients are combined. Keep adding

more icing sugar until the mixture forms a thick paste.

4 Sprinkle a work surface with icing sugar. Scrape the sugarpaste out of the bowl and knead well with more icing sugar until the paste becomes pliable and no longer sticks to the work surface.

5 Seal the paste in a food-grade polythene bag when you are not using it to prevent it forming a crust (see notes on storage below).

Colouring and storing sugarpaste

Homemade or shop-bought sugarpaste can be coloured and stored in exactly the same way as for modelling paste. Guidelines can be found on page 28.

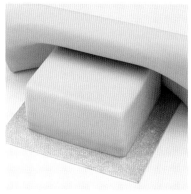

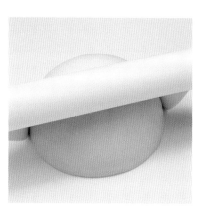

Modelling paste

It is important to use a good modelling paste when it comes to making figurines. I prefer to use a paste that contains CMC gum (carboxymethyl cellulose): this not only gives the paste good texture and pliability but also helps it hold its shape. There are many different brands on the market but I would always recommend using a paste that you are familiar with and that you feel comfortable using.

To make the figurines in this book I have used SK Sugar Florist Paste (SFP) as it is pliable and dries firm, giving a smooth finish. If you require the paste to be slightly softer, you can mix SFP 50:50 with any other modelling paste. However if you can't get hold of flower paste or you would prefer to make your own, you can follow the recipe below.

Ingredients

50ml (1¾fl oz) water

7g (½tbsp) unflavoured gelatine powder

30g (1oz) white vegetable fat

120g (4¼oz) glucose syrup

5ml (1tsp) SK Glycerine*

10ml (2tsp) clear vanilla essence

50g (1¾oz) egg white, at room temperature (I use SK Fortified Albumen and water to make up the 50g (1¾oz))**

1kg–1.25kg (2lb 3¼oz–2lb 12oz) icing/confectioners' sugar (you may need extra, see note on page 42)

15ml (1tbsp) SK CMC Gum

50g (1¾oz) cornflour/corn starch/maize starch

Equipment

Heatproof bowl

Bain marie

Whisk

Sieve

Sealable food-grade polythene bag

1 Place the water in a heatproof bowl. Sprinkle the gelatine over the water and leave it to soak for about five minutes. Place the bowl over a pan of simmering water, making sure the bowl isn't touching the water. Stir until the gelatine is completely dissolved and has become transparent.

2 Melt the white vegetable fat in a bain marie (double boiler) or a microwave. While the bowl is still over the bain marie, add the melted vegetable fat, glucose, glycerine (if needed) and vanilla essence to the gelatine. Whisk thoroughly until all the ingredients are combined. Be careful not to overheat the mixture at this point: never bring the gelatine to the boil.

3 Remove the bowl from the heat and stir in the egg whites or reconstituted albumen. The mixture has to be warm when the whites go in; they will curdle if the gelatine mix is too hot.

4 Sift 500g (1lb 1¾oz) of icing sugar into a bowl with the CMC and the cornflour then mix in the gelatine. Keep adding more icing sugar until the mixture forms a thick, sticky paste.

5 Sprinkle a work surface with icing sugar. Scrape the modelling paste out of the bowl and knead well with more icing sugar until the paste becomes pliable and no longer sticks to the work surface.

6 Seal the paste in a food-grade polythene bag when you are not using it to prevent it forming a crust (see notes on storage overleaf).

Basic modelling guidelines and tips for using modelling paste can be found on pages 45 to 55.

*Avoid using glycerine in extremely humid weather conditions.

**The Food Standards Agency recommends using only pasteurised egg in any food that will not be cooked (or only lightly cooked).

If you decide to use fresh egg white always use eggs bearing the Lion mark, which guarantees that they have been produced to the highest standards of food safety. All Lion Quality eggs come from British hens vaccinated against salmonella, are fully traceable and have a 'best before' date on the shell as a guarantee of freshness. This is particularly important for cake makers and decorators as you may well use eggs for baking and preparing icings, marzipans and cake fillings.

Colouring sugarpaste and modelling paste

A wide range of paste, liquid and dust food colourings is available from sugarcraft suppliers (see page 256), so you can be as creative as you like with your sugar models. Squires Kitchen makes a wide range of food colours which do not contain glycerine so won't affect the consistency of your paste when dry (see page 52).

I recommend using paste food colours to achieve both light and dark hues; liquid food colours can be used for pastel tones only where a small amount of colour needs to be added, but should not be used if you want to achieve an intense colour as adding too much of it will make the paste too soft and sticky.

Paste food colours are concentrated, so only add a tiny amount of colour at a time using the tip of a cocktail stick until the desired colour is achieved. Blend the colour into the paste by kneading well. Let the paste rest in an airtight, food-grade polythene bag for a couple of hours before use to allow the colour to develop.

How to colour a large amount of sugarpaste (e.g. when covering a cake):

First take a small piece of sugarpaste and add colour to it using the tip of a cocktail stick until a high intensity of the desired hue is produced, e.g. deep red.

Gradually add small portions of this intensely coloured piece of paste into the large amount of sugarpaste until you achieve your chosen colour, e.g. deep red added to white sugarpaste will create a light pink (rose).

This method makes the colour easier to blend and allows for more gradual colouring, meaning that you are less likely to ruin it by adding too much colour straight from the pot to a large amount of white paste.

How to store sugarpaste, modelling paste and pastillage

Once the paste is coloured as required and ready to use, rub the surface with vegetable fat to prevent the paste from forming a crust and leave it to rest in an airtight food-grade polythene bag. Store the sealed bag of paste in a plastic container to keep it moist for longer.

Once it is sealed, homemade sugarpaste, modelling paste and pastillage can be kept as follows:

- At room temperature for up to a month.
- In the fridge for up to two months.
- In the freezer for up to six months.

Take the paste out of the fridge or freezer and allow it to reach room temperature. Knead the paste well to achieve pliability before use.

If you are using ready-made pastes, check the pack for storage guidelines.

TUTOR TIP

Do not wrap sugarpaste in cling film as it is slightly porous and therefore doesn't stop the paste from getting a crust.

Royal icing

Royal icing is one of the most basic recipes in cake decorating yet is so useful for its endless possibilities when decorating cakes and cookies. I have used Instant Mix Royal Icing from Squires Kitchen throughout the book, but if you prefer to make your own I would recommend the following recipe. Make sure all the bowls and spatulas used for making royal icing are completely clean and grease-free before you start, otherwise the icing will not reach a good consistency. When making my own royal icing I make it up to firm-peak consistency then let it down with cooled, boiled water as required.

Ingredients

40g (1½oz) egg white, at room temperature (I use SK Fortified Albumen and water to make up 40g (1½oz) following instructions on the pack)*

250g–300g (8¾oz–10½oz) icing/confectioners' sugar (depending on the size of the egg white)

5ml (1tsp) strained fresh lemon juice

Equipment

Stand mixer with paddle attachment

Rubber spatula

Airtight plastic container

Cling film

Kitchen paper

*See guidelines on page 27 regarding the use of egg in food that will not be cooked.

1   Place the egg whites in an electric mixer fitted with a paddle attachment. Beat the whites at a medium speed to break them slightly. If you are using dried albumen powder, follow the instructions on the pack to reconstitute it and beat as explained above.

2   Spoon the sifted icing sugar into the egg whites (or reconstituted albumen) while mixing at a slow to medium speed. Mix until they have turned creamy, then add the lemon juice. Add more icing sugar until the icing forms stiff peaks that do not bend over. This is firm-peak consistency.

3   Place the royal icing in an airtight plastic container and cover it with cling film before sealing the lid to prevent it from drying out. A damp piece of kitchen paper can be placed on top of the film to keep it moist.

Consistencies

You will need varying consistencies of royal icing depending on how you wish to use it:

Firm/stiff peaks: for sticking figurines onto a cake; for piping hair, borders and basketweave effects; and for stencilling.

> ### TUTOR TIP
>
> Add a little sieved icing sugar to soft-peak royal icing and re-beat until it forms stiff peaks.

Soft peak/medium consistency: to fill eye sockets and draw lines, dots and borders on cakes. Make the icing following the recipe above and add enough pre-boiled water so that it forms bent peaks when lifted with a palette knife.

Run-out/flooding consistency: for filling spaces between piped lines or for coating cakes and cupcakes. Start with stiff-peak icing and add a teaspoon at a time of cold, pre-boiled water to make the icing thin enough so that it smooths out on its own on a work surface within 10–15 seconds.

Firm/stiff peaks

Soft peaks/medium consistency

Run-out/flooding consistency

TUTOR TIP

Fresh egg whites can be kept in a jar in the fridge for up to 15 days. Some of the water in the whites will evaporate: this will strengthen the egg whites and make them more suitable for use in royal icing.

Colouring royal icing

Colour royal icing with paste or liquid food colours. If you are using paste colours, dip a cocktail stick into the pot, transfer the colour to a bowl of icing and mix in with a palette knife. Add a little food colour at a time until you have achieved the colour you require. For liquid colours use the point of a knife or a pipette to add droplets of colour into the icing and mix well as before.

Once you have coloured the icing, keep the bowl covered with cling film and a damp kitchen towel to prevent the icing from forming a crust.

How to store royal icing

Royal icing can be stored in the fridge for up to a week if you are using fresh eggs. After a couple of days in the fridge you may find that the icing has separated with a thick layer of sugar on the top and a watery consistency underneath. To fix this, take the royal icing out of the fridge and let it come to room temperature. Take it out of the container, making sure that you do not scrape any dry icing from the sides into the mixture. Re-beat it in the mixer until you achieve the original consistency.

TUTOR TIP

When you want to colour the icing a dark colour, it is advisable to colour it in advance so it has time to fully develop.

How to pipe run-outs

To create a run-out, fit a paper piping bag with a no. 1 nozzle, fill it with medium-consistency royal icing in your chosen colour and pipe an outline around each biscuit. Let down the royal icing to run-out consistency (see page 29), place in a piping bag with a no. 2 nozzle and flood the area inside the outline with the runny icing.

If you want to add more than one colour to a run-out decoration, simply pipe the second colour onto the run-out while it is still wet. Gently tap the decoration on a work surface to ensure the colours settle evenly.

Allow the icing to dry in a warm, dry place. Make sure the food colours you are using don't contain glycerine as this will prevent the icing from drying fully.

Run-outs can be piped directly onto a biscuit or, alternatively, you can pipe them onto a piece of cellophane as an off-piece decoration. Tape a piece of cellophane to a work surface and slide a template under it, if required. Grease the cellophane with white vegetable fat, pipe the run-out onto it and leave it to dry under the heat of a lamp. Once dry, you can then stick the run-out onto a cake or biscuit with a little royal icing.

Pastillage

The quickest and easiest product to use when making pastillage is SK Instant Mix Pastillage. As well as being easy to make you are also guaranteed the same consistency every time. However, if I ever need to make my own pastillage, I always use the following recipe.

Ingredients

80g (2¾oz) egg whites, at room temperature (I use SK Fortified Albumen and water to make up the 80g (2¾oz) following instructions on the pack)*

1kg (2lb 3¼oz) icing/confectioners' sugar, plus extra if needed (see tip below)

50g (1¾oz) cornflour

5ml (1tsp) SK CMC Gum

Clear vanilla essence

Melted white vegetable fat

Equipment

2 large mixing bowls

Wooden spoon

Sealable food-grade plastic bags

*See note on page 27 regarding the use of egg in food that will not be cooked.

1 Place the egg whites into a large bowl.

2 In another bowl sift half the icing sugar with the CMC gum and cornflour then pour this into the bowl of egg whites. Mix with a wooden spoon until you get a soft, stretchy dough.

3 At this point take the dough out of the bowl and knead it on a clean work surface with more icing sugar until it is pliable and no longer sticks to the work surface.

4 Rub the surface of the pastillage with a little melted vegetable fat to prevent it from forming a crust. Store in an airtight food-grade plastic bag. Do not leave pastillage unwrapped as it dries very quickly.

How to use pastillage

1 Roll out some pastillage on a work surface dusted with cornflour. To achieve an even thickness you may find it easiest to use spacers (picture A).

2 Transfer the pastillage to a chopping board lightly dusted with cornflour, texture if needed and cut out the shape required using a template. Use a sharp, plain-bladed knife to make a neat, straight edge (picture B). To cut circles use a round cutter dusted with a little cornflour.

3 Remove the excess paste from around the edge and leave the

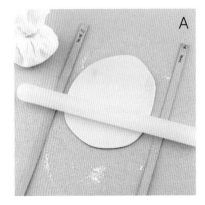

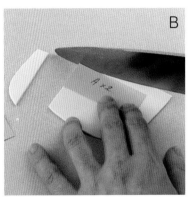

TUTOR TIPS

Bear in mind that the amount of sugar given in the recipes is only a guide. You may need to add extra icing sugar depending on the type of sugar you are using and the weather conditions (e.g. add more icing sugar in humid climates).

Do not roll out too much pastillage at a time as it dries quickly; aim to roll out just enough for the size of the template you are using.

For curved shapes such as cylinders it is best to use pastillage that contains CMC or gum tragacanth. The gum will give extra strength to the paste and will allow it to be wrapped around the former without losing its shape.

Using spacers of the required depth is the best way to achieve an even thickness when rolling out paste. I usually find the following sizes useful: 2mm, 3mm, 4mm, 5mm, 1cm and 1.5cm (¹⁄₁₆", ⅛", just over ⅛", ³⁄₁₆", ⅜" and ⁹⁄₁₆"). To achieve a greater thickness such as 3cm (1³⁄₁₆") you can stack them on top of each other. You will find different spacers available from sugarcraft and chocolate suppliers (see page 256).

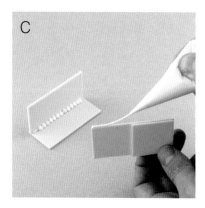

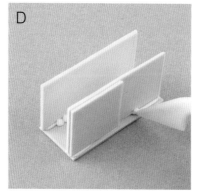

piece of pastillage to dry on the chopping board. Flip the piece of pastillage over once it is dry on one side to allow it to dry evenly on both sides. Drying time will depend on the thickness and size of the piece of pastillage and the weather conditions (if conditions are humid it will take longer to dry).

How to stick pieces of dry pastillage together

1   Fill a paper piping bag with soft-peak royal icing, snip off the very end and pipe a line of icing onto the side of the shape that is to be glued in place (picture C).

2   Place the piece in the required position and remove the excess royal icing with the pointed end of a modelling tool or a clean paintbrush (picture D).

3   Once all the pieces are assembled, leave to dry completely.

Colouring pastillage

Pastillage can be coloured like any other paste (see page 28) but you should bear in mind that extra colour has to be added as it will lighten as it dries. When pastillage pieces are fully dry they can be painted using liquid food colours, edible metallic paint or metallic dust food colours diluted with a few drops of clear alcohol.

How to make pastillage rocks

By heating pastillage in a microwave, you can easily create realistic rock shapes from sugar. These are useful when you want to create a rocky, stony or coral effect on a celebration cake (see In the Dead of Night on page 180).

1   Roll approximately 20g (¾oz) of pastillage into a ball and place in a small microwaveable bowl. Heat in a microwave for a minute on full power. The piece of pastillage should triple in volume once it has been heated.

2   Remove the bowl from the microwave and leave the pastillage to stand for a few minutes. To release the pastillage from the bowl, scrape the sides with a knife or a small spatula. Leave to cool.

3   Once cold, break the pastillage into random pieces to create natural-looking rock shapes. Arrange the rocks on your cake, stacking them together if necessary, and secure with dots of royal icing.

Edible (sugar) glue

Edible glue is available to buy from sugarcraft suppliers, however if you would like to make your own, mix one level teaspoon of CMC gum with 150ml (5¼fl oz) of cooled, boiled water and a few drops of white vinegar. Let the mix rest for an hour until it becomes gel-like. If you need to adjust the consistency add extra water to make it runnier, or more CMC to make it thicker.

Edible glue can be stored in a jar with a lid and kept in the fridge for up to a month.

How to use softened paste as glue

Softened sugar paste makes a strong edible glue that is ideal for sticking dry pieces of paste together: this method works with pastillage, flower paste and modelling paste. I use softened sugarpaste to secure the cake tiers when stacking a cake. I would only advise using softened pastillage in very humid weather conditions as it dries quicker than other pastes which contain glycerine (and therefore take longer to dry).

1 Dip a small piece of sugar paste into a bowl of cooled, boiled water then spread it on a work surface with a spatula until it forms a creamy, tacky consistency. Make sure to use the same colour paste as the pieces you are going to stick together so it blends in.

2 Dab a small amount of softened paste onto the desired area and stick the pieces together. You may need to hold the pieces in place for a few moments to secure them. Remove any excess softened paste with a damp paintbrush to achieve a neat finish.

How to use edible glue

Edible glue is used for sticking pieces of fresh paste together. The glue will only work if one or both of the modelled pieces is still soft, so stick them together before they dry completely.

Use a paintbrush to dab a small amount of edible glue on the surface and remove the excess with your finger so that you are left with a sticky surface. Do not use too much glue otherwise the pieces may slide out of place.

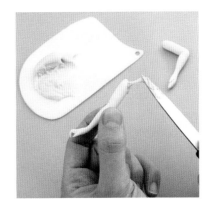

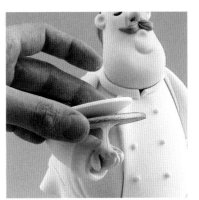

PREPARING AND COVERING CAKES FOR DECORATION

Layering, filling and covering a cake

Following this technique, you can combine different sponges and fillings of your choice for round, square and other shaped cakes.

Ingredients

3 x 15cm (6") round or square sponge layers (see pages 9 to 10)

1 x 15cm (6") round or square brownie layer (optional, see page 16)

150ml (5¼fl oz) sugar syrup (see page 22)

250g (8¾oz) buttercream (see page 20)

150g (5¼oz) dark chocolate ganache (see page 23) (optional)

Brandy or any other spirit of your choice (optional)

600g (1lb 5¼oz) marzipan (optional)

600g (1lb 5¼oz) sugarpaste

Equipment

Basic equipment (see pages 6 to 7)

Pastry brush

15cm (6") round or square cake card

23cm (9") round or square cake drum/board

Cling film

Cake smoothers

Turntable (optional)

TUTOR TIP

The method I use for layering a cake means that you flip the cake over after you've stacked and crumb-coated it; the flatter layer at the bottom will become the top, giving a neater finish.

1 Place a layer of sponge onto a cake card and brush the surface with a little sugar syrup. Spread a layer of buttercream over it and place another layer on top. Continue to stack the remaining layers of sponge in the same way. Stick a 15cm (6") round or square cake card to the top of the cake with a dab of the filling and press down gently. Wrap the cake in cling film and chill in the fridge overnight.

TUTOR TIP

If you want to use brownie for the base layer, spread dark chocolate ganache over the third sponge layer and place the layer of brownie on top instead.

2 Trim the sides of the cake with a serrated knife, if necessary, to make sharp, straight edges. Spread a thin layer of buttercream over the sides of the cake with a palette knife to seal the crumb. Chill in the fridge to let the buttercream set, then apply a second layer to give a smooth and neat finish.

3 Use the cake card to help you flip the cake over, then place it back on the same cake card. The flatter, bottom layer is now at the top of the cake. Spread a layer of buttercream over the top to seal it, refrigerate the cake, then apply a second layer. Return the cake to the fridge until you are ready to cover it.

4 If you choose to use a marzipan coating, roll out 600g (1lb 5¼oz) of marzipan on a work surface lightly dusted with icing sugar to 3mm (⅛") thick. Fold the marzipan over the rolling pin, then lift it over the cake and unroll the marzipan gently over the top of the cake. Adjust the paste at the corners to make sure they are neat, then gently run the palm of your hand over the top and down the sides of the cake to remove any air bubbles.

5 Gently rub over the top and sides of the cake with two cake smoothers to create straight edges, stick down the marzipan and give a neat finish. Trim the excess marzipan from around the base with a plain-bladed knife.

6 Allow the marzipan to firm up for a couple of hours or overnight at room temperature before coating the cake with sugarpaste. Brush the marzipan with brandy or pre-boiled water to make the surface sticky, then set aside.

7 Take 600g (1lb 5¼oz) of sugarpaste and knead until it is soft and pliable. Cover the cake in the same way as for the marzipan layer.

TUTOR TIP

I recommend that you layer and fill the cake a few days before you cover it: this will allow the flavour to mature and ensure it is evenly moist.

How to line a cake with a sponge sheet

Lining a cake with a sponge sheet is a technique that I use regularly when layering a large round or square sponge cake with any soft or creamy filling. This technique allows you to get a clean, neat finish on the edge and sides of the cake once it is covered with sugarpaste, and also gives you the option to omit the marzipan covering which is not always to everyone's taste.

If you would prefer to prepare the cake in the traditional way there is no need to bake the sponge sheet to line the cake. Likewise if you are making a small cake you won't need the sponge sheet around the outside to keep its shape, so simply spread the top and sides with a thin layer of buttercream from step 9.

Please note that the quantities given are for a 20cm (8") round or square cake.

Ingredients

40cm x 30cm (16" x 12") vanilla sponge sheet (3 egg recipe) (see pages 12 to 13)*

3 x 20.5cm (8") round or square sponge cake layers (see pages 9 to 10)

300ml (10½fl oz) sugar syrup (see page 22)

300g (10½oz) filling, e.g. ganache (see pages 23 to 25)

150g (5¼oz) ganache or buttercream for the crumb coat

Equipment

Acetate sheet

20.5cm (8") round or square cake tin for lining the cake

Pastry brush

20.5cm (8") cake card

28cm (11") round cake drum or stainless steel tray to use as base for crumb-coating the cake

Cling film

Palette knife

Plastic scraper

Turntable

*One sponge sheet cut lengthways into three strips allows you to line two 20cm (8") round or square tins, approximately 10cm (4") in height.

1   Line the tin or ring used for baking the cake with a strip of acetate of the height required. For a square cake with straight corners, cut the acetate into four pieces and stick them to the inner sides of the tin with a dab of filling.

2   Place a strip of the vanilla sponge sheet all the way around the inside of the tin with the brown crust facing inwards. For a square shape with straight corners, cut the sponge into four pieces, then place and stick them to the acetate sheet with a dab of filling.

3   Place a layer of vanilla sponge at the bottom and brush with sugar syrup. Trim the sides of the sponge layer slightly to fit in the shape if required.

4   Spread a layer of your chosen filling on top and onto the sides of the sponge sheet lining the cake.

5   Repeat the layering process until you reach the height required.

6   Finish the cake with a layer of sponge on the top and brush with syrup.

7   Stick a cake card onto the top layer of sponge with a dab of the filling and wrap the cake in cling film. Store in the fridge until needed.

8   Flip the cake over onto the cake drum to release it from the tin. Remove the acetate carefully.

9   To crumb-coat the cake, use a palette knife to spread a layer of buttercream onto the top and sides of the cake. This seals the cake and gives an even surface for the sugarpaste or marzipan to stick to.

10   Remove the excess buttercream with a plastic side scraper: the easiest way to do this is to place the cake onto a turntable and rotate the cake whilst holding the scraper against the side of the cake.

11   Chill the cake for a few hours to allow the buttercream to firm. If you leave the cake overnight make sure you cover it with cling film to protect it from any unwanted fridge odours. Before coating the cake, apply another thin layer of buttercream to help the sugarpaste stick.

TUTOR TIP

I recommend that you layer the cake with the filling three days before you decorate it. The cake will mature in flavour and will be evenly moist.

How to make a dome-shaped cake

With the amount of ingredients given below you can make either a 15cm or 18cm (6" or 7") diameter dome-shaped cake with an approximate height of 8cm (3¹/₈"). This shape is used in the Pigs Might Fly project, starting on page 79.

Ingredients

30cm x 40cm (12" x 16") thin sheet of light sponge (made with 3 eggs, see pages 12 to 13)

30cm x 40cm (12" x 16") thick sheet of light sponge (made with 5 eggs, see page 12)

100g (3½oz) lemon curd or 250g (8¾oz) strawberry jam

100ml (3½fl oz) sugar syrup

250g (8¾oz) buttercream

500g (1lb 1¾oz) marzipan (optional)

25ml (just over ¾fl oz) brandy

500g (1lb 1¾oz) sugarpaste

Equipment

15cm (6") dome-shaped cake tin

10cm (4") round cutter, or similar size round plastic container

Cling film

15cm (6") round cake card

Plain-bladed knife

Palette knife

Pastry brush

TUTOR TIP

As there are many layers to this cake, I like to combine different fillings. I find that filling alternate layers with strawberry jam and lemon curd (see page 25) adds a fresh, fruity taste to the sponge but you can use any filling of your choice. You can also use different flavours of buttercream (see page 20) to add another twist to the cake.

TUTOR TIP

For a cake with a firmer crumb, you can replace the thick sheet of light sponge with a sheet of butter sponge instead (see recipe on pages 9 to 10).

1 Place the dome-shaped cake tin on a cutter or similar to give it stability whilst you assemble the cake. Cover the inside of the tin with a large piece of cling film that comes over the edges.

2 Cut out a circle that is 25.5cm (10") in diameter from the thin sheet of sponge, then cut out a segment so it will fit comfortably inside the tin. Arrange the sheet inside the tin with the crust facing upwards, then trim any sponge that is overlapping to make it fit neatly in the tin.

3 Cut out five discs from the thicker sheet of sponge that are 6cm, 8cm, 10cm, 12cm and 15cm (2³/₈", 3¹/₈", 4", 4¾" and 7") in diameter.

4 Use a palette knife to spread a layer of buttercream over the sponge sheet in the tin. Spread a thin layer of jam over the smallest sponge disc and place it in the bottom of the tin with the jam side down. Press it down gently and use a pastry brush to cover the surface with sugar syrup. Spread more buttercream on top of the first disc, cover the 8cm (3¹/₈") disc in jam and place on top. Repeat the same layering technique with the remaining sponge discs in ascending size order. Once you have put the final disc on top, fold the extra cling film in to cover the sponge and store in the fridge overnight.

5 Remove from the fridge, then stick a 15cm (6") cake card on top with some buttercream. Carefully flip the cake over to release it from the mould. Remove the cling film, crumb-coat it and leave in the fridge until you are ready to cover it.

6 Cover the cake with 500g (1lb 1¾oz) of marzipan if desired, and 500g (1lb 1¾oz) of sugarpaste (see page 34).

TUTOR TIP

I recommend coating the cake with a thin layer of marzipan to help the cake keep its structure, especially when you are using light sponge cake. You can omit the marzipan layer if you are using butter sponge discs instead, as the firmer consistency will make the cake more stable.

If you are using an 18cm (7") dome-shaped tin, you will need a 28cm (11") diameter layer of sponge to line the tin and discs 8cm, 10cm, 12cm, 15cm and 18cm (3¹/₈", 4", 4¾" and 7") in diameter.

Covering a straight-edged cake with marzipan

If you require a cake with a sharp top edge, a marzipan layer will help to create straight edges underneath the sugarpaste coating.

Edibles

Cake, filled and crumb-coated (see page 34)

Marzipan

Icing/confectioners' sugar in shaker

SK Sugarpaste

Clear alcohol (e.g. gin or vodka)

Equipment

Large rolling pin

Large cake drum/board (bigger than the cake size)

Plain-bladed knife

Greaseproof paper

Cake smoothers

Cake card the same size as the cake

Pastry brush

1 Remove the crumb-coated cake from the fridge.

2 Roll out some marzipan on a work surface dusted with icing sugar to a thickness of approximately 3mm (1/8"). Transfer the rolled marzipan to a cake board (that is bigger than the cake to be coated) dusted with icing sugar. Place the cake upside down onto the marzipan and trim to size around the bottom edge using a plain-bladed knife.

3 To cover the side of the cake, cut a strip of greaseproof paper to the same height and circumference as the cake. Roll out a piece of marzipan and use the paper template to cut it to the required height and length. Roll up the marzipan strip and stick it to the side of the cake. Unroll the paste around the cake and trim away the excess marzipan neatly at the join.

4 Using two smoothers, press the sides down gently to achieve an even surface and create a neat, straight edge at the bottom.

5 Stick a cake card the size of the cake on top of the cake with a little buttercream and flip the cake back over. Leave the marzipan to firm up before covering with sugarpaste.

6 Dampen the surface of the marzipan with clear alcohol using a pastry brush and cover the cake with sugarpaste as described on page 34.

TUTOR TIP

If you don't like marzipan you can omit this stage completely, or replace the marzipan with sugarpaste. However, I like to use marzipan because it gives a nice shape to the cake and keeps it moist.

Covering a cake drum (board) with sugarpaste

To give your cakes a professional finish, place them on a cake board or drum covered with sugarpaste and edged with ribbon.

Edibles

Edible glue

Sugarpaste

Icing/confectioners' sugar in shaker

Equipment

Large paintbrush (sugarcraft use only)

Rolling pin

Cake drum (board)

Pizza wheel

Ribbon

Non-toxic glue stick

1 Brush the surface of the cake drum with a little edible glue.

2 Knead the required quantity of sugarpaste until it becomes pliable. Roll out the paste on a work surface dusted with icing sugar to a thickness of approximately 4mm (1/8") and to the size of the board that you need to cover. Fold the paste over the rolling pin and place it gently on the board.

3 Rub a smoother over the surface to stick the paste to the board and remove any imperfections.

4 Turn the board over so it is sugarpaste side down, then use a sharp knife or a pizza wheel to neatly trim away the excess paste from around the edges. Flip the board up the right way again.

5 Secure a length of ribbon onto the edge of the board with a non-toxic glue stick, taking care to ensure that the glue does not come into contact with the sugarpaste. Make a slight overlap at the join then position this at the back when you place your cake onto the board.

Dowelling a cake

If you are making a stacked cake with more than one tier you will need to dowel the lower tiers to prevent the cake from sinking. Dowels will also support the weight of a large, heavy figurine and prevent it from sinking into the cake.

Edibles

Cakes, prepared and covered with sugarpaste, placed on cake cards of the same size

Clear alcohol (e.g. gin or vodka) or boiling water

SK Food Colour Pen (any colour)

Royal icing or softened sugarpaste (to secure the cakes together)

Equipment

Dowelling template

Plastic cake dowels

Craft knife

1 Place each cake onto a thin cake card, usually of the same size so it cannot be seen, and cover in the usual way (see page 34).

2 Using a dowelling template or your own template made from greaseproof paper, mark where you would like the dowels to go. Use three dowels for smaller cakes and four for larger cakes so that they have enough support. They should be equally spaced around the central point but within the size and shape of the tier above.

3 Sterilise all the plastic dowels before use by wiping them with clear alcohol or submerging them in boiling water. Allow to dry before use.

4 Push a dowel down into the cake until it touches the board at the base. Mark the dowel level with the surface of the sugarpaste using a food colour pen. Repeat with the other dowels in the same tier then remove them and cut them to size using a craft knife.

5 Insert the dowels back into the cake. When you have dowelled all the upper tiers (except the top one), carefully stack them, using a little softened sugarpaste or royal icing to stick them together.

TUTOR TIP

If the height of the marks on the dowels differs, cut them all to the height of the tallest mark to ensure that the stacked tiers remain level.

How to cover a polystyrene dummy

Polystyrene dummy cakes are extremely useful in modelling: I often use them to support cake-top figures as they are firmer than a real cake and you can insert barbecue skewers into them easily, rather than into a cake. They are readily available from sugarcraft suppliers (see page 256).

Polystyrene shapes have several other useful purposes in modelling: they are used as supports for figurines; can be covered with sugarpaste to make parts of a figure lighter (such as the sphere shape for the toy soldier's head on page 44); are used as a base to transport figurines on; and can be used as formers for pastillage pieces.

Edibles

Sugarpaste

Edible glue

Equipment

Round or square polystyrene dummy

Paintbrush: no. 10

Rolling pin

Cake smoothers

Pizza wheel

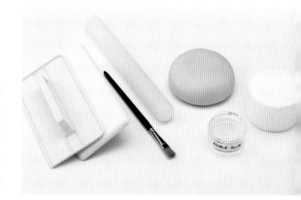

1 Brush the surface of the dummy with a thin layer of edible glue.

2 Knead the required quantity of sugarpaste until it becomes pliable. Roll out the paste on a surface dusted with icing sugar to a thickness of approximately 4mm ($^1/_8$") so it is big enough to cover the top and sides of the dummy. Lift and drape the paste gently over the top of the dummy.

 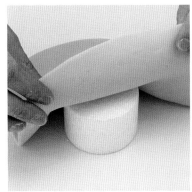

TUTOR TIP

It is a good idea to add a pinch of CMC if the paste is quite soft, especially when you are covering a square dummy, as the sharp edges may tear the paste.

3 Carefully lift the paste away from the sides of the dummy to open out any folds, then use the palms of your hands to smooth the paste down the sides of the dummy.

4 Trim the excess from around the base of the dummy with a sharp knife or pizza wheel. If you are covering a small, round dummy, place a round cutter with a slightly larger diameter over the dummy and use it to trim the excess paste from around the base and achieve a neat edge.

5 Rub over the dummy gently with a cake smoother in each hand to remove any imperfections from the paste. Allow the paste to dry for a couple of days before inserting any figurine into the top to ensure it won't sink into the paste.

 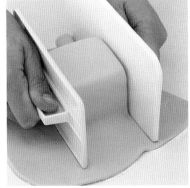

How to cover a polystyrene ball with sugarpaste

Polystyrene balls are useful when you want to create a large, round head shape that is not too heavy, especially when you are creating caricature figures where the head is larger than the body. They are also ideal when you are making large-scale pieces of work.

You will need

A polystyrene ball in the size required

A ball of modelling paste the same size

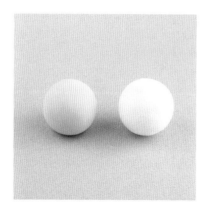

1   Place the ball of modelling paste in one hand and flatten it with the palm of your other hand.

2   Spread a little edible glue over the flattened paste with your fingertip, rubbing the surface until it is tacky.

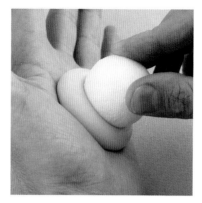

3   Press the polystyrene ball onto the tacky surface. Roll the ball between the palms of your hands in a circular motion, pushing the paste halfway up the surface of the polystyrene ball and keeping the paste an even thickness.

4   Hold the ball between the palm and thumb of one hand and push the paste around the ball with your other palm towards the exposed end.

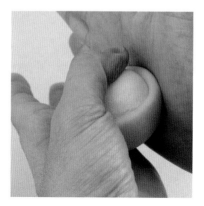
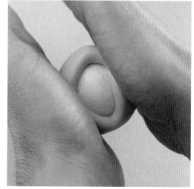

5   Keep rolling and pushing the paste up with the heels of your hands until you have covered the polystyrene ball completely.

6   Finally, roll the ball between the palms of your hands in a circular motion to get a smooth and crack-free surface.

MODELLING TIPS AND TECHNIQUES

Modelling basic shapes

Making your figurines smooth and crack-free can be difficult if you are not used to modelling. Always make sure you use the right modelling paste (see page 27) and follow these guidelines to make sure your models have a smooth, professional finish.

Ball

Take a piece of modelling paste between your fingers and thumbs and start to stretch and fold the paste to give it a soft and pliable consistency (picture A).

Hold the paste between the palms of your hands and press firmly. Simultaneously squeeze and roll the paste in circular movements in order to smooth out any cracks on the surface of the paste (picture B). Release the pressure but keep moving your hands in a circular motion until you get a smooth ball shape (picture C).

The ball is the most important basic shape to master as, when you start to model, every other shape will emerge from this first ball shape.

Teardrop

Roll a smooth ball then open out your hands as shown and roll the ball up and down to create a pointed end (picture D).

Pear shape

Roll a smooth ball and place it in the palm of one hand. Press and roll the side of your other hand up and down on one half of the ball to create a neck shape (pictures E and F).

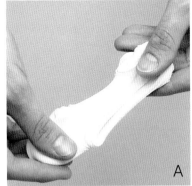
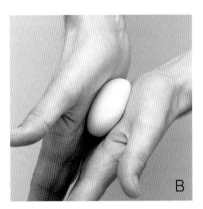

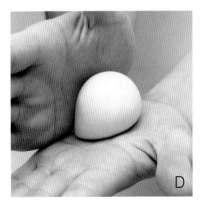

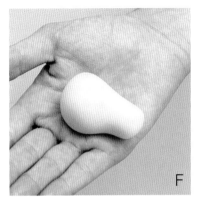

Tips for using modelling paste

- Rub a little white vegetable fat into the palms of your hands to prevent the paste from sticking to them.

- If the paste is sticky you can either knead a little extra icing sugar or a pinch of CMC in to the paste to adjust its consistency, especially when the piece needs to be strong.

- If the paste is too hard, knead in a little vegetable fat to make it pliable and stretchy again. A few drops of pre-boiled water can also be added to replenish lost moisture.

- If the paste has developed a dry outer crust, just peel it off with a sharp knife so that you can save the moist piece inside. This usually happens when the paste has not been stored properly in an airtight food-grade plastic bag.

- Keep the paste in the fridge when you are not using it, always sealed in a food-grade plastic bag. This is particularly important if you live in a hot and humid climate.

- If the paste seems too soft and doesn't hold its shape, add pinches of CMC to it until you achieve a firmer consistency.

- In extremely humid weather conditions do not use any paste or food colours that contain glycerine (also known as glycerol). Glycerine absorbs the moisture in the air and will prevent the paste from drying properly.

- If you find that the paste dries quickly whilst you are modelling, add a paste that contains glycerine, such as sugarpaste/rolled fondant which is usually used for covering cakes. The glycerine in the sugarpaste will help the paste to retain moisture for longer.

- The best way to find out how the paste works in specific weather conditions and individual cases is to use it. Trial and error will allow you to make the best decisions when using the paste, so allow plenty of time to practise.

Proportions for cute characters

When modelling characters the proportions of the figurines affect whether they look cute (larger head) or more realistic (smaller head).

If you make the head (A) roughly the same size as the torso (B) you will end up with a cute-looking character: this basic rule applies to most of the figures modelled in this book. You can vary this head:torso ratio if you want to create a specific type of figure, but the volume of both the head and the torso should be roughly the same if you want to create cute human or animal characters.

From the drawing you can see how I would create a male character with the head the same size as the torso. For a female figure, simply make the waist thinner and add breasts.

When creating a human-like character, take the modelled head or torso as a unit of measurement to help you define the length of limbs, as well as the overall height of the figure. A good height for a human-like character is five or six heads high. The legs are two-and-a-half heads long. Finally, note that the arms should fall slightly higher than the knees when they are attached.

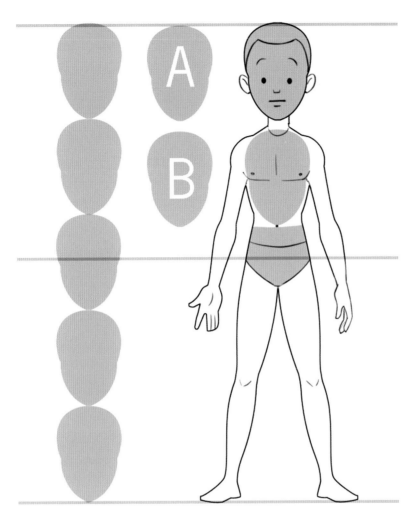

As well as experimenting with different head:torso ratios you can make the legs, arms or neck longer to stylize the character. It is important that you take these proportions as a guide only and do not feel constrained by them when creating your own figures. I would always encourage you to discover your own cute proportions for modelling and to use the ones I have suggested only as a starting point.

You can portray different ages simply by moving the eyes. Once you have made the head draw an imaginary line across the middle of the face. To make a young person place the eyes below this line and for an older character place the eyes on or above the line. As a rule the lower the eyes are from the middle line the younger the character looks; the higher they are above the line the older the character looks.

The eyebrows are part of an imaginary circle that sits around the eye: this imaginary circle can be stretched or squashed to achieve different expressions as shown below.

Finally, the height of the ears should be between the eyes and the base of the nose.

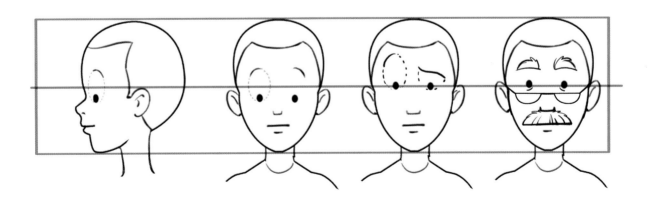

How to create different facial expressions

It is easy to achieve a range of facial expressions by simply adjusting the shape and positioning of the mouth, eyes and eyebrows, as I have demonstrated with the Illusionist and bunnies below.

Angry

For an angry expression, make the mouth slanted, opening one side very slightly. Push out the lower lip with the edge of a Dresden tool. Position the eyebrows just above the eyes, giving them an arched, angular shape. Bags under the eyes and frown lines also help to make the figure look angry.

Confused

For a confused expression, make the mouth a crescent shape so the corners of the mouth are turned down. Open the mouth slightly and push out the lower lip with edge of the Dresden tool. Position the eyebrows higher up the forehead and make sure they are slanted downwards.

Shocked/surprised

If you want to create a shocked or surprised look, use the handle of a paintbrush or a barbecue skewer to open up the mouth into an elongated 'O' shape. Position the eyebrows at the top of the forehead and make the eyes very wide.

Happy

To make your figure look happy, create a smile by pushing the edge of a round cutter into the face. To open up the mouth, push the paste down with the rounded side of a Dresden tool. Use a ball tool to make dimples then add teeth, if desired. Add the eyes, either open or closed. The eyebrows should be raised and sit high up the forehead.

How to make arms and hands

Edibles

Modelling paste (see projects for specific amounts)

Equipment

Craft knife

SK Cutting Tool (optional)

Arms

1   Roll some skin-coloured modelling paste into a sausage. Continue to roll and taper the sausage towards one end, using the side of your hand to create the wrist. Make sure to leave a piece of paste at the end for the hand.

2   Use your index finger to flatten the paste slightly at the end of the arm into a paddle shape. Cut a V-shape into one side of the paste with a craft knife to bring out the thumb.

3   Roll your index finger gently across the middle of the sausage to separate the upper arm and forearm. If you need to bend the arm, make an indent at the inner elbow and wrist with a plastic cutting tool: this will help you move the arm to the required angle. Bend the arm into position, then use your index fingers to push the paste towards the point of the elbow to help sharpen it.

Hands

1   To make a hand which you can attach to the end of a sleeve, roll some skin-coloured modelling paste into a bowling pin shape. Press the larger end into a paddle shape with your index finger and bring out the thumb as shown in the step picture.

2   To define the fingers, push the edge of a cutting tool into the end of the hand, starting with a mark in the middle of the hand, then add another line on each side.

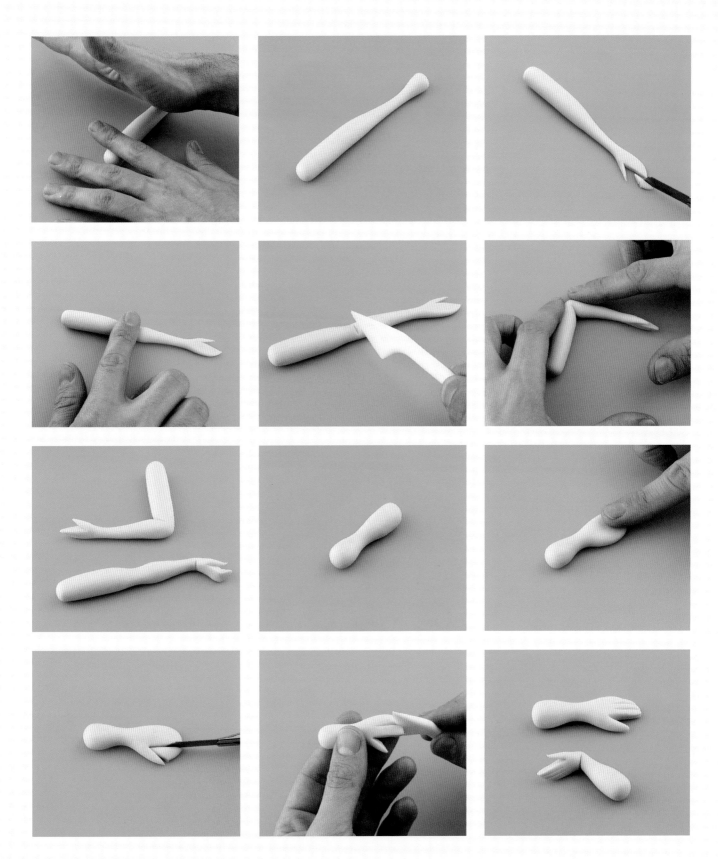

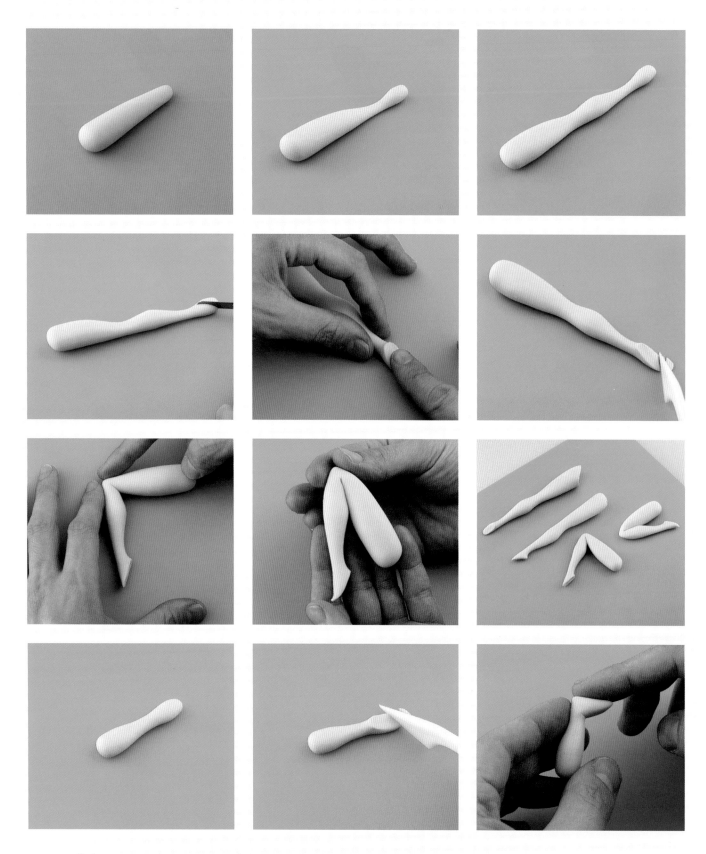

How to make legs and feet

Edibles

Modelling paste (see projects for specific amounts)

Equipment

Craft knife

SK Cutting Tool (optional)

Legs

1 Roll a ball of skin-coloured modelling paste into a sausage that tapers towards one end.

2 Press and roll the paste with the side of your hand just above the tapered end of the sausage to define the ankle. Make sure to leave a piece of paste at the end for the foot.

3 Press and roll the paste again with the side of your hand in the middle of the leg to separate the thigh from the calf.

4 Place the leg on its side and trim the foot at an angle using a craft knife.

5 Gently hold the ankle between your fingers, then use your index finger on the other hand to push the paste up towards the calf and create the heel. If the foot starts to widen, pinch the sides slightly to make it narrower. Trim the end of the foot at an angle with a cutting tool to make a line for the toes.

6 If you need to bend the leg, make an indent in the back of the knee with a cutting tool: this mark will help you move the leg to the required angle. Bend the leg into position, then use your index fingers to push the paste towards the kneecap to help sharpen the joint.

Feet

1 To make a foot which you can attach to the end of a pair of trousers, start off with a bowling pin shape and follow step 5 for the legs above.

2 If you need to bend the foot, mark an indentation at the ankle with a plastic cutting tool and bend forward. Squeeze the paste between your index fingers to help define the heel shape.

How to make ears

I prefer to insert the ears into the head, rather than just gluing them to the sides of the head, as this means that they are more secure and less likely to fall off.

Edibles

Small amount of modelling paste

Equipment

Paintbrush/barbecue skewer

Ball tool

1 Use the handle of a paintbrush or a skewer to make a hole in each side of the head, following the eye line as a guide. Brush a little edible glue in each hole.

2 Roll two small pinches of skin-coloured sugarpaste into teardrop shapes and stick the pointed ends into the sockets.

3 Pinch the teardrops between your thumb and index finger to flatten them down slightly, then push a ball tool into the middle of each ear to shape them.

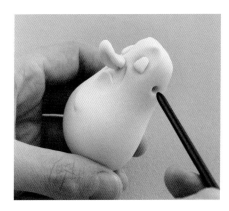
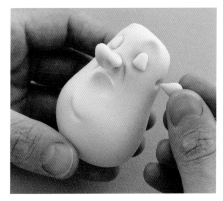
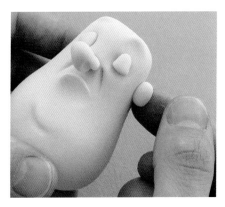
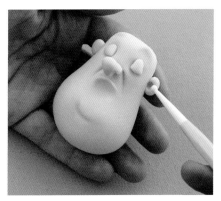

Use of colour

I have used SK Professional Paste Food Colours to create all of the projects in this book as their range covers the complete colour wheel. If you are not familiar with the range or you are using a different brand you can use the list below to find out how to mix generic colours to achieve your desired colour.

SK Colours	Generic Colours	SK Colours	Generic Colours
Dark Forest	Green + a touch of red or orange + a touch of blue or black	Poppy	Red + a touch of yellow or orange
Leaf Green	Yellow + a touch of green + a touch of orange	Poinsettia	Red + a touch of blue or violet
Holly/Ivy	Green + a touch of red or orange	Fuchsia	Pink + a touch of violet
Vine	Green + a touch of yellow	Rose	Pink
Sunny Lime	Yellow + a touch of green	Cyclamen	Red + a touch of lilac or violet
Cactus	Green + a touch of blue	Plum, Thrift, Violet	Violet
Fern	Green + yellow	Lilac	Lilac
Yucca	Dark green	Bordeaux	Burgundy
Mint	Green	Gentian	Blue
Olive	Green + a touch of orange	Hyacinth	Dark blue
Daffodil	Yellow	Hydrangea/Bluegrass	Blue + a touch of green
Sunflower	Yellow + a touch of orange	Bluebell, Wisteria	Blue + a touch of violet
Marigold	Yellow + a touch of red	Teddy Bear Brown	Brown + a touch of yellow
Berberis	Orange	Chestnut	Brown
Nasturium	Orange + a touch of red	Bulrush	Dark brown
Terracotta	Red + a touch of green or brown	Jet Black	Black
		Cream	White + a touch of yellow + a touch of brown
		Edelweiss	White

How to make different skin tones

For a lighter skin tone, I usually colour White SFP with Teddy Bear Brown or, depending on the character, I also mix in a touch of Berberis/Nasturtium, Pink/Fuchsia or Poppy paste food colours. These colours bring warmth to the skin tone and allow you to create the ideal colour for your figure. I also try to balance the colour of the skin tone with the colour palette used in the rest of the project.

For a mid-tone skin colour, I would add a touch of Poppy and a touch of Sunflower to White SFP.

For a darker skin tone, I tend to colour White SFP with Warm Brown paste food colour or I add a touch of Poppy as well to achieve a richer tone. Depending on the figure you want to create, you could alternatively use dark brown food colour and a touch of green to create a slightly different, darker tone.

Guidelines for colouring modelling paste, pastillage and royal icing can be found on pages 26 to 32.

DARK FOREST LEAF GREEN HOLLY/IVY VINE SUNNY LIME CACTUS

FERN YUCCA MINT OLIVE DAFFODIL SUNFLOWER

MARIGOLD BERBERIS NASTURTIUM TERRACOTTA POPPY POINSETTIA

FUCHSIA ROSE CYCLAMEN PLUM THRIFT VIOLET

LILAC BORDEAUX GENTIAN HYACINTH HYDRANGEA BLUEGRASS

BLUEBELL WISTERIA TEDDY BEAR BROWN CHESTNUT BULRUSH JET BLACK

Painting and colouring techniques

The different effects that can be created using edible colours are endless. A few of the techniques that I've used in this book are described here: these can be used on virtually any sugar piece to really bring it to life.

Airbrushing

If you have an airbrush you need to use liquid food colours with it. If the colour is too bright, just add a few drops of cooled, boiled water to dilute it. Place the piece to be sprayed over a spare piece of paper and airbrush from a distance to prevent patchiness. Apply a thin layer of colour at a time until you achieve the shade you require. Always start with soft colours and add more layers to build up darker colours. If you do not have an airbrush, similar subtle effects can be created by dusting colour onto the surface of your work (see below).

Splashing technique

I love using this technique as you don't need to have an airbrush. Dilute some liquid or paste food colour with several drops of cooled, boiled water in a saucer. To create the 'splash' effect, dip a new, unused toothbrush into the diluted food colour and flick the bristles with your thumb in order to splash colour all over the piece. Do not overload the toothbrush otherwise it won't colour the piece evenly. When applying the colour, position the toothbrush a few centimetres away from the object and push the bristles backwards using your thumb. This technique will give your piece more texture and you can achieve different effects by altering the consistency of the food colour. A more watery colour will result in larger, heavier droplets; a thicker consistency will create finer droplets.

Metallic colours

Tip some metallic food colour into a saucer. Add a few drops of clear alcohol to make the consistency you need for painting and brush evenly over the piece of work. To achieve an even finish you may need to apply more than one layer of metallic paint, allowing each layer to dry fully before applying the next one. The alcohol will evaporate quickly so keep adding it as needed.

Dusting

Dip a dry, soft, round paintbrush into the dust food colour and rub the bristles on a piece of kitchen paper to remove any excess dust. Removing this excess colour will give you more control when you apply the dust to the sugar surface. I also find it useful to mix the dust with a little cornflour to ensure that the colour covers the sugar surface evenly. I use this technique when dusting figures' cheeks with Pastel Pink dust food colour.

Transporting sugar figurines

Once you have made your sugar models you need to make sure you transport them safely to the venue where the cake will be served. These hints should help you avoid damaging your work in transit, especially if you are travelling long distances.

• Place the figurine, which must be fully dry, in a cake box which has a piece of polystyrene or foam in the bottom. You can also stick several cocktail sticks into the polystyrene around the figurine to stop it rolling about.

• Depending on the type of figure you are transporting you can also fill in the spaces between the polystyrene base and the figure itself with soft material such as pieces of polystyrene or foam pad. This should reduce the risk of breakages, especially of more fragile pieces such as necks and arms. Look at the shape and dimensions of the figurine to see how you can support the whole structure.

• Once you have arrived at your destination, secure the figurine to the cake, pastillage base or dummy cake support with a dot of ready-made stiff-peak royal icing or softened paste. If the figurine is slim and tall do not remove the skewer that supports the whole structure. Make sure that the recipient is aware of any skewers or other inedible

items you have used to support your figures so that they can be removed safely before the cake is served.

• It is also advisable to use a dummy cake to support slender figures rather than a real cake so that the skewer remains stable throughout the whole event. Before serving the cake, the dummy cake and the figurine should be removed as one piece.

• Always make spares of any pieces that you think are likely to get damaged, such as little flowers or other small, fragile objects, and take them with you. I usually take spare pieces of paste just in case I have to fix something to the piece upon arrival.

• All these hints apply to sugar characters that are fragile and more likely to break during transportation. If you don't have to take the cake anywhere or if you are making more robust figurines you may not have to take any precautions, simply place them onto the cake when they are finished.

MONTY THE SHEEPDOG

This adorable Old English sheepdog puppy is the perfect cake for anyone who has their own four-legged friend. He can be personalised to suit the recipient by changing the letter on the nametag and changing the colour of the fur.

EDIBLES

15cm (6") round sponge, layered and filled

200g (7oz) sponge cake mix, baked in a condensed milk tin lined with baking parchment

SK Sugarpaste (rolled fondant):

  400g (14oz) baby blue (Bridal White sugarpaste + Hyacinth)

  500g (1lb 1¾oz) Bridal White

  20g (¾oz) blue-green (Bridal White sugarpaste + Bluegrass)

  100g (3½oz) grey (Bridal White sugarpaste + a pinch of Tuxedo Black sugarpaste)

  20g (¾oz) light blue (Bridal White sugarpaste + Hydrangea)

  350g (12¼oz) light turquoise (Bridal White sugarpaste + touch of Gentian)

  10g (¼oz) ruby (Bridal White sugarpaste + Cyclamen)

  30g (1oz) Tuxedo Black

SK Professional Paste Food Colours: Bluegrass, Cyclamen (ruby), Gentian (ice blue), Hyacinth, Hydrangea

SK Professional Dust Food Colour: Edelweiss (white)

SK Designer Pastel Dust Food Colour: Pastel Pink

SK Designer Metallic Lustre Dust Food Colour: Silver

SK Professional Liquid Food Colour: Hyacinth

SK Instant Mix Royal Icing:

  50g (1¾oz) white (uncoloured)

  100g (3½oz) light turquoise (touch of Gentian)

SK CMC Gum

EQUIPMENT

Basic equipment (see pages 6 to 7)

23cm (9") square cake drum (board)

Plastic disposable piping bags

Piping nozzles: nos. 5, 7

20cm (7¾") spare cake card, dusted with icing sugar

Pizza wheel

Round cutters: 2cm, 3cm (¾", 1⅛")

Square cutters: 1.5cm, 2cm (⅝", ¾")

New vegetable brush

92cm x 1cm width (37" x ⅜") satin ribbon: pale blue

Templates (see page 246)

CAKE DRUM

1 Roll out 300g (10½oz) of baby blue sugarpaste and cover the square cake drum (see page 41). Use the edge of a clean ruler to emboss two lines across the board and two lines down the board to divide it into 7.5cm (3") square tiles. Mix some Hyacinth liquid food colour with a few drops of cooled, boiled water then dip a toothbrush into the mixture and use it to flick the colour randomly over the board (see page 54). Repeat the same technique using Edelweiss dust food colour diluted in cooled, boiled water. Trim the board with a pale blue ribbon and set aside to dry.

TUTOR TIP

I prefer to use dust food colour diluted in a few drops of cooled, boiled water rather than paste food colour, as the solution tends to dry quicker. I also recommend that you wear gloves when using this technique to avoid staining your hands.

BASKET

2 Place the basket top template on the top of the 15cm (6") round cake and trim it to size using a serrated knife. Position the basket base template on the cake and trim the cake sides

TUTOR TIP

Instead of baking a cake for the basket, you could use crisped rice cereal mix instead and mould it into shape (see page 19).

at an angle to create an upside-down basket shape. Crumb-coat the cake and leave to chill in the fridge for a couple of hours.

3 Roll out some baby blue sugarpaste to 2mm (1/16") thick, fold it over a rolling pin and lay it over the 20cm (7¾") cake card which should be lightly dusted with icing sugar. Place the basket cake onto the sugarpaste with the larger side down and trim around the edge of the cake with a pizza wheel.

4 Roll out some light turquoise sugarpaste to 2mm (1/16") thick and cover the rest of the cake. Trim the excess paste from around the base of the cake with a pizza wheel and allow the paste to dry.

5 Tape a cellophane sheet onto a large cake card and place the coated cake onto it so the basket shape is still upside down. Make up some royal icing to firm-peak consistency, leave half white and colour the other half with a touch of Gentian to make a light turquoise colour. Fit one piping bag with a no. 5 nozzle and fill it with the white icing. Fit another bag with a no. 7 nozzle and fill it with the light turquoise icing.

TUTOR TIP

The cellophane will stop the icing from sticking to the board and, once the icing has dried, you can easily peel the cellophane sheet from the cake without tearing the piped lines.

6 Pipe a vertical line from the top edge to the bottom edge of the cake with the white royal icing. Use the light turquoise royal icing to pipe a short

horizontal line across the top of the vertical white line, then leave a gap that is the same thickness as the first line. Continue down the side of the cake, gradually increasing the length of each horizontal line.

7 Pipe another vertical line next to the first, then start to pipe down the side of the cake with the blue icing in the same way as before, fitting each blue line in the gaps to create a basket weave effect. Continue all the way around the cake to create the basket.

8 Roll out some light turquoise sugarpaste, cut out an oval shape using the basket base template as a guide and place it onto the cake. Once the basket is flipped over, this layer of sugarpaste will act as a cushion and stop the piped lines touching the work surface. When the icing has dried, remove the tape from the cellophane sheet, place another cake card on top of the basket and flip the cake over. Gently peel away the acetate sheet.

9 Roll two thin sausages of light turquoise sugarpaste that are the same length as the rim of the basket. Mark lines along each sausage with the sharp edge of a Dresden tool to add texture, then twist the two sausages together to create a rope and secure around the top of the cake with edible glue.

10 To make the handles, knead some light turquoise sugarpaste with a pinch of CMC to strengthen the paste. Roll two long, thin sausages and twist them together as before. Cut the rope in half, bend each section around a 3cm (1⅛") round cutter to curve the handles and leave them to dry.

SHEEPDOG

Body

11 Trim the cylinder-shaped cake to make it approximately 12.5cm tall x 6cm diameter (5" x 2³⁄₈"). Shape the top into a dome, then cut the cake into four layers and fill with ganache or buttercream (see page 34). Crumb-coat the cake and leave to chill for an hour in the fridge.

TUTOR TIP

Alternatively, you could model the same shape out of crisped rice cereal mix if you'd prefer.

12 To cover the cake, thinly roll out a wide strip of Bridal White sugarpaste that is approximately 23cm long x 16cm wide (9" x 6½"). Place the cake on its side at one end and roll it along the paste until the sides are completely covered. Trim the excess paste at the join and stand the cake upright. Gather the paste at the top and trim away any excess with a pair of scissors. Smooth down the paste with the palm of your hand and allow to firm up.

13 Roll approximately 40g (1½oz) of Bridal White sugarpaste into a sausage and split it in half. Model each piece into a flattened teardrop shape, then attach them around either side of the bottom of the cylinder. Position them so the pointed end is facing backwards at an angle. These will act as fillers to give shape to the legs.

14 Roll out 100g (3½oz) of grey sugarpaste to 3mm (¹⁄₈") thick and cut around the template for the grey strip of hair. Wrap it around the base

of the body so both ends meet at the front and cover the legs. Trim away any excess paste if necessary. Repeat with 100g (3½oz) of Bridal White sugarpaste and the template for the white hair. Wrap the paste around the top of the body so it sits above the grey paste, then trim any excess paste from the front.

Front legs

15 Roll some Bridal White sugarpaste into a thick sausage and split it in half. Narrow each sausage towards one end, leaving a thicker piece of paste at the end for the paw. Mark a line just before the thicker end with the edge of a Dresden tool and bend the paw to 90°. Repeat for the second leg, then secure them to the front of the body and mark three lines down each paw with the blade of a knife. Trim the top of the legs into a V-shape where the fur on the chest will fit later.

Head

16 To make the head, roll approximately 100g (3½oz) of Bridal White sugarpaste into a ball and flatten the top to create a dome shape. Secure to the front of the top of the cylinder.

17 Push a ball tool into the paste to open up the mouth and bring out the lower lip at the same time. Press the blunt side of a 2cm (¾") round cutter above the mouth to make a smile, then push a small ball tool into each corner of the mouth to make dimples. Run your finger over the paste to soften any marks left by the ball tool and define the cheeks. Roll out a small piece of ruby sugarpaste very thinly, cut out the shape of the mouth using a cutting wheel and secure it inside the mouth.

18 For the muzzle, roll a small piece of Bridal White sugarpaste into an oval shape and attach it above the mouth with a little edible glue. Draw a line down the centre of the muzzle with a Dresden tool. Roll a small piece of Tuxedo Black sugarpaste into a teardrop shape and stick it to the muzzle with the pointed end facing downwards. Pinch the nose between your fingers slightly and open up the nostrils with a small ball tool.

19 Mix some Bridal White and ruby sugarpaste to make a light pink colour for the tongue, then roll the paste into an oval and flatten it slightly. Stick it into the bottom of the mouth and mark a line down the middle. Brush the cheeks with Pastel Pink dust food colour using a soft paintbrush.

20 For the chest, roll some Bridal White sugarpaste into a sausage with pointed ends and flatten one side against the work surface. Attach it between the head and the legs to fill out the chest area, then add texture across the chest with the edge of a Dresden tool and blend in the joins.

21 Roll two long teardrops of grey sugarpaste, flatten them slightly and attach them to either side of the head for the ears.

22 For the floppy hair on the head, roll some Bridal White sugarpaste into several different-sized teardrops and flatten them down with the palm of your hand. Make a few snips into the ends of the paste with a pair of scissors to create loose strands. Mark lines down the paste with the edge of the Dresden tool to add texture and attach them over the head with edible glue.

23 Roll several smaller sausages of Bridal White sugarpaste

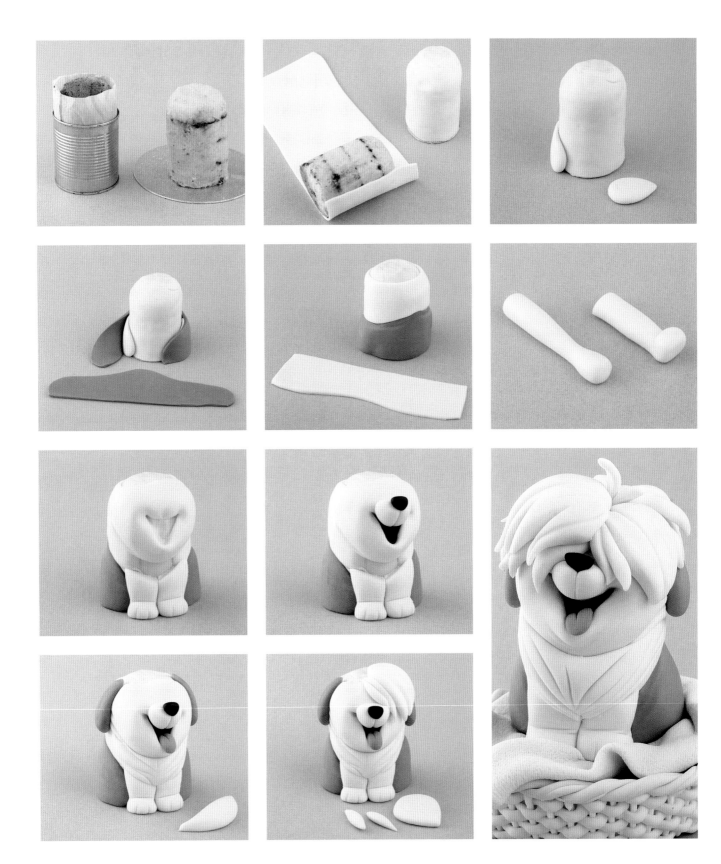

and taper the ends to create the loose strands of hair at the front. Secure them to the front of the head so they come down over the muzzle and cover the eye line.

24 Knead a small piece of Bridal White sugarpaste with a generous pinch of CMC and roll three long teardrop shapes for the loose strands of hair sticking up on top of the head. Flatten them down a little and leave them to dry on their side in a slightly curved position. Once they have firmed up, secure them upright to the top of the head.

Tail

25 Roll 20g (¾oz) of Bridal White sugarpaste into a ball and make a smaller ball from some grey sugarpaste. Press the two balls together and roll them in your palms to merge the two colours into one ball. Roll the ball into an elongated pear shape, tapering the wider end into a point. Mark lines along the paste to add texture then let the paste firm up.

TAG

26 Knead a small piece of Bridal White sugarpaste with a generous pinch of CMC and roll it out to 2mm (1/16") thick. Cut out a 2cm (¾") square with a cutter, then emboss a smaller square shape in the centre using a 1.5cm (5/8") cutter. Turn the tag 45° so it is a diamond shape. Make a hole in the top corner with the tip of a barbecue skewer or a small CelStick. Thread a thin sausage of Bridal White sugarpaste through the hole to make a loop.

27 Fill a small paper piping bag with uncoloured royal icing, snip off the very tip of the bag and pipe the letter of your choice onto the tag. Once the tag has dried, use a paintbrush to paint it with Silver lustre dust food colour diluted with a few drops of clear alcohol.

BALLS

28 Roll 15g (½oz) of blue-green sugarpaste and 15g (½oz) of light blue sugarpaste into balls and mark a line around the middle of each one with the edge of a Dresden tool. Insert a barbecue skewer into each ball and leave them to firm in a piece of polystyrene so they keep their shape.

ASSEMBLY

29 Position the basket on the cake drum and secure in place with a dot of royal icing. Attach the handles to each side of the basket with dots of light turquoise royal icing.

30 For the blanket, roll out 150g (5¼oz) of light turquoise sugarpaste to 3mm (1/8") thick and cut out a rectangle. Press the bristles of a new vegetable brush all over the paste to give it texture, then fold the edges of the paste under to create a hem. Arrange the blanket loosely on the basket and position the dog on top while the paste is still soft. Attach the tail to the basket with a touch of softened grey sugarpaste.

31 Secure one of the balls on the basket and the other to the board with dots of royal icing. Roll a very thin sausage of blue-green sugarpaste and attach it around the join between the head and the chest. Stick the tag to the dog's chest with a dot of royal icing.

TUTOR TIP

If you are making this cake for someone you know, pipe their initial onto the dog tag for an extra special touch.

DOG TAG BISCUITS

Pipe the run-out initials on a piece of cellophane following the instructions on page 30 and leave to dry.

Bake 35 5cm (2") square chocolate biscuits following the recipe on page 18.

Fit a paper piping bag with a no. 1 nozzle, fill with medium-consistency white royal icing and pipe an outline around each of the biscuits. Let down some of the icing to run-out consistency and use the runny icing and a no. 2 nozzle to flood inside the outline (see page 30). Let the icing dry.

Pipe a square border around the biscuit just inside the original outline, using the same medium-consistency icing and a no. 1 nozzle. Turn the biscuit at a 45° angle to make a diamond shape, then secure a piped initial in the centre with royal icing.

Once dry, mix some Silver lustre dust with clear alcohol and paint over the surface of the biscuit.

BUON APPETITO!

Crisped rice cereal mix is ideal for modelling this rather portly chef, allowing the character to be large yet lightweight. You can customise this figurine by changing the local cuisine he is serving up; pasta is the dish of the day for this proud Italian chef.

EDIBLES

16.5cm round x 7cm deep (6½" x 2¾") cake, filled and crumb-coated (see page 34)

SK Sugarpaste (rolled fondant):

  1kg (2lb 3¼oz) Bridal White

  200g (7oz) pale green (Bridal White + touch of Dark Forest)

SK Sugar Florist Paste (SFP, gum paste):

  50g (1¾oz) Black

  100g (3½oz) dark blue (Bluebell SFP + pinch of Black SFP)

  50g (1¾oz) grey (White SFP + touch of Blackberry)

  20g (¾oz) pale yellow (White SFP + touch of Marigold)

  30g (1oz) salmon pink (White SFP + touch of Berberis)

  150g (5¼oz) skin tone (White SFP + touch of Teddy Bear Brown + touch of Pink)

  300g (10½oz) White

SK Professional Paste Food Colours: Berberis, Blackberry (black), Marigold (tangerine), Teddy Bear Brown

SK Designer Paste Food Colour: Dark Forest

SK Quality Food Colour (QFC) Paste: Pink

SK Instant Mix Pastillage:

  150g (5¼oz) white (uncoloured)

  200g (7oz) pale green (touch of Dark Forest)

SK Professional Dust Food Colours: Nasturtium (peach), Poinsettia (Christmas red)

SK Designer Pastel Dust Food Colour: Pale Peach

SK Designer Metallic Lustre Dust Food Colour: Silver

SK Professional Liquid Food Colour: Blackberry (Black)

SK Professional Food Colour Pen: Black

Half quantity of crisped rice cereal mix (see page 19)

SK CMC Gum

EQUIPMENT

Basic equipment (see pages 6 to 7)

23cm (9") round cake drum (board)

16.5cm (6½") round cake card

7cm round x 6cm deep (2¾" x 2³/₈") polystyrene dummy

Spare polystyrene dummy

Professional chocolate half-shell mould: 10cm (4") long (optional)

Stanley knife

Round cutters: 2cm, 3.5cm, 4.5cm, 5.5cm, 6.5cm, 7cm (¾", 1³/₈", 1¾", 2¼", 2½", 2¾")

New vegetable brush

73cm x 15mm width (29" x ⁵/₈") satin ribbon: black

Templates (see page 247)

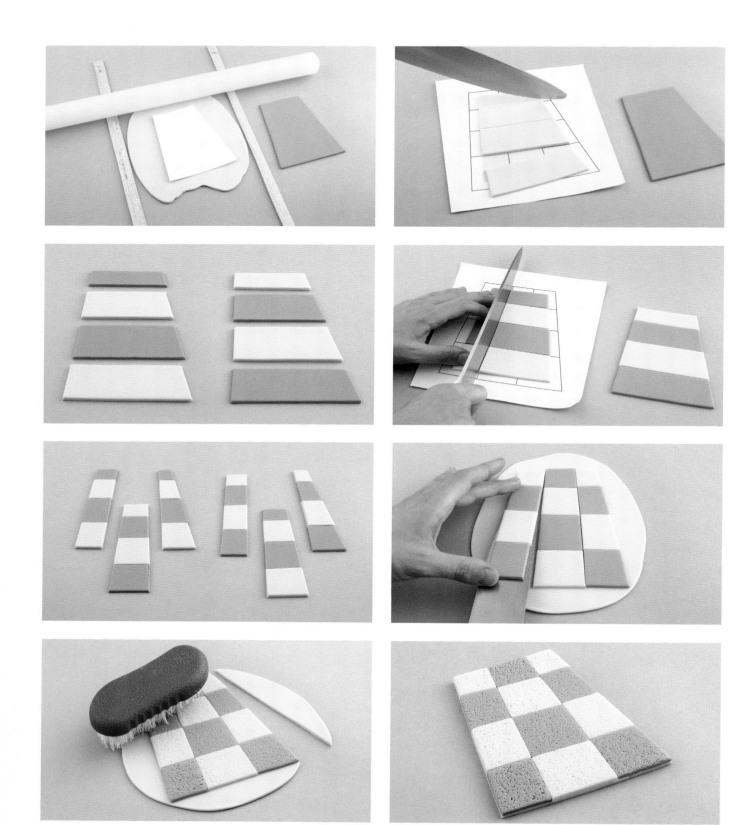

CHEQUERED FLOOR

1 Mix 100g (3½oz) of white pastillage with 100g (3½oz) of White SFP to make a strong paste. Split the paste into two equal pieces, then colour one half with a touch of Dark Forest paste food colour and the other half with more Dark Forest colour to achieve a darker shade of green.

2 Roll out each half to 4mm (³/₁₆") thick on a surface lightly dusted with cornflour. Cut out the outline of the floor from each piece following the template provided. Place each floor piece onto the grid provided and cut across the horizontal lines. Once you have cut them both into strips, swap two strips of one colour with the other. Place each floor piece over the grid again and cut along the vertical lines. Swap the central strip of one floor with the central strip of the other.

3 For the backing, roll out the leftover paste to 3mm (¹/₈") thick and make it slightly bigger than the size of the floor. Brush the top of the paste with edible glue and lift the floor strips onto the paste using a spatula or a palette knife, making sure to keep the pattern the same. Press a vegetable brush into the paste to give it some texture, if desired. Trim the sides with a sharp knife for a neat, clean finish and allow to dry completely.

4 Roll out 200g (7oz) of the paler green pastillage on a surface lightly dusted with cornflour to approximately

1cm (³/₈") thick. Cut out the base shape using the template provided and allow to dry overnight.

5 Once the pieces are completely dry, secure the floor on top of the base with some softened pastillage.

CHEF

Torso

6 Make up half a quantity of the crisped rice cereal mix following the recipe on page 19.

7 Lightly grease a 10cm (4") long half-shell mould and fill it at least 2cm (¾") over the rim to make the chef's prominent belly. Press on the mix to flatten it down then release the shape from the mould. Trim straight across the bottom with a sharp knife, making the torso approximately the same shape as the template provided.

TUTOR TIP

If you don't have a half-shell mould, you can shape the torso by hand. Simply start off with a ball of crisped rice cereal mix and slowly mould it into the shape of the template provided, pressing the mix on the work surface to achieve a flat back and a rounded top.

8 Knead 250g (8¾oz) of Bridal White sugarpaste with a generous pinch of CMC, roll it out to 4mm (³/₁₆") thick and slightly larger than the torso template. Brush the paste with edible glue and press the back of the torso onto it. Trim away any excess paste with a cutting wheel.

TUTOR TIP

When making an irregular chequered floor using this method, you will end up with two chequered pieces. It is a good idea to keep the second piece as a spare in case the first one breaks.

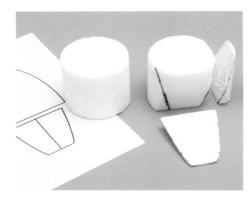

9 Roll out the leftover paste to the same thickness and drape it over the top. Smooth out the paste with the palm of your hand and neatly trim any excess from around the base. Set aside to dry.

Legs

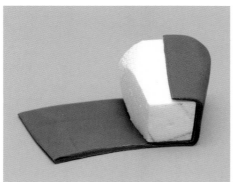

10 Use the template to mark out the trapezium shape of the legs on the 7cm x 6cm (2¾" x 2⅜") cylindrical polystyrene dummy. Carve the dummy into shape with a Stanley knife following the marks.

TUTOR TIP

The template provided is only to be used as a guide as you might need to adjust the size and shape of the legs according to the size of the torso you have made.

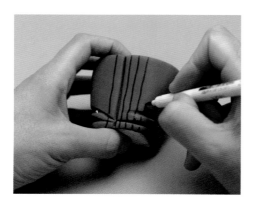

11 Roll out the dark blue SFP to 5mm (¼") thick. Cut out a strip of paste to cover the legs following the template provided. Brush the paste with edible glue and wrap it around the legs so the ends meet at the back. Trim any excess paste with a knife to neaten the join. Use the length of a skewer to indent a central vertical line down the back and front to divide the legs. Draw a few creases around the bottom of the trousers using the back of a cutting tool and allow to firm up.

TUTOR TIP

Alternatively, you can model the legs from crisped rice cereal mix if you'd prefer to make the whole figurine from edible materials.

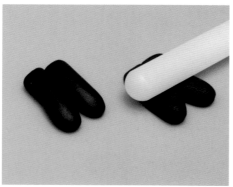

12 Draw vertical lines down the trousers with a Black food colour pen and allow to dry completely.

Shoes

13 Roll some Black SFP into a wide sausage and cut it in half for the shoes, making sure they are in proportion to the base of the legs. Place the pieces side by side and stick them together with edible glue. Press a small rolling pin into the top of the shoes at the back to give shape and create a small groove for the legs to sit in. Use a Dresden tool to mark a sole line around the bottom of each shoe. Brush over the groove with a little edible glue and press the legs into it so they sit comfortably on the shoes. Leave to dry completely.

14 Insert two barbecue skewers into the shoes and up through the legs, leaving a piece protruding from the bottom. Spread a little softened pastillage over the base of the shoes and push the skewers down into the chequered floor and through the pastillage base.

TUTOR TIP

If the floor and pastillage base are too hard to pierce with a skewer, use a corkscrew or the tip of a pair of scissors to create holes to insert the skewers through.

Head

15 Roll 80g (2¾oz) of skin tone SFP into a pear shape that is slightly elongated at the top to match the size of the template provided. Push a ball tool into the upper half of the head to open up the eye sockets. Gently run your fingertip over the edges to smooth them down slightly.

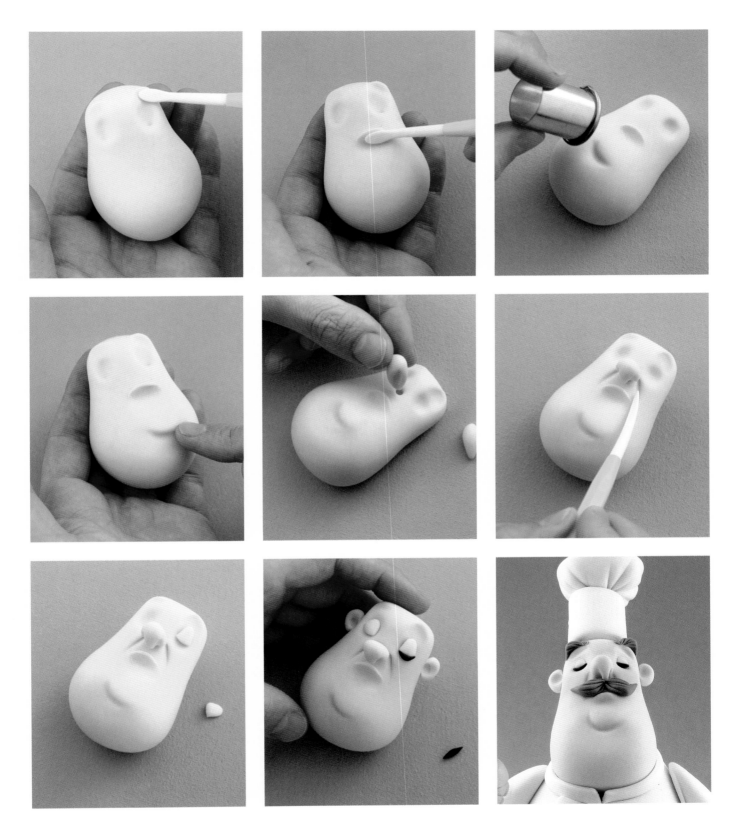

Push the rounded side of the Dresden tool into the paste above the eyes to bring out the eyebrows.

16 Using a Dresden tool, stroke the paste gently upwards to bring out the lower lip. Mark on the chin using the blunt end of a 2cm (¾") round cutter. Gently run your finger underneath the mark to push down the paste and define the chin.

17 Roll a piece of skin tone SFP into a small teardrop shape and push the handle of a paintbrush lengthways into it to open up the nostrils. Make a hole just below the eyes with the tip of a barbecue skewer, insert the smaller end of the nose into it and secure with a little edible glue. Mark slightly curved expression lines on either side of the nose using the edge of a Dresden tool.

18 For the closed eyelids, roll two tiny ovals of skin tone SFP, flatten them down slightly and trim one end with a round cutter. Secure inside the eye sockets with edible glue. Roll two tiny sausages of Black SFP with tapered ends and attach them just underneath the base of the eyelids.

19 Make and attach the ears as explained on page 51. Allow the head to firm up enough to handle.

20 Mix Pale Peach dust food colour with a little cornflour and use a soft brush to dust it over the cheeks.

Make and attach the ears as explained on page 51.

TUTOR TIP

Simply follow the diagram of the head to help you position the facial details. Note how all the facial features fall on the upper half of the face to accentuate the chef's double chin.

Hat

21 Roll some White SFP into a sausage that is approximately 3cm (1⅛") long and trim both ends straight to create a cylinder. Allow to firm up.

22 Roll a large teardrop of White SFP and secure it on top of the cylinder with edible glue. Draw crease lines from the bottom to the top of the teardrop using a Dresden tool.

Tray

23 Roll out some white pastillage to 3mm (⅛") thick on a surface lightly dusted with cornflour and cut out a 7cm (2¾") circle with a round cutter. Emboss an inner circle with the blunt side of a 6.5cm (2½") round cutter and set aside to dry.

24 Dilute some Silver lustre dust food colour with a few drops of clear alcohol and paint the tray with the mixture. Add a touch of Blackberry liquid food colour to the mixture and apply a second coat to give the tray some depth.

Dish

25 Roll out a small piece of white pastillage to 2mm (¹/₁₆") thick on a surface lightly dusted with cornflour. Cut out with a 5.5cm (2¼") round cutter, then place the circle onto a 4.5cm (1¾") round cutter and push in the centre with your finger to make it concave. Set aside to dry.

Assembly

26 Gently push the torso down through the two skewers

protruding from the legs and secure in place with softened pastillage.

27 Roll out 100g (3½oz) of White SFP to 3mm (⅛") thick and cut out the jacket shape using the template provided. Brush the torso with edible glue, then wrap the jacket around the body from the back, bringing the ends round to the front so they sit to one side and overlap slightly.

TUTOR TIP

The template provided is only to be used as a guide: you may need to adjust the size and shape of the jacket to fit the torso you have made.

28 Use the handle of a paintbrush to mark a faint line around the waist where the apron string will be attached later. Gently gather the paste around the bottom and sides of the jacket to give it some movement. Use a 3.5cm (1⅜") round cutter to cut a hole from the paste at the top of the jacket slightly towards the front of the body. Add creases down the sides with the handle of a paintbrush.

29 For the buttons, roll six tiny pieces of White SFP into teardrops. Use the tip of a barbecue skewer to make six small holes down the front of the jacket in two rows of three. Stick the buttons into the holes with a little edible glue.

30 Insert a skewer into the top of the torso and gently push the head down onto it, positioning the head so it is tilted backwards slightly. Secure in place with a little edible glue.

31 For the collar, cut out a very thin strip of White SFP and cut the

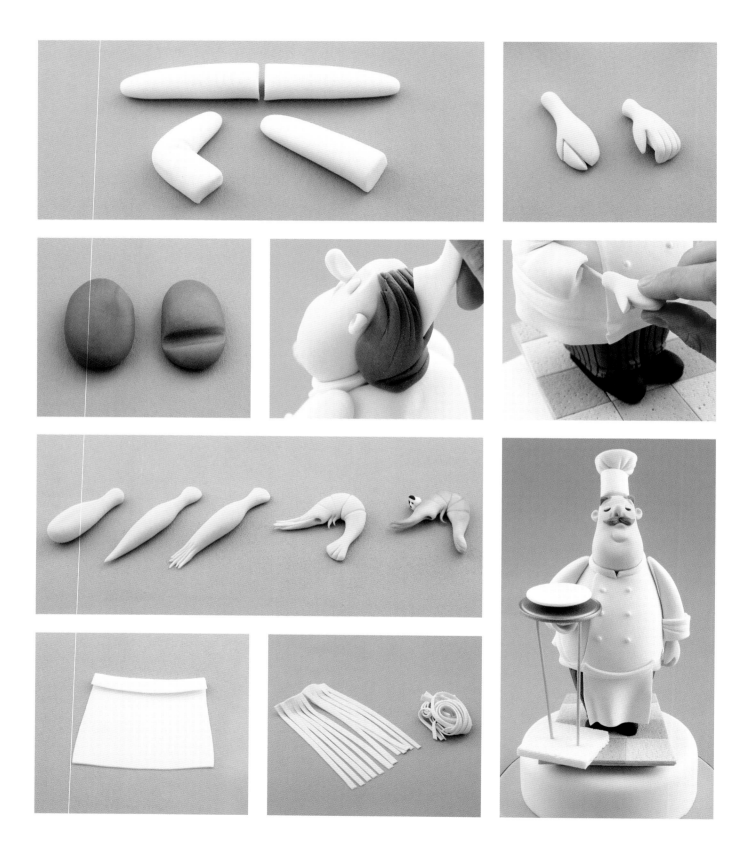

ends at a slight angle. Secure it around the base of the head so that the ends come together at the front.

Arms

32 Roll 80g (2¾oz) of White SFP into a thick sausage that tapers slightly at either end and cut it in half. The length of the arms should be approximately the same as the distance from the neck to the waistline. Attach the left arm so it is hanging straight by the side of the body. For the right arm, mark and bend halfway along the paste at a 90° angle and attach to the other side with edible glue.

Hands

33 Make two hands as explained on page 48 using skin tone SFP. Make the fingers on the right hand straight and the fingers on the left hand slightly bent. Allow to firm up.

34 Once both hands have firmed, secure the left hand inside the sleeve with a little softened white pastillage. For the right hand, insert a cocktail stick into the sleeve first, push the hand onto it and secure in place with a little softened pastillage. Attach a 1.5cm (⅝") wide strip of White SFP around the end of each sleeve to make the cuffs. Use a Dresden tool to add crease lines across them.

Hair

35 Roll a small piece of grey SFP into an oval shape that is big enough to cover the back of the head and thick enough to fill out the head shape. Use the handle of a paintbrush to make a groove near the bottom end

of the oval. Bend the paste at the mark and stick to the back of the head. Mark hair lines vertically down the paste with a cutting tool.

SHRIMP

36 Roll some salmon pink SFP into a bowling pin shape. Narrow the thicker part to a point for the head, flatten it down slightly and mark lines down it with the edge of a Dresden tool. Mark shorter lines along the tail, draw a line across the middle of the body and bend into a C-shape. Mark a few more lines around the body with the edge of a Dresden tool and use the handle of a paintbrush to open up the mouth. Using a small pair of scissors, make two small cuts just behind the mouth to bring out the little arms.

37 Use a soft brush to dust the back, head and tail with Nasturtium dust food colour. Finish with a coat of Poinsettia dust food colour to bring out the colour of the shrimp.

38 Roll two very small balls of White SFP for the eyeballs and attach them to the top of the head. Use Black SFP to make two thin sausages with pointed ends and stick them to the top of the eyeballs. Draw on the two little dots for the pupils using a Black food colour pen. Allow to dry.

FINISHING TOUCHES

39 Roll out a thin sheet of White SFP and cut out a trapezium shape for the apron, making it big enough to cover the front of the legs. Fold the top edge down to create a hem and attach the apron to the front of the jacket so it hangs over the legs. Glue a very thin strip of White SFP around the

waist to create the apron string following the mark you made earlier.

40 Insert a cocktail stick into the top of the head and gently push the hat down onto it. Secure it in place with softened pastillage. Model two small crescent shapes for the eyebrows and two sausages with tapered ends for the moustache from some grey SFP and draw hair lines across them using the edge of a Dresden tool. Attach two for the eyebrows and two to the upper lip for the moustache.

41 Secure the dish onto the silver tray then attach the tray to the chef's right hand with a little softened pastillage. Use barbecue skewers to hold the tray in place until fully dry.

42 Roll out some pale yellow SFP into a thin sheet then make some long cuts along it with a cutting wheel to create a fringe effect. Roll up the fringed paste into a loose ball to make the fettuccini pasta. Dab a little edible glue on the plate and arrange the pasta on it. Secure the shrimp on top of the pasta so that its tail is tangled up in it.

CAKE AND CAKE DRUM

43 Cover the cake with Bridal White sugarpaste (see page 34) then dowel the cake (see page 42).

44 Cover the cake drum with Bridal White sugarpaste coloured with a touch of Dark Forest paste colour (see page 41). Secure the cake in the centre of the cake drum and trim the edge with a black ribbon.

45 Place the figurine in the centre of the cake and secure in place with softened pastillage.

CHEF BISCUITS

Bake 30 6cm (2³/₈") round biscuits following the recipe provided on page 18.

Make up some medium-consistency royal icing and colour it with a touch of Nasturtium paste food colour. Fit a piping bag with a no. 1 nozzle, fill the bag with icing and pipe an outline around the biscuits. Let down the icing to run-out consistency, fit a piping bag with a no. 2 nozzle and fill with the icing. Flood inside the outline with the runny icing then allow to dry (see page 30).

Model the nose, moustache and eyebrows in the same way as for the chef on the main cake, then attach them to the biscuit with a little edible glue. For the eyes, draw two curved lines on either side of the nose with a Black food colour pen. Dust the cheeks and nose with Nasturtium dust food colour. Dilute a little Nasturtium liquid food colour with a few drops of cooled, boiled water and paint on a curved line for the chin using a fine paintbrush.

PIGS MIGHT FLY

Prepare to amaze your friends and family with this flying pig figurine! The fun and colourful cartoon style of this cake makes it great for children's birthday parties – everyone is bound to fall in love with the little piggy pilot. This cake is a reminder that the sky's the limit when it comes to being imaginative with your sugar modelling skills.

EDIBLES

15cm x 8cm (6" x 3¹/₈") dome-shaped cake, filled and crumb-coated (see page 38)

SK Sugarpaste (rolled fondant):

400g (14oz) light blue (Bridal White sugarpaste + touch of Gentian)

200g (7oz) scarlet red (Bridal White sugarpaste + Fuchsia + touch of Poppy)

400g (14oz) sky blue (Bridal White sugarpaste + Hyacinth)

SK Sugar Florist Paste (SFP, gum paste):

10g (¼oz) Black

30g (1oz) deep blue-green (White SFP + Bluegrass)

30g (1oz) deep orange (White SFP + Nasturtium)

30g (1oz) pale blue-green (White SFP + touch of Bluegrass)

100g (3½oz) pale peach (White SFP + touch of Nasturtium)

30g (1oz) soft beige (White SFP + touch of Chestnut)

50g (1¾oz) terracotta (White SFP + Terracotta)

50g (1¾oz) White

SK Instant Mix Pastillage:

100g (3½oz) orange (Nasturtium)

100g (3½oz) palest blue (touch of Gentian)

100g (3½oz) SK Instant Mix Royal Icing

SK Professional Paste Food Colours: Bluegrass, Chestnut (soft beige), Fuchsia, Gentian (ice blue), Hyacinth, Nasturtium (peach), Poppy

SK Designer Paste Food Colour: Terracotta

SK Professional Dust Food Colour: Fuchsia

SK Designer Pastel Dust Food Colour: Pastel Pink

SK Professional Food Colour Pen: Black

SK CMC Gum

EQUIPMENT

Basic equipment (see pages 6 to 7)

25.5cm (10") square cake drum (board)

20.5cm (8") round or square polystyrene dummy

4cm x 4cm x 16.5cm (1½" x 1½" x 6½") rectangular polystyrene block

Round cutters: 1cm, 1.5cm, 4cm, 5cm (³/₈", ⁵/₈", 1½", 2")

Small, plastic drinks bottle lid

Stanley knife

Bulbous cone tool

Piece of thin card, e.g. from a cereal box or cake box

Thick cardboard

Non-toxic glue stick

1m x 15mm width (39" x ⁵/₈") grosgrain ribbon: blue and white striped

Templates (see page 246)

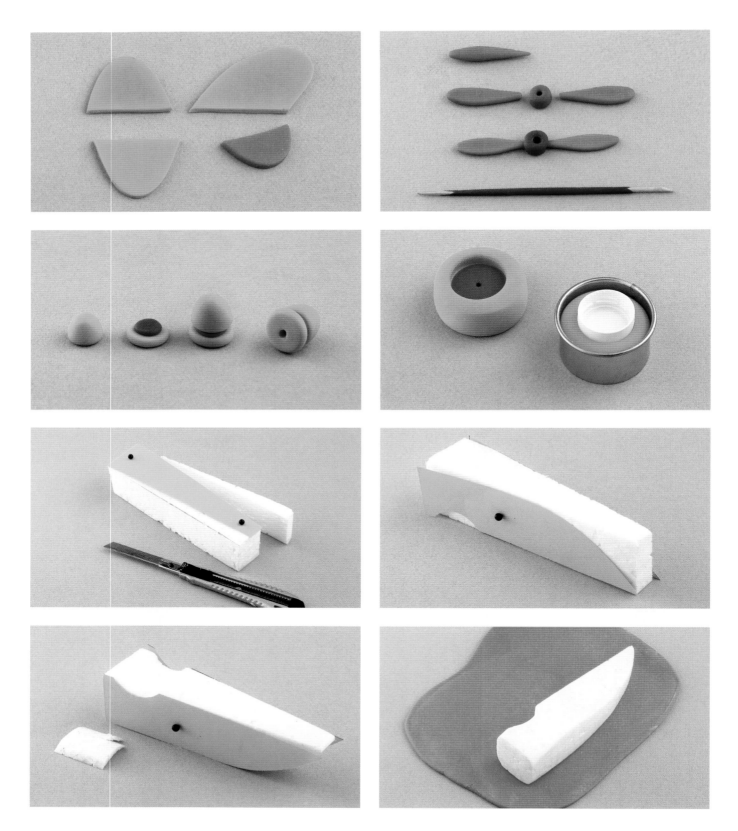

TEMPLATES

1 Trace all the templates onto a thin piece of card and cut them out with a pair of scissors.

AEROPLANE

Stabilizers

2 Roll out the orange pastillage to a 4mm (³/₁₆") thickness and cut out one vertical stabilizer (A) and two horizontal stabilizers (B). Colour a small piece of leftover orange pastillage with a touch of Poppy red paste food colour to achieve a deeper shade. Cut out the second vertical stabilizer (C) from the deep orange paste. Leave all the pieces to dry on a flat surface.

Propeller

3 For the blades, roll some deep orange SFP into two long teardrops following the template as a guide. Flatten them slightly with a cake smoother then trim the pointed end straight with a sharp knife. Leave to dry.

4 For the hub, roll out a small piece of terracotta SFP to 1cm (³/₈") thick and cut out a 1.5cm (⁵/₈") circle using a round cutter. Pierce the centre with the handle of a paintbrush and use the tip of a Dresden tool to make two indents on opposite sides where the blades will be inserted. Allow to firm up.

5 Once the blades are completely dry, insert the straight end into the sides of the hub and secure them in place with a little softened deep orange paste. Dust the blades with Fuchsia dust food colour when they are completely dry.

6 To make the central axis, moisten a 16cm (6¼") long barbecue skewer with edible glue and thread a small ball of terracotta SFP onto it. Use your palms to roll the paste along the length of the skewer and allow to dry.

7 To make the nose cone, roll a small ball of orange SFP into a rounded cone shape. Roll another small ball of paste and flatten it between your fingers to make the base. Once both pieces are firm enough to handle, stick them together with a fresh circle of terracotta SFP that is slightly smaller than the base. Pierce the bottom of the cone with the handle of a paintbrush to create a hole where the central axis will be inserted.

Engine

8 Roll 55g–60g (2oz) of orange pastillage into a ball and place it inside a 5cm (2") round cutter that has been lightly dusted with cornflour. Slightly flatten the top of the paste with the heel of your hand then push a small plastic drinks bottle lid into the paste to hollow out the centre. Remove the paste from the cutter and leave to dry.

9 Roll out some terracotta SFP very thinly and cut out a circle the same size as the bottle lid. Secure the paste in the base of the hole. Make a hole through the centre of the engine with a paintbrush handle.

Fuselage

10 Place the top fuselage template (D) onto the polystyrene block and secure it in place with round-headed pins. Following the template, use a Stanley knife to trim down the

sides of the block to make it wedge-shaped. Remove the template and pins when you have finished.

11 Secure the side fuselage templates (E) to either side of the polystyrene wedge with round-headed pins. Trim along the top edge of the template to create the curve underneath the fuselage. Turn the block over and cut into the polystyrene to make a groove for the cockpit. Again, remove the template and pins once you have finished.

12 Brush the polystyrene shape with edible glue and put to one side. Roll out 150g (5¼oz) of scarlet red sugarpaste to approximately 4mm (³/₁₆") thick. Lay the polystyrene shape on its side on the sheet of paste and fold the sugarpaste over the polystyrene so the

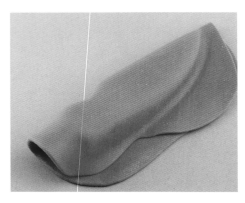

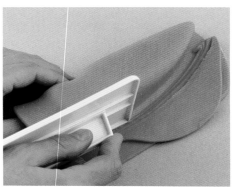

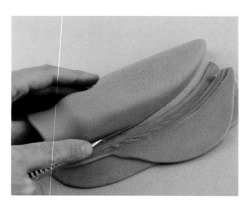

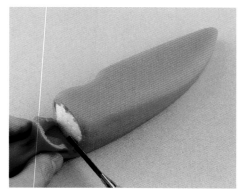

join will be at the bottom of the fuselage. Run the edge of a cake smoother over the join to seal it and help stick the paste to the polystyrene. Trim away the excess paste from around the fuselage with a Stanley knife to achieve a neat finish.

13 While the paste is still soft, use the edge of a Dresden tool to mark lines along both sides of the fuselage. Allow the fuselage to dry on the side that will face the back of the cake.

TUTOR TIP

I have carved the fuselage out of a polystyrene block, but if you wanted to make the plane edible, you could make the fuselage from crisped rice cereal mix instead (see page 19).

Wings

14 Knead the sugarpaste trimmings from the fuselage with a touch of Nasturtium paste food colour to create a slightly deeper shade. Add a generous pinch of CMC gum to the paste in order to strengthen it, then roll it out to 4mm (3/16") thick. Cut out the wings following the template provided, then remove a 1cm (3/8") circle from the middle with a round cutter. This is where you will insert a plastic dowel to secure the plane onto the cake.

TUTOR TIP

If you are working in extremely humid conditions, it is advisable to use pastillage for the wings to give them maximum strength as they will support the fuselage once the plane is placed on the cake.

15 Secure the fuselage centrally on top of the wings with royal icing or some softened deep orange paste. Allow the wings to dry at an angle: place a piece of thick cardboard underneath each wing and keep them in place with either a cutter or a piece of foam/ polystyrene until completely dry.

Assembly

16 Colour some royal icing the same colour as the fuselage using Fuchsia and a touch of Poppy paste food colour. Fill a paper piping bag with the icing and snip off the very tip of the bag. Pipe a line of royal icing along the flat edge of the vertical stabilizer (C) and secure under the tail of the fuselage. Brush away any excess royal icing for a clean finish and support with a piece of polystyrene until dry.

17 Attach the vertical stabilizer (A) to the top of the fuselage and keep it in place with a barbecue skewer. Secure the horizontal stabilizers (B) either side and support each piece with a block of polystyrene until completely dry.

18 Stick the engine to the front of the fuselage with a dab of royal icing. Insert the central axis through the hole in the engine and push it halfway into the fuselage, leaving a small piece sticking out. Leave to dry.

19 Once the whole aeroplane has completely dried, roll out a very thin sheet of terracotta SFP and cut out a rectangle that is approximately 3cm x 3.5cm (1 1/8" x 1 3/8") in size. Place this in the cockpit area and attach with a little edible glue. Roll a thin sausage of deep orange SFP and attach it around the edge of the cockpit. Push the propeller onto the central axis, followed by the nose cone.

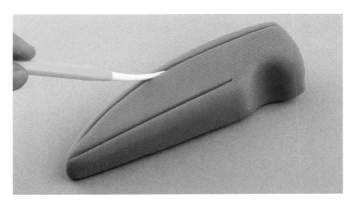

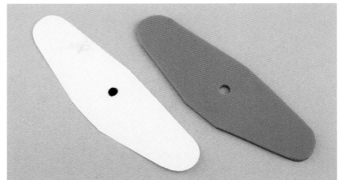

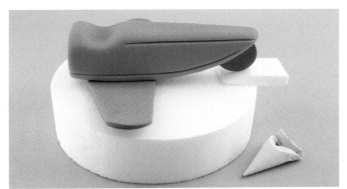

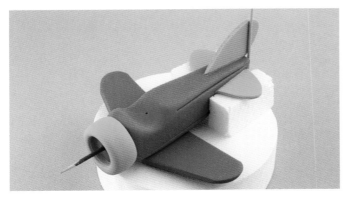

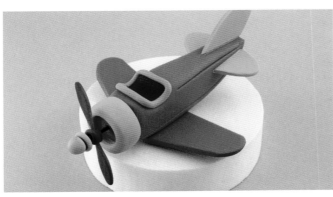

PIG

Head

20 Roll 30g (1oz) of pale peach SFP into an oval shape using the diagram of the head for reference.

21 Open up the mouth following the technique on page 115. Push a small ball tool into each corner of the mouth to make dimples then run your finger over the paste to soften any marks left by the tool. Use the edge of a Dresden tool to create a curved line beneath the mouth and bring out the lower lip.

22 For the snout, roll a small oval of pale peach SFP and attach it above the smile with a little edible glue. Open up the nostrils with the tip of a cocktail stick.

23 To make the eyes, use a Dresden tool to indent two small, curved lines either side of the top of the snout. Brush the cheeks and snout with Pastel Pink dust food colour using a soft paintbrush.

24 Roll out a small pinch of terracotta SFP very thinly, cut the paste into the same shape as the mouth and secure it inside. Mix some White and terracotta SFP to make a paler shade, then roll the paste into a tiny oval and glue into the bottom of the mouth. Flatten down the tongue and mark a line down the middle.

25 For the eyelashes, roll two very small, tapered sausages of Black SFP and secure them over the eye marks. Allow the head to firm up overnight.

Aviator helmet

26 Roll out some soft beige SFP and cut out a circle with a 4cm (1½") round cutter. Brush the back of the head with a little edible glue and wrap the paste around the head with the palm of your hand. Insert a cocktail stick into the base of the head so you can hold it comfortably whilst working on the rest of the details.

27 To make the flaps, cut out a strip of soft beige SFP that is approximately 5cm long x 1.5cm wide (2" x ⅝") in size with rounded ends. Cut the paste in half widthways and attach each piece to the sides of the helmet. Use a Dresden tool to mark a few creases at the joins and give each flap a little movement. Roll a thin sausage of soft beige SFP and secure across the front of the helmet, then attach a tiny ball to each flap.

28 For the goggles, roll two small ovals of pale blue-green SFP then hollow out the centre of each one using a small ball tool. Fill in the holes with smaller ovals of White SFP. Roll out the deep blue-green SFP thinly, cut out a very narrow strip that is long enough to fit around the back of the head and secure it in place. Take a pinch of deep blue-green SFP and roll it into a tiny oval, secure the goggles to the top of the head and place the oval of paste between them.

Ears

29 Roll some pale peach SFP into two small teardrop shapes and flatten them slightly with your fingers. Press a bulbous cone tool down the length of each ear and cut them straight across the bottom. Fix the ears to the aviator helmet with a little edible glue, so they sit just behind the goggles.

Torso

30 Roll 15g (½oz) of pale peach SFP into a smooth ball, then roll out some White SFP very thinly and cut out a semicircle for the tummy that is roughly the same size as the side of the ball. Secure the White SFP to the ball with a little edible glue. Press down on the front and back of the ball to give the torso shape. Trim any excess paste from the bottom of the ball to make the body relative in size to the cockpit. Stick the torso into the cockpit while the paste is still fresh.

31 For the neck, roll a small piece of pale peach SFP into a ball and flatten it down between your fingers. Secure to the top of the torso and insert a cocktail stick into the neck and down through the torso and fuselage, leaving the cocktail stick protruding from the top. Allow to firm up.

Arms

32 Roll some pale peach SFP into two sausages and taper one end slightly to create the wrist, leaving a small piece of paste at the end. Snip into the end of the arms with a small pair of scissors to make the trotters. Leave one of the arms straight, bend the other slightly at the elbow and allow to dry.

33 Attach the arms to either side of the torso with a little edible glue. The straight arm should reach upwards and the bent arm should sit over the edge of the cockpit.

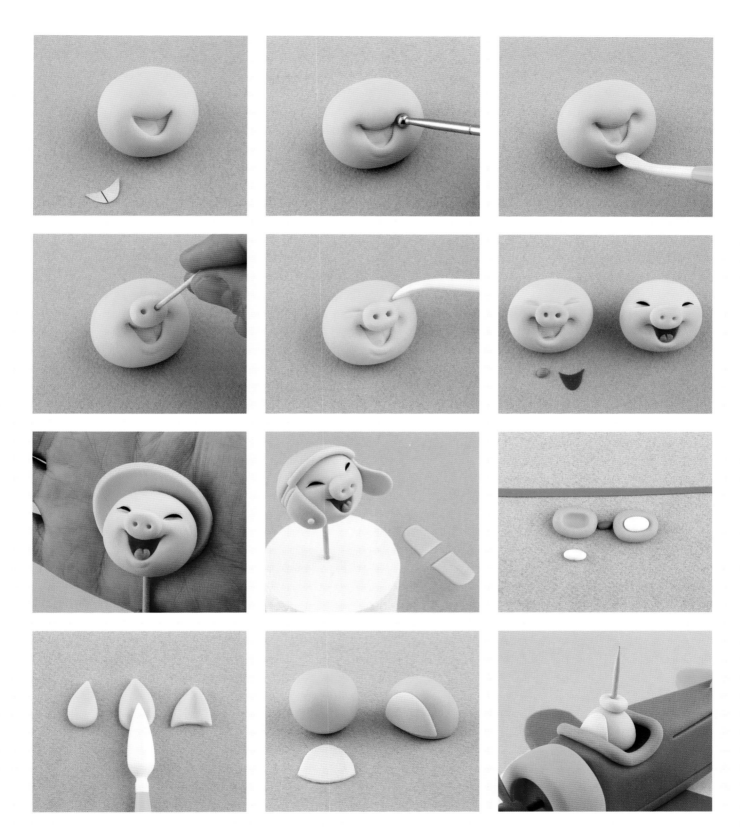

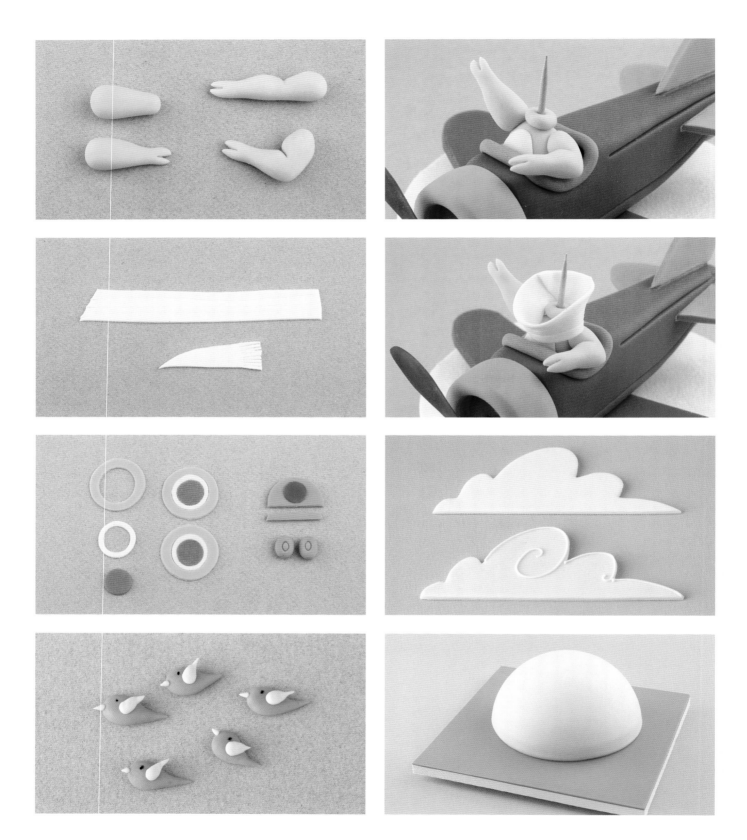

Scarf

34 Cut out a strip of White SFP that is approximately 5cm (2") long x 1.5cm (⁵/₈") wide, mark a few lines along the paste with a Dresden tool and secure around the pig's neck. Push the head gently onto the skewer, so it is slightly tilted to one side. Cut another piece of thinly rolled White SFP into a long triangular shape and make several cuts in the shorter end with a small pair of scissors. Secure this piece over the pig's shoulder as if it is being blown by the wind.

35 Use the leftover colours of SFP to make the decorative details on the plane. Use different sizes of round cutters to make the targets and the wing design. Roll very small balls of paste and attach them to the fuselage and tail to add detail.

CLOUDS

36 Roll out the pale blue pastillage to 4mm (³/₁₆") thick and cut out the cloud shapes using the templates provided and a craft knife. Once dry, fill a paper piping bag with white off-peak royal icing and pipe a swirly outline around each of the clouds.

BIRDS

37 Roll pinches of deep blue-green SFP into small teardrops and flatten them down slightly. Colour some off-peak royal icing with a touch of Bluegrass paste food colour and fill a paper piping bag with the icing. Snip the tip off the bag and pipe a leaf shape for the wing and a small triangle for the beak. Use a Black food colour pen to draw on the eye. Allow to dry flat.

CAKE AND CAKE DRUM

38 Cover the dome-shaped cake with light blue sugarpaste (see page 38) and the cake drum with sky blue sugarpaste (see page 41). Secure the cake in the centre of the drum and trim the cake drum with the striped ribbon.

39 Insert a dowel slightly off-centre into the cake until it reaches the cake board, leaving a piece of dowel sticking out. This is the main dowel into which the aeroplane will be skewered: the dowel should go through the hole in the bottom of the wings and into the fuselage. Insert two more dowels on either side of the main supporting dowel, where the wings of the aeroplane will sit over the cake. Place a small piece of pale blue sugarpaste under the fuselage to help lift up the back of the plane.

TUTOR TIP

These extra dowels will help support the wings if you are transporting the cake and prevent the topper from sinking into it.

40 Place the clouds around the cake drum so they sit behind each other and give depth to the scene. Pipe a line of beads with royal icing behind each cloud to secure them firmly to the board.

CLOUD BISCUITS

Make up the biscuit dough following the recipe on page 18, then cut out 25 cloud-shaped biscuits using the template on page 246 and bake.

Once the biscuits have cooled, colour some medium-consistency royal icing with a touch of Hydrangea paste food colour, fit a piping bag with a no. 1 nozzle and fill with the icing. Pipe an outline around each of the biscuits. Let down the icing to run-out consistency and place in a piping bag fitted with a no. 2 nozzle. Flood inside the outline of the biscuit and leave to dry.

Colour some more medium-consistency royal icing with Hyacinth paste food colour, then use a no. 1 nozzle to pipe a swirly outline over the edge of the clouds. Leave to dry.

Model the little birds following the instructions on page 89 and attach them to the biscuits with dots of royal icing.

THE HAPPY FOX

Fresh from frolicking in the autumn leaves, this cheery critter's picture-perfect smile would make him a fun addition to a celebration cake.

EDIBLES

200g (7oz) SK Instant Mix Pastillage

SK Sugar Florist Paste (SFP, gum paste):

    50g (1¾oz) Black SFP

    200g (7oz) burnt orange (White SFP + Berberis)

    5g (just under ¼oz) light pink (White SFP + touch of Poppy)

    95g (3¼oz) off-white (White SFP + touch of Berberis)

    25g (just over ¾oz) poppy red (White SFP + Poppy)

    25g (just over ¾oz) soft beige (White SFP + Chestnut)

    25g (just over ¾oz) tangerine (White SFP + Marigold)

    25g (just over ¾oz) terracotta (White SFP + Terracotta)

SK Professional Paste Food Colours: Berberis, Chestnut, Marigold, Poppy

SK Professional Liquid Food Colour: Teddy Bear Brown

SK Designer Paste Food Colour: Terracotta

SK Professional Dust Food Colours: Bulrush, Chestnut, Poppy

EQUIPMENT

Basic equipment (see pages 6 to 7)

Rectangular dummy: 18cm x 15cm x 3cm deep (7" x 6" x 1⅛")

New vegetable brush

Curved former, e.g. food-grade cardboard tube

Bulbous cone modelling tool

Rose leaf cutter set (FMM)

Rose leaf cutter set (TT)

SK Great Impressions Briar Rose Leaf Veiner Set

Template (see page 252)

TREE STUMP

1 Use the template to carve a tree stump shape from the polystyrene dummy using a sharp knife.

2 Make up 200g (7oz) of pastillage according to the packet instructions. Dust a non-stick board with cornflour and roll out the paste into a 3mm (1/8") thick sheet. Brush the top of the polystyrene with edible glue, turn it over and press it down on the pastillage. Trim away the excess paste from the top edge with a sharp knife and flip the stump over again. Texture the paste by drawing a knife repeatedly from the centre to the edge of the stump. Draw concentric circles over the top.

3 To cover the sides, roll out a 4cm (1½") wide strip of pastillage. Add texture to the paste by drawing a number of parallel lines along its side using the blade of a plain knife. Fix the strip around the edge of the carved dummy using edible glue. Use a new vegetable brush to push the paste into all the crevices and add some extra texture. If the stump will be placed on a cake, cover the bottom with pastillage, otherwise you can leave it uncovered. Leave the paste to dry for a few hours before painting it.

BARK PIECES

4 Roll out the pastillage off-cuts and cut out five or six irregular rectangle shapes. Use a sharp knife and vegetable brush to add texture to the bark pieces in the same way as for the tree stump. Leave the pieces to dry on a curved former, such as a food-grade cardboard tube, to give them a slight curve.

5 Once the tree stump and bark pieces are completely dry, paint them with Teddy Bear Brown liquid food colour. Apply more than one coat in certain areas to deepen the colour and create some variation.

LEAVES AND BERRIES

6 To make the leaves, roll out the soft beige, tangerine and terracotta SFP individually on a non-stick board lightly greased with white vegetable fat. Cut out a variety of different-sized leaves using the rose leaf cutters and a cutting wheel tool for the long, thin ones. Add veining details using a rose leaf veiner then pinch along the central vein to add some movement. Set the leaves aside to dry.

7 Once dry, dust the leaves with Bulrush, Chestnut and Poppy dust food colours to create a selection of different autumnal shades.

8 To make the berries, roll small pieces of poppy red paste into balls and allow them to dry.

FOX

Body

9 Roll some burnt orange SFP into a bottle shape, lay the bottle on its side and flatten it slightly. Press the sides in slightly to square off the edges. Mark a curved line for the hind legs on either side of the body using a Dresden tool. Insert a wooden barbecue skewer into the neck and all the way down through the body, then leave the model to dry slightly.

10 To make the fur on the belly and chest, roll some off-white SFP into a thick sausage shape with a pointed end. Continue to roll the paste 1/3 from the pointed end to make it thinner. Press the thinner side with the palm of your hand to flatten it down.

11 Skewer the body into a spare dummy and attach the off-white fur section to the front of the body with a little edible glue. Use a Dresden tool to mark some fine lines over the chest, then set the model aside while you start work on the head.

Head

12 Roll some burnt orange SFP into a cone shape then roll a little less off-white SFP into a second, slightly smaller cone. Stick the two pieces together with a little edible glue, lining up the two points at the front to create a snout.

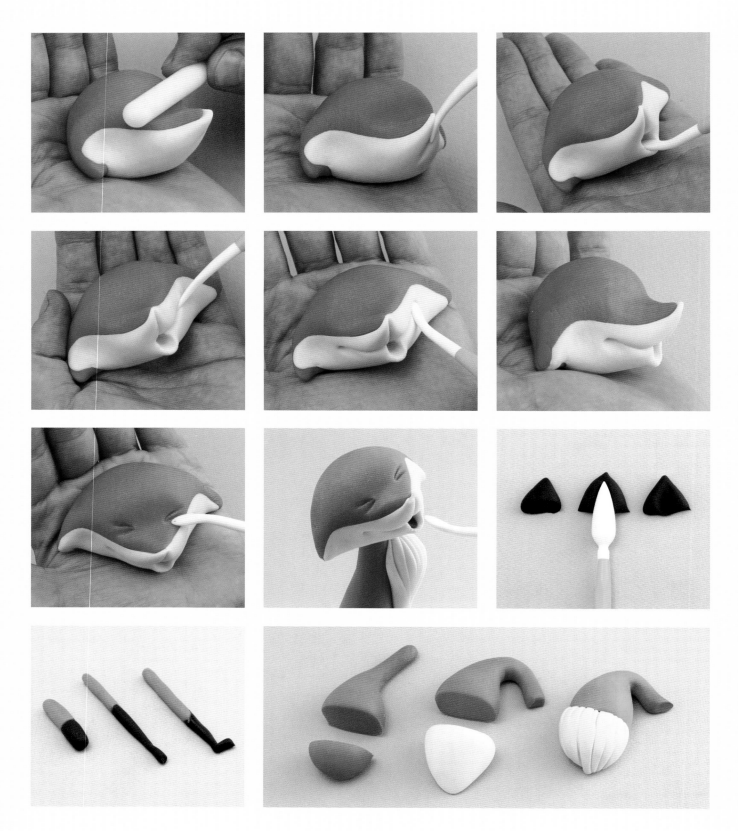

13 Squeeze the paste gently at each side of the snout with your thumbs, stroking the paste out towards the sides to define the shape of the head. Pinch out the snout with your thumb and index finger to flatten its sides, then create a curve by rolling a CelStick above the nose and over the middle of the face. Draw a line on the lower part of the snout with the edge of a Dresden tool, then use the rounded end to open the mouth and extend the lower lip.

14 For the smile, draw a line with the edge of a Dresden tool from the mouth to each cheek, then push the rounded end into either side of the mouth to make a pair of dimples.

15 To make the eyes, draw two small, curved lines on either side of the face with a Dresden tool.

16 Push the head onto the skewer which runs through the body, tilting it slightly to one side. Roll a tiny piece of terracotta SFP into a ball and push it into the fox's mouth with a Dresden tool. Roll out a tiny piece of light pink paste and push it into the mouth.

17 Make a row of teeth by rolling a tiny, thin sausage of off-white SFP with pointed ends. Glue it into the lower part of the mouth, pushing up the ends to make fangs.

18 For the nose, roll a tiny piece of Black SFP into a teardrop shape and fix it onto the top of the snout using edible glue. Flatten the top of the teardrop in line with the snout.

19 For the eyebrows, roll two tiny pieces of off-white paste into sausages with pointed ends and fix them in place above the eyes with edible glue. Add some texture with a Dresden tool.

20 To make the eyelashes, roll two tiny pieces of Black SFP into thin sausages with pointed ends and fix them into the two uppermost curved lines on the face with edible glue.

21 Mix a small amount of Poppy dust food colour with some cornflour then dust it over the cheeks.

Ears

22 Roll some Black SFP into two cone shapes and trim away the bases to create a straight edge. Press a bulbous cone tool into the middle of each ear, then fix to each side of the head with a little edible glue.

Legs

23 To make each of the front legs, stick a piece of burnt orange SFP and a piece of Black SFP together then roll them out into a thin sausage, leaving a piece of Black paste at the end for the foot. Bend the end of the black section at a right angle to the leg, bringing the heel back slightly. Secure the legs behind the chest fur, curving round to the front of the body.

24 For the back legs, roll two tiny pieces of Black SFP into long, thin teardrop shapes. Draw two small lines in the thicker end of each leg for the toes. Attach underneath either side of the front of the body with a little edible glue.

Tail

25 Roll some burnt orange SFP into a bottle shape then trim away the wider end with a knife. Curve the narrow top section back on itself to

form a tight bend. Roll some off-white SFP into a cone shape and fix this to the end of the tail with edible glue. Use a Dresden tool to add a furry texture to the off-white section then leave the tail to dry in the same position.

TUTOR TIP

As the tail is quite big, it is best to stick it straight onto the tree stump to avoid breakages.

ASSEMBLY

26 Once the fox is finished, fix him to the tree stump with some softened SFP. Scatter the leaves and bark pieces around the stump to create an autumnal scene.

AUTUMN LEAF BISCUITS

Make up some vanilla and chocolate biscuit dough following the recipes provided on page 18. Cut out approximately 20 maple leaves and 30 slim leaves using different leaf-shaped cookie cutters, then bake.

Once the biscuits have cooled, colour three batches of medium-consistency royal icing with Teddy Bear Brown, Terracotta and Berberis paste food colours respectively. Place each colour of icing in a piping bag fitted with a no. 1 nozzle and use them to pipe an outline around each of the cookies,

using a different colour for each leaf design (see page 30). Let down the icing to run-out consistency then flood the biscuits with the same colour icing as used for the outline and leave to dry.

Pipe lines for the leaf veins using medium-consistency royal icing coloured with Terracotta paste food colour and a no. 1 nozzle. Pipe dots of Poppy-coloured run-out icing randomly over some of the leaves and allow to dry. To finish, splash Poppy and Terracotta food colour over the cookies using the method described on page 54.

TOY SOLDIER

This toy soldier is brought to life with only a few geometric shapes – and perhaps a bit of winding up! The friendly figurine would make any child's day and is perfect for finishing off a birthday or christening cake.

EDIBLES

SK Sugarpaste (rolled fondant):

  200g (7oz) Bridal White

SK Sugar Florist Paste (SFP, gum paste):

  100g (3½oz) Black

  30g (1oz) blue-green (White SFP + Bluegrass)

  100g (3½oz) dark blue (White SFP + Bluebell)

  100g (3½oz) light blue (White SFP + Hydrangea)

  30g (1oz) red (White SFP + Poppy)

  50g (1¾oz) reddish terracotta (White SFP + Terracotta + touch of Poppy)

  100g (3½oz) skin tone (White SFP + touch of Teddy Bear Brown + touch of Pink)

  50g (1¾oz) terracotta (White SFP + Terracotta)

  30g (1oz) yellow (Marigold SFP)

SK Professional Paste Food Colours: Blackberry (black), Bluegrass, Edelweiss (white), Hydrangea, Poppy, Teddy Bear Brown

SK Quality Food Colour (QFC) Paste: Pink

SK Designer Paste Food Colour: Terracotta

SK Instant Mix Pastillage:

  50g (1¾oz) white (uncoloured)

SK Instant Royal Icing Mix:

  50g (1¾oz) white (uncoloured)

SK Designer Pastel Dust Food Colour: Pale Peach

SK Professional Liquid Food Colour: Blackberry (black)

SK Designer Metallic Lustre Dust Food Colour: Silver

SK CMC Gum

EQUIPMENT

Basic equipment (see pages 6 to 7)

6cm (2³/₈") cube straight-edge dummy

3cm (1¹/₈") polystyrene ball

Spare polystyrene dummy

Round cutters: 5mm, 1cm, 1.5cm, 3cm, 3.5cm, 4cm, 4.5cm, 5cm ($1/4$", $3/8$", $5/8$", $1^1/8$", $1^3/8$", $1^1/2$", $1^3/4$", 2")

3cm (1¹/₈") diameter cylindrical former, e.g. plastic cocktail stick container

Templates (see page 248)

DIE (BASE FOR TOY SOLDIER)

1 Cover the 6cm (2³/₈") cube dummy with Bridal White sugarpaste (see pages 42 to 43). While the paste covering is still fresh, press a small ball tool into the sides to create the correct amount of circular 'pips' on the die. Fill in the holes with very small balls of blue-green SFP, then press with a ball tool to flatten them down. Allow the die to dry for a few days.

TROUSERS

2 Knead 60g (2oz) of dark blue SFP with a pinch of CMC. Roll the paste into a thick sausage and use two cake smoothers to flatten the top and sides, using the template as a size guide. Trim the ends with a sharp knife to the exact length of the template. Press a skewer down the middle of both the front and back to divide the two legs. Leave to dry flat for a couple of hours.

TORSO

3 Knead 30g (1oz) of light blue SFP with a pinch of CMC. Roll the paste into a teardrop shape: press lightly on the narrower part to make it flat and bring out the bulbous end to create the belly of the toy soldier. Cut straight edges at the bottom and top of the shape with a small, sharp knife and make sure that the wider end is the same width as the legs. Mark a line down the middle of the front using the back of a knife. Secure the torso to the top of the legs with edible glue, while they are still drying in a flat position.

4 For the neck, roll a tiny piece of Black SFP into a sausage, cut the ends to make them straight and mark a line down the middle with the back of a knife. Attach to the top of the torso with edible glue. Insert a cocktail stick down through the neck and torso, leaving a small piece protruding from the neck to support the head later on.

SHOES

5 Roll some Black SFP into a short sausage and divide it into two equal pieces. Leave one end rounded and the opposite end flat on each half then flatten slightly. Use edible glue to attach the shoes to the legs while they are still drying in a flat position. Push a skewer lengthways into the bottom of the shoes up through the legs and halfway up the torso. It is important to let this whole piece dry overnight on a flat surface.

HEAD

6 Cover a 3cm (1¹/₈") diameter polystyrene ball with 30g–35g (1oz–1¼oz) of the skin tone SFP, following the technique on page 44.

TUTOR TIP

If you do not have a polystyrene ball to hand, simply roll 60g (2oz) of skin-coloured SFP into a ball that is approximately 4cm (1½") in diameter.

7 To make the mouth, push a 3cm (1¹/₈") round cutter into the lower half of the ball to create a wide, curved smile and press a 1.5cm (⁵/₈") round cutter underneath for the lower lip. Run your finger underneath the lower lip to bring it out further.

8 For the eyes, make two very small holes with a small ball tool along the middle line of the face. Fill in the holes with two very small pieces of Black SFP. Use a fine paintbrush to add a dot of white paste food colour to highlight the eyes.

9 For the nose, roll out a small piece of skin tone SFP into a wedge shape, then cut out a strip with a sharp knife. Cut the nose to length, making the ends straight. Secure between the eyes with a little edible glue.

10 Roll two balls of skin tone SFP and flatten into discs for the ears. Attach the ears to each side of the face just below eye level using edible glue. Emboss a circle inside the ear using a 5mm (¼") round cutter and pierce the centre of each ear with a cocktail stick.

11 Mix some Pale Peach dust food colour with a little cornflour and use a soft brush to dust it over the cheeks.

12 For the eyebrows, roll two small pieces of Black SFP into slightly curved teardrops and attach above each eye with a little edible glue. Leave the head to dry completely overnight.

13 To make the hair, roll out some Black SFP to 4mm (³/₁₆") thick and cut out a 5cm (2") circle using a round cutter. Glue over the back of the head and trim away any excess paste if necessary. For the sideburns, roll two small teardrop shapes of Black SFP and stick them in front of each ear.

DRUM

14 To create the main body of the drum, roll out some reddish terracotta SFP to 3mm ($^1/_8$") thick and cut out a strip using the template provided. Wrap the strip around a 3.5cm ($1^3/_8$") round cutter and trim the ends if necessary. Once the paste has firmed up after a couple of minutes, remove the cutter and allow to dry completely.

15 Roll out some yellow SFP thinly and cut out several strips that are approximately 2cm ($^3/_4$") long. Stick down the sides of the drum with edible glue and trim to size if necessary.

16 For the top of the drum, mix the SFP used for the main body with a little White SFP to create a slightly lighter colour. Roll the paste to 3mm ($^1/_8$") thick and cut out a 4cm ($1^1/_2$") circle using a cutter. While the paste is still soft, emboss with the blunt edge of a 3cm ($1^1/_8$") round cutter to create an inner circle. Leave to dry then stick onto the top of the main body with royal icing.

17 For the base of the drum, roll out some terracotta SFP to 3mm ($^1/_8$") thick and cut out a 4.5cm ($1^3/_4$") round circle using a cutter. Attach the drum to this lower lid with edible glue and leave to dry on a flat surface.

18 To make the hoop around the head of the drum, roll out some terracotta SFP to 2mm ($^1/_{16}$") thick and cut out a 3mm ($^1/_8$") wide strip. Secure it around the upper lid.

19 Paint two cocktail sticks with Blackberry liquid food colour and leave to dry. Roll two small balls of blue-green SFP and attach them to the end of the sticks.

HAT

20 Roll out some dark blue SFP on a non-stick board to 2mm ($^1/_{16}$") thick and cut out a rectangle using the template provided. Lightly dust the paste with cornflour and place around a round former that is approximately 3cm ($1^1/_8$") in diameter, such as a plastic cocktail stick container or a small rolling pin, to create a neat cylinder. Join the ends at the back neatly, trimming off any excess if necessary. Leave the paste to dry before removing the former.

21 Roll out some dark blue SFP more thinly and cut out a circle that is the same diameter as the cylinder. Glue the SFP cylinder onto the circle, trim off any excess paste if necessary and leave to dry on a flat surface. Once dried, turn upside down to make the rest of the hat.

22 For the peak, roll out some Black SFP to 3mm thick ($^1/_8$") and cut out a crescent shape following the template provided. Attach to the base at the front of the hat with edible glue and leave to dry.

23 For the flower decoration, roll a little piece of yellow SFP into a ball and flatten it down slightly. Mark lines across the paste with the blade of a knife to divide it into petals. Make a small hole in the centre of the flower and fill with a small ball of Black SFP to finish. Attach to the front of the hat.

24 For the feather decoration, roll a small piece of Black SFP into a flattened teardrop shape and attach it above the flower.

WIND-UP KEY

25 Make up some pastillage and roll it out on a non-stick board to 3mm ($1/8$") thick. Cut out the two wings of the key using the templates provided. While the paste is still soft, gently press a medium ball tool into each piece and set aside to dry.

26 For the shank of the key, roll some pastillage into a sausage the same size as the template provided. Leave to dry.

27 Once the three pieces have dried out completely, stick them together with a little royal icing in a piping bag. Remove any excess royal icing with a dry brush to leave clean joins.

28 For the nut, roll out a small piece of pastillage and cut out a thin strip. Make several marks along the strip and attach it around the end of the key shank with a little edible glue. Leave to dry.

29 Once the key is dry, dilute some Silver lustre dust food colour in a few drops of clear alcohol and paint over it. If necessary, apply a second layer after the first has dried.

ARMS AND HANDS

30 To make the first arm, roll some light blue SFP into a sausage that tapers slightly at one end. Cut to the length required to fit the size of the body. Mark and bend at the elbow then hollow out the wider end with the handle of a paintbrush. Repeat to make the second arm and leave to dry on a flat surface. Roll two tiny balls of yellow SFP and attach one to each sleeve as a button.

31 For the hands, roll two small balls of skin tone SFP and press them on one side with a small ball tool to create the palm of the hand. Make a tiny hole with a skewer in the top of the hands and mark a line from the hole halfway down the palm to create the thumb. Glue the hands to the arms with edible glue and leave to dry overnight.

ASSEMBLY

32 Push the skewer protruding from the feet into a spare polystyrene dummy in order to keep the figure upright while you assemble it. Insert a barbecue skewer into the base of the head at a slight angle and remove to leave a hole. Push the head down onto the cocktail stick protruding from the neck and secure in place with softened skin tone SFP. Support the head in place with temporary skewers until fully dried.

33 For the belt, roll out a piece of Black SFP thinly and cut out a strip that is just over 1cm ($3/8$") wide. Glue it around the bottom of the torso from the back to the front, trimming off the excess at the join with a pair of scissors.

34 Roll out some yellow SFP and cut out two narrow stripes that are the same length as the legs.

Stick the strips down either side of the trousers.

35 For the bottom of the jacket, thinly roll out some light blue SFP and cut a strip that is just under 1cm ($3/8$") wide and as long as the belt. Attach the strip around the hips so it sits just underneath the belt and joins at the front. Trim the ends at an angle to give the illusion that the jacket is slightly open.

36 To make the buckle, roll a small ball of yellow SFP and flatten it slightly. Make a hole in the centre with a small ball tool and fill it with a tiny piece of Black SFP. Attach to the front of the belt with edible glue. Roll two tiny ovals of yellow SFP and attach to the front of the jacket for the buttons.

37 To secure the hat on top of the head, cut out a circle of Black SFP that is slightly smaller than the diameter of the hat and glue it on top of the head. Moisten inside the base of the hat with edible glue and place it on the round piece of paste in the required position.

38 Roll a small sausage of dark blue SFP, brush it with edible glue and use it to secure the drum to the legs. Stack pieces of polystyrene underneath the drum to help support it in position until it has dried completely.

39 Attach the wind-up key to the back of the torso using a very small piece of softened pastillage and support with a skewer until dry.

40 Secure the arms to the torso with a very small amount of softened light blue SFP, use skewers to support them in position and leave to dry.

FINISHING TOUCHES

41 Roll out some dark blue SFP to 5mm (¼") thick and cut out two crescent shapes using a 1cm (³/₈") round cutter. Attach them over the top of the shoulders with edible glue. Cover the join between the hand and the arm with a thin sausage of dark blue SFP then gently insert a drumstick into each hand.

42 For the strap of the drum, roll out some reddish terracotta SFP and cut out a 5mm (¼") wide strip. Attach to the right side of the drum, bring it around the neck and tuck the strip under the left arm. Stick another strip just below the left arm, finishing on the left-hand side of the drum. Add a small circle of red SFP where the end of each strap meets the drum and finish with a smaller ball of yellow SFP on top.

43 Pierce the die with a barbecue skewer where you want to position the figurine. Once the whole soldier has completely dried, take it out of the temporary dummy, cover the bottom of the shoes with softened pastillage and push the skewer into the hole in the die.

TOY SOLDIER BISCUITS

For these coordinating biscuits, you will need to prepare the piped flowers before you make the biscuits (see instructions for making off-pieces on page 30). Colour some medium-consistency royal icing with Sunflower and a touch of Poppy paste food colours. Place it in a piping bag fitted with a no. 1 nozzle and pipe eight teardrops meeting at a central point on a square of wax paper. While the icing is still wet, pipe a dot of black run-out icing in the centre and leave the flower to dry.

Make up the biscuit dough following the recipe on page 18, cut out 30 6cm (2³/₈") circles and bake. Once cool, colour some medium-consistency royal icing with Gentian paste food colour, fit a piping bag with a no. 1 nozzle and fill with the blue icing. Pipe around the outline of the biscuits.

Let down the blue icing to make it run-out consistency, fit a piping bag with a no. 2 nozzle and fill the bag with the icing. Flood inside the outline, then leave the icing to dry (see page 30). Secure a flower in the centre of each cookie with a dot of royal icing.

QUEEN OF THE KITCHEN

This kitsch kitchen scene is a great celebration cake for any mum, grandma, sister or friend who loves to bake. With a nostalgic, vintage design it's the perfect tribute to anyone who is the undisputed queen of her own kitchen.

EDIBLES

16.5cm square x 7cm deep (6½" x 2¾") cake, filled and crumb-coated (see page 34)

SK Sugarpaste (rolled fondant):

200g (7oz) Bridal White

700g (1lb 8¾oz) pale blue (Bridal White sugarpaste + touch of Wisteria)

SK Sugar Florist Paste (SFP, gum paste):

50g (1¾oz) blue-green (White SFP + Bluegrass)

10g (¼oz) dark brown (Bulrush SFP)

10g (¼oz) deep orange (White SFP + Berberis)

10g (¼oz) light turquoise (White SFP + touch of Hydrangea)

200g (7oz) palest blue (White SFP + touch of Hyacinth)

30g (1oz) peach (White SFP + touch of Marigold + touch of Pink)

100g (3½oz) reddish terracotta (White SFP + Terracotta + touch of Poppy)

100g (3½oz) ruby (Cyclamen SFP)

100g (3½oz) skin tone (White SFP + touch of Teddy Bear Brown + touch of Pink)

50g (1¾oz) White

SK Instant Mix Pastillage:

30g (1oz) blue-grey (Wisteria)

100g (3½oz) pale blue (touch of Wisteria)

100g (3½oz) ruby (Cyclamen)

50g (1¾oz) white (uncoloured)

SK Professional Paste Food Colours: Berberis, Bluegrass, Cyclamen (ruby), Fuchsia, Hyacinth, Hydrangea, Marigold (tangerine), Poppy, Teddy Bear Brown, Wisteria

SK Designer Paste Food Colour: Terracotta

SK Quality Food Colour (QFC) Paste: Pink

SK Professional Liquid Food Colours: Bulrush (dark brown), Hyacinth

SK Designer Pastel Dust Food Colour: Pastel Pink

SK Instant Mix Royal Icing:

150g (5¼oz) white (uncoloured)

30g (1oz) pink (Fuchsia)

SK Professional Food Colour Pen: Brown

SK CMC Gum

EQUIPMENT

Basic equipment (see pages 6 to 7)

20.5cm (8") square cake drum (board)

16.5cm (6½") square cake card

Spare cake card

Spare polystyrene dummy

Piece of thin card, e.g. from a cereal box or cake box

Round cutters: 5mm, 1cm, 1.5cm, 2cm, 4cm (¼", ⅜", ⅝", ¾", 1½")

Round piping nozzle: no. 3

Square cutter: 8mm (⅜")

Small lily of the valley cutter (TT)

Tweezers (optional)

18-gauge floral wire: white

85cm x 15mm width (33½" x ⅝") satin ribbon: navy blue

67cm x 5mm width (26" x ¼") satin ribbon: navy blue

Templates (see page 248)

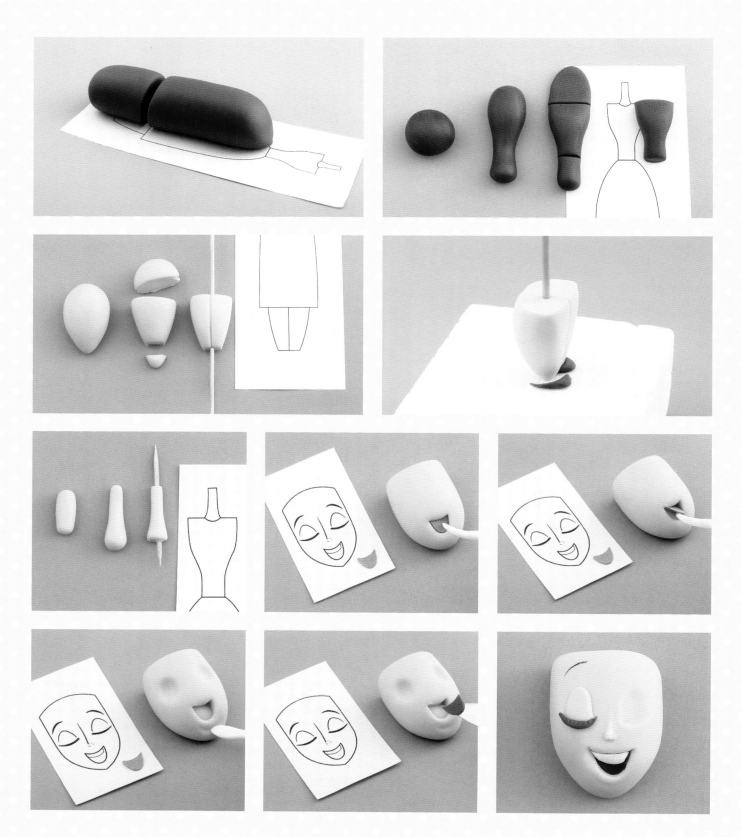

HOUSEWIFE

Skirt

1 Knead 100g (3½oz) of ruby pastillage with 100g (3½oz) of ruby SFP then add a generous pinch of CMC to make a stronger modelling paste. Roll the modelling paste into a long, thick sausage following the width of the template as a guide. Slightly flatten the sausage on one side, round off the top end and use a knife to cut the bottom edge straight. The rounded side will form the back of the skirt and the flatter side will be the front.

TUTOR TIP

The extra pinch of CMC will help strengthen the paste and speed up its drying time.

2 Insert a lightly greased skewer in through the bottom of the skirt, almost ¾ of the way up its length. Allow to firm up overnight then push the skewer protruding from the skirt into a spare polystyrene dummy.

TUTOR TIP

It is advisable to grease the skewer with a little white vegetable fat before inserting it into the skirt, as this will make it easier to remove later.

Torso

3 Roll a 20g (¾oz) ball of ruby modelling paste into the shape of a bowling pin. Press down on the thicker end with the heel of your hand to flatten it slightly. Use a knife to cut the paste straight at both ends following the torso template provided. Insert a cocktail stick into the bottom of the torso then remove to make a hole. Pierce another hole in the top of the torso where the neck will be inserted later. Allow to firm up.

Legs

4 Roll 30g (1oz) of skin tone SFP into a long teardrop and flatten it down slightly with your hand. Use a knife to cut both ends straight to make a trapezium shape following the template provided. Insert a skewer into the paste lengthways, making sure to leave a long piece of skewer protruding from the bottom to help support the figurine when it is inserted into the cake. Press the length of a skewer into the front and back of the paste to indent a vertical line, dividing the legs. Once firm enough to handle, insert the legs into a piece of spare polystyrene.

5 Roll two very small sausages of reddish terracotta SFP. Make the ends pointed and secure around the front of each leg for the shoes. Set aside to dry.

Neck

6 Roll a small piece of skin tone SFP into an elongated pear shape and cut the ends straight following the template provided. Insert a cocktail stick into the neck lengthways and allow to firm up.

Head

7 Roll approximately 25g (just over ¾oz) of skin tone SFP into a teardrop shape. Flatten down the top slightly and press the sides to square them off, following the template provided for the head shape.

8 To open up the mouth, cut out the shape of the smile from a piece of card first. Place the cardboard piece on the lower half of the face and gently push it into the paste with the tip of a Dresden tool. To remove, simply push down on one of the corners to lift the opposite side and carefully lift away with a pair of tweezers or a Dresden tool.

9 Gently press a small ball tool into the upper half of the face to make the eye sockets. Bring out the lower lip by pressing the paste underneath the mouth with the rounded edge of a Dresden tool.

10 Roll out a very small piece of reddish terracotta SFP and use a cutting wheel and the card template to cut out the shape of the smile. Lift the paste on the tip of a small knife and secure inside the mouth. Roll out a very small piece of White SFP thinly and cut out a crescent shape for the teeth with a 1cm (³/8") round cutter. Cut one side straight and secure in the top of the mouth.

11 Roll a very thin, long teardrop from some skin tone SFP for the nose and secure between the eyes. Carefully pinch the bridge and cut the bottom of the nose straight.

12 For the closed eyelids, roll two tiny ovals of skin tone SFP and flatten them down slightly with your finger. Trim one end of the lids using a 1cm (³/8") round cutter and secure into the eye sockets. Roll two very small, pointed sausages from a piece of Bulrush-coloured SFP and attach them just underneath the eyelids to make the eyelashes. Use a fine paintbrush and Bulrush liquid food colour to paint the eyebrows towards the top of the face.

13 Mix Pastel Pink dust food colour with some cornflour and brush it over the cheeks using a soft paintbrush. Allow the head to dry overnight, or until firm enough to handle.

TUTOR TIP
_____

Simply follow the head diagram to decide where to position the facial details.

Skirt pattern

14 Push a cocktail stick vertically into the top of the skirt towards the flatter side (remember that the flat side will be the front).

15 Thinly roll out some reddish terracotta SFP and cut out rings of different sizes using 5mm, 1cm, 1.5cm and 2cm (1/4", 3/8", 5/8" and 3/4") round cutters. Shape the circles into ovals and attach them randomly over the skirt, including off the edge.

16 Place 30g (1oz) of pink royal icing into a small paper piping bag and snip off the tip. Pipe circles either on the inside or outside of the rings. Pipe tiny dots of pink royal icing over the skirt. Cut out very small circles of deep orange SFP with a no. 3 round piping nozzle and stick them over the

TUTOR TIP
_____

In order to pipe more comfortably, you may find it easier to remove the skirt from the polystyrene base and hold it by the skewer protruding from the base.

skirt to finish the pattern. Alternatively, you can roll very small pinches of deep orange paste into balls and flatten them with your finger.

17 Push the torso down onto the cocktail stick protruding from the top of the skirt and position it so that it is facing slightly to the right. Secure in place with a little softened ruby modelling paste. Insert the neck down onto the top of the torso and secure with a little softened skin tone SFP.

Arms

18 Make two arms following the instructions on page 48. The arms should be fairly thick but in proportion to the rest of the body: make sure the elbows sit just above waist level. Mark with a Dresden tool at the elbow. Bend the left arm at a 90° angle and have the hand flat as shown in the picture. Allow the arm to dry on its side with the thumb facing upwards. Insert a cocktail stick into the forearm to help the arm support the weight of the tray and cake. Snip off the end of the cocktail stick with a small pair of pliers.

19 Bend the right arm slightly at the elbow and bend the hand gently backwards. Allow both arms to dry completely.

Tray

20 Thinly roll out a small amount of white pastillage, cut out a 4cm (1½") circle and allow to dry on a flat surface.

Collar

21 Take a very small piece of reddish terracotta SFP and roll it into a thin sausage with pointed ends. Position the collar around the neck so the pointed ends join at the back. Flatten the collar slightly and make a V-shaped cut at the front to shape.

Apron

22 To make the apron pattern, roll out some White SFP very thinly and cut out a thin strip and several circles using a 5mm (1/4") round cutter. Set aside and cover with food-grade plastic to prevent the pieces from drying out.

23 Roll out some peach SFP very thinly, lay the white strip across the top of the paste and spread the dots out evenly. Roll over the paste again to merge the pattern and cut out the shape of the apron following the template provided. Secure a strip of White SFP across the bottom of the apron and use the handle of a paintbrush to give it a frilly finish. Use the tip of a no. 3 piping nozzle to emboss tiny circles just above the frilled edge.

24 Attach the apron to the front of the body: make some loose folds at the bottom of the apron and leave the top part slack as shown in the picture.

25 Cut out a very narrow strip of White SFP and secure it around the waist to create the apron strings. Place another strip of the same size around the neck and secure the ends to the top of the apron. Finish the apron by securing a White SFP bow to the back of the body.

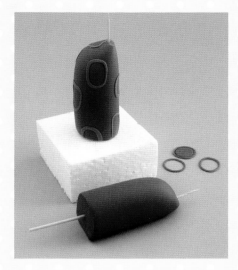
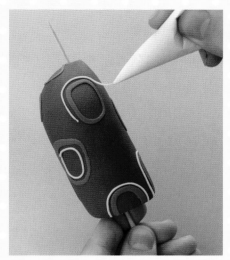
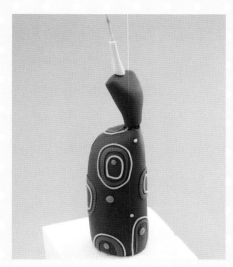
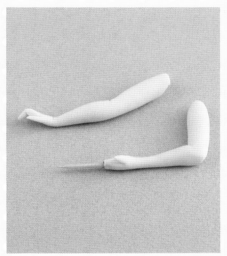
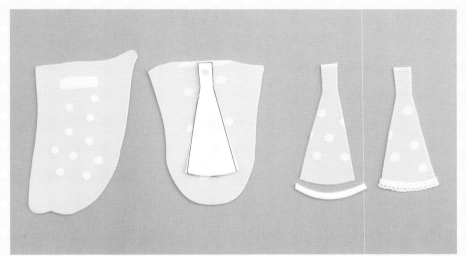
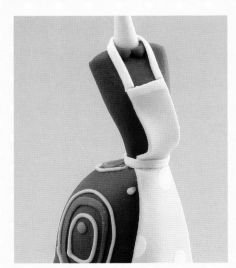
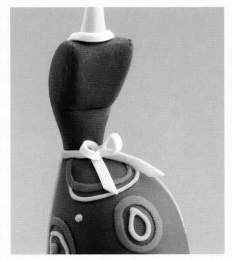

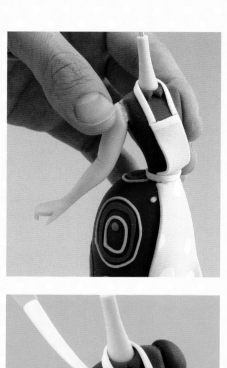
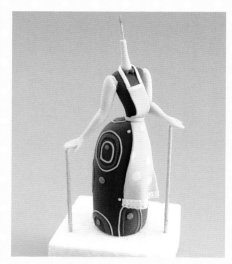

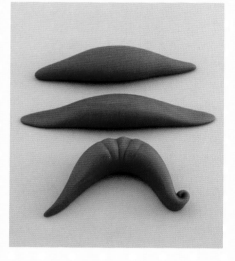

Assembly

26 Attach the arms to the sides of the torso with softened skin tone SFP and leave to dry completely, using barbecue skewers to support them. Remove any excess paste from the joins with a paintbrush for a neat finish.

27 For the sleeves, roll out some reddish terracotta SFP and cut out a 2.5cm (1") circle using the cutter. Divide the circle in half and place each half over the shoulders so the cut side makes the bottom edge of the sleeve. Gently stroke the paste around the curve of the shoulder and use edible glue to secure. Push the edge of a Dresden tool into the join to neaten it and trim away any excess paste with a craft knife.

28 Roll a small piece of reddish terracotta SFP into a teardrop shape that is large enough to cover the back of the head and fill out the head shape. Flatten it down slightly with your fingers and attach to the back of the head, from the nape upwards. Gently push the head down onto the skewer

protruding from the top of the neck and secure in place. Allow to dry before adding the rest of the hair.

29 Roll a sausage of reddish terracotta SFP that tapers at both ends and flatten the ends with the heel of your hand, leaving the middle section quite thick. Bend the sausage into a C-shape and use the edge of a Dresden tool to make indents across the middle section. Roll up the ends slightly and secure to the top of the head with a little edible glue. Make small teardrop shapes from the same colour paste and attach them over the forehead for the fringe.

30 For the hairband, roll a very small piece of deep orange SFP into a thin sausage that is pointed at both ends and attach it at the join between the fringe and the rest of the hair.

31 Remove the figurine from the polystyrene base, then twist and pull the skewer protruding from the bottom of the skirt to remove it. Push the figurine down onto the skewer in the top of the legs and secure with some

softened skin tone SFP. Attach the tray to the left hand with some softened skin tone SFP and support with skewers, if necessary, until fully dry.

32 Make a small flower using the lily of the valley cutter and White SFP then attach it to the right of the hairband. Allow the whole figurine to dry completely.

VINTAGE CABINET

33 Following the cabinet templates, roll out the pale blue pastillage to the thickness required and cut out each piece. Leave them on a flat surface to dry completely.

34 For the legs, cut an 18-gauge floral wire into four pieces that are 4.5cm (1¾") long and moisten them with edible glue. Push a ball of blue-grey pastillage onto each piece of wire and roll the paste along it using your palms. Continue until you have made a narrow cone shape that covers the whole length of the wire. Trim any excess paste from either end and allow to dry completely.

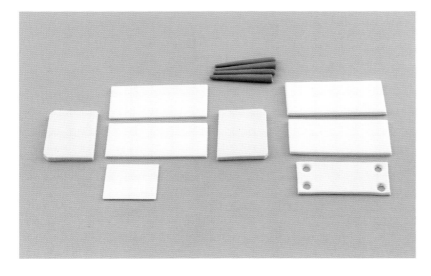

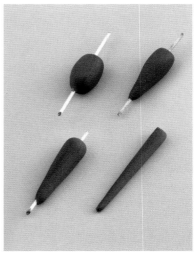

Important note: In order to make the legs of the cabinet very thin, I have had to use wire rather than cocktail sticks. As the wire is inedible, make sure that you remove the cake topper before it is served.

35 Fill a paper piping bag with firm-peak royal icing, snip off the tip of the bag and use the icing to glue the pieces of the cabinet together. Attach the front door (C) to the front of the cabinet (A1). Lay the top of the cabinet (B1) flat on a surface and glue the front and back pieces (A1 and A2) to the longer sides at a 90° angle. Reinforce the joins on the inside with dots of royal icing. Remove any excess icing with the tip of a knife to neaten the joins on the outside. Secure the bottom of the cabinet (B2) on top of the sides and allow to dry for a few minutes. Lay the cabinet on a thin piece of pastillage to raise it while you work and attach the sides (D1 and D2) with the rounded corners at the front. Secure the leg reinforcement (E) on top and attach the legs in the sockets at a slight angle. Allow to dry completely before turning the cabinet upright. Attach two very small strips of blue-grey pastillage to the doors.

MODEL CAKES AND STANDS

36 For the bottom tier, lightly dust a 2cm (¾") round cutter with a little cornflour. Roll a ball of palest blue SFP and place it inside the cutter. Push a large ball tool into the paste to hollow out the inside and create a cylindrical shape as shown in picture. Repeat for the middle tier using a 1.5cm (⅝") round cutter. Roll out some palest blue SFP to the same thickness as the height of the other two tiers and cut out a cylinder with a 1cm (⅜") cutter for the top tier.

37 Once all tiers are dry, stack them on top of each other and stick them together with run-out consistency icing. Allow the run-out icing to drip down the sides of the cake. Finish with a small ball of light turquoise SFP.

38 Repeat steps 36–37 to make another tiered cake, this time from White SFP. Cut out a flower shape from light turquoise SFP using a small lily of the valley cutter and soften the edges with a ball tool. Fold the flower in half and pinch at the base. Place on top of the cake.

39 Use white pastillage to model a small cone shape for the base of the cake stand and cut out a 3cm (1⅛") circle for the plate. Once dry, attach the plate to the base with a dot of softened pastillage and allow to dry completely.

40 Model a small piece of light Hydrangea SFP into a thick ring shape and draw lines round the sides with the edge of a Dresden tool. Once firm, dip it in white run-out consistency icing and leave to dry.

41 To make the tea towels and cloths, roll out some pale blue SFP very thinly and cut out three rectangles. Paint over the paste using Hyacinth liquid food colour and a fine paintbrush and fold loosely before arranging on the cake.

KITCHEN FLOOR

42 Roll out 100g (3½oz) of palest blue SFP to 2mm (1/16") thick and cut out a 16cm (6¼") square using the template provided. Mark a grid on the paste using a blade tool and a clean ruler: each line should be 2cm (¾") apart to make equal squares.

43 To create the pattern, cut out circles from each square on the grid using a 1.5cm (⅝") round cutter. Roll out some White SFP to the same thickness as the floor, cut out the same amount of circles and fill in the gaps. Cut out diamond shapes from the corners using an 8mm (⅜") square cutter. Fill the gaps with squares of blue-green SFP in the same way. Use a ruler and a blade tool to mark out the tiles again. Draw dots and dashes over the tiles with a Brown food colour pen to create a symmetrical pattern.

TUTOR TIP

When making a tiled floor, make sure the paste is fresh enough that all the 'patchwork' pieces stick together without the need for edible glue.

44 Roll out some pale blue SFP to 2mm (1/16") thick and cut out another 16cm (6¼") square. Brush the surface with edible glue, lift the tiled floor on a cake card and place it on top of the second square.

45 While the floor is still soft, place the cabinet in position and gently push it into the paste to make grooves; this will give the cabinet more stability once it is glued in place. Take care, however, not to push the legs through the tiled floor as they must not come into contact with the cake. Pierce the tiled floor with a barbecue skewer where you will insert the character later and leave to dry.

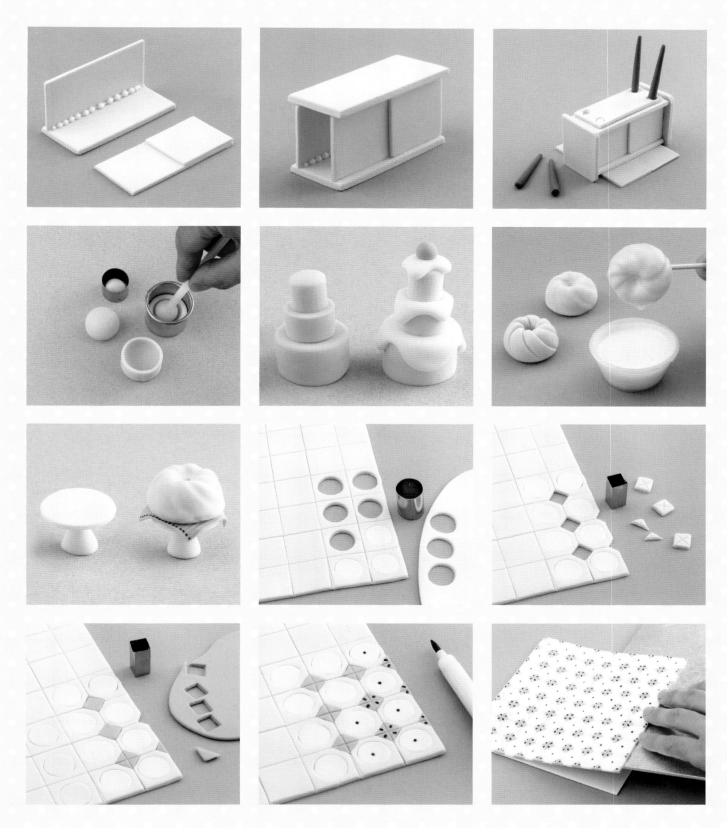

CAKE AND CAKE DRUM

46 Cover the cake with pale blue sugarpaste (see page 34) and trim with the 5mm (¼") navy blue ribbon.

47 Cover the cake drum with Bridal White sugarpaste (see page 41) and secure the cake in the centre. Finish the cake board with the 15mm (⁵⁄₈") navy blue ribbon.

CAKE ASSEMBLY

48 Secure the tiled floor to the centre of the cake with royal icing then stick the cabinet in the grooves with dots of royal icing or softened pastillage. Attach the cake stands, cakes and cloths on top of the cabinet with dots of royal icing. Position a folded kitchen cloth on the tiled floor.

49 Once the figurine has completely dried, take it out of the temporary dummy, cover the bottom of the feet with softened SFP to act as a glue and push the skewer into the pre-made hole in the floor. Place the cake on the tray in her hand.

TUTOR TIP

If you are transporting the cake, it is best to attach the figurine upon arrival to prevent breakages (see page 55).

TILE BISCUITS

Bake 35 5cm (2") square biscuits following the recipe provided on page 18.

Colour some medium-consistency royal icing with a touch of Bluegrass paste food colour, fit a piping bag with a no. 1 nozzle and fill with the pale blue icing. Pipe an outline around each of the square biscuits, then let down the remaining icing to run-out consistency. Flood inside the outline with the blue runny icing and a no. 2 nozzle (see page 30).

While the icing is still wet, use some white run-out icing and a no. 2 nozzle to pipe four evenly spaced white dots on each biscuit. Gently tap the biscuit on the work surface to smooth out the icing and blend the two colours. Colour some run-out icing with Hydrangea and a touch of Black paste food colours and pipe teardrops around the circles to create a repeated pattern on each tile. Drop a dot of the darker icing into the centre of the white circles and leave to dry.

SOLAR SUPERHERO

Fans of comics and sci-fi movies will appreciate this fantastic superhero figurine that seems to defy gravity. This exciting cake design shows you how to use airbrush colours to make vivid scenes and achieve a real depth of colour. You can have lots of fun experimenting with colours and designs to create your very own superhero.

EDIBLES

18cm x 10cm (7" x 4") dome-shaped cake, filled and crumb-coated (see page 38)

SK Sugarpaste (rolled fondant):

    800g (1lb 12oz) Bridal White

SK Sugar Florist Paste (SFP, gum paste):

    400g (14oz) skin tone (White SFP + touch of Nasturtium)

SK Instant Mix Pastillage:

    100g (3½oz) white (uncoloured)

SK Instant Mix Royal Icing:

    100g (3½oz) pale orange (touch of Nasturtium)

SK Professional Paste Food Colour: Nasturtium

SK Professional Liquid Food Colours: Bulrush, Nasturtium, Poinsettia, Sunflower

SK CMC Gum

EQUIPMENT

Basic equipment (see pages 6 to 7)

28cm (11") square cake drum (board)

18cm (7") round cake card

20.5cm (8") round or square polystyrene dummy

Round piping nozzles: nos. 4, 16

Savoy piping nozzle: 10mm (3/8")

Masking tape

1m x 15mm width (39" x 5/8") satin ribbon: burgundy

Airbrush

Templates (see page 249)

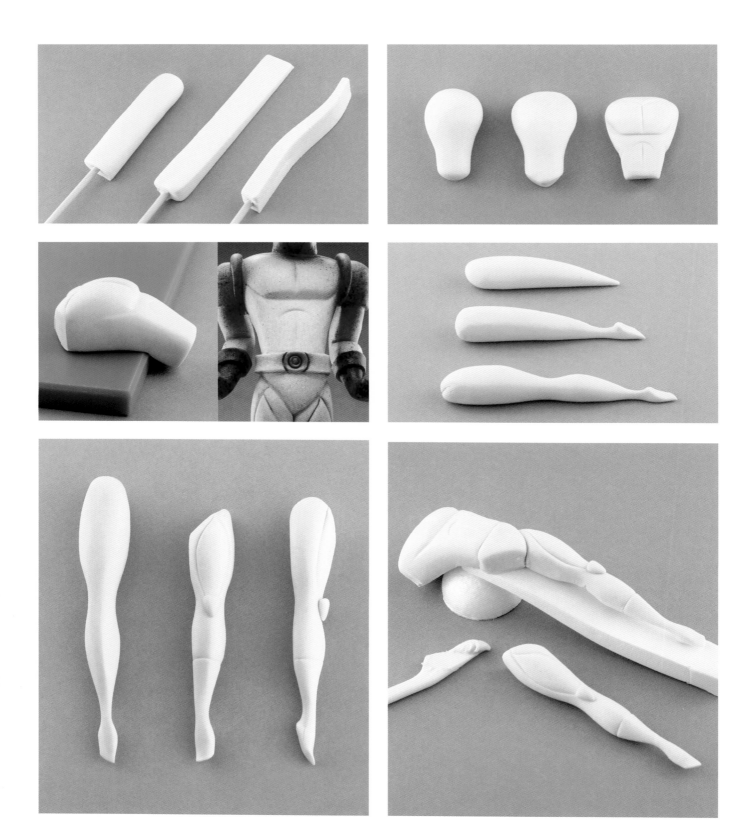

PASTILLAGE SUPPORT

1 Roll 100g (3½oz) of white pastillage into a long sausage that is the same width as the front support template. Insert a dowel halfway up the support, leaving approximately 10cm (4") protruding from the base. Press the top and sides with cake smoothers to thin the paste slightly towards the top of the support to make it into a wedge and achieve the length required. Cut the sides straight with a sharp knife to make the paste fit the template.

2 Turn the support on its side and bend the paste into shape following the support profile template. Allow the paste to dry.

TUTOR TIP

Prepare the pastillage support in advance as you need it to be completely dry before you start modelling the superhero.

SUPERHERO

Torso

3 Roll 80g (2¾oz) of skin tone SFP into a pear shape. Press the top of the thicker end with the side of your hand to bring out the chest and widen the shoulder line. Flatten the other end slightly so it is the same thickness as the body template provided. Use a sharp knife to trim the bottom end straight, then follow the template to cut the top into the shape of the shoulder line.

4 Press the side of a cake smoother across the middle of the paste to bring out the chest (pectorals) and lower the stomach simultaneously. Use the edge of a cake smoother to define the sides of the chest and accentuate the 'lat' muscles. Use a Dresden tool to mark on the collar bone, stomach and abdominal muscles and a line down the chest, following the lines on the template. Position the torso with the waist over the edge of a non-stick board to give the back a slight curve and allow to firm up.

Legs

5 Roll 80g (2¾oz) of skin tone SFP into a sausage and cut it in half. Roll both pieces into long cones and model them into legs (see page 51) that are the same size as the template. Pinch along the shins to create a sharp edge, then roll tiny piece of skin tone SFP into a triangular shape and attach it to the knee with a little edible glue. Use the edge of a Dresden tool and the template to mark lines on the legs for the boots and thighs. Position the legs with the kneecaps facing upwards and leave them to firm up.

6 Before the legs and torso dry out completely, attach the lower half of the torso to the top of the pastillage support and secure with a little softened skin tone SFP. Raise the top end of the pastillage support with a piece of polystyrene or similar, in order to allow the torso to hang over the end. Roll 10g (¼oz) of skin tone SFP into a triangular shape for the hips following the template as a guide, and attach to the pastillage support just below the torso. Secure both legs to the hips and the pastillage support with a little softened SFP. Use the templates to help you position the legs and torso on the pastillage support.

Arms

7 Roll 40g (1½oz) of skin tone SFP into a sausage, divide it in two

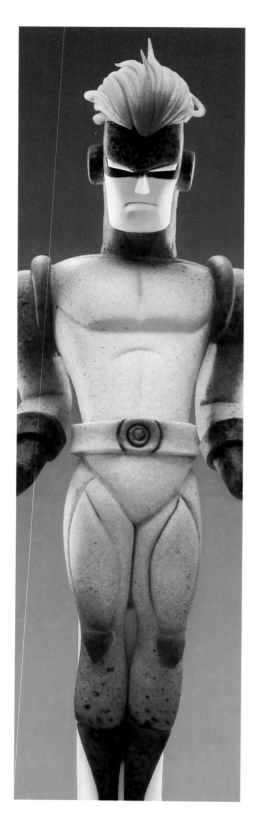

and model each piece into an arm (see page 50) using the templates as a guide. You do not need to model an open hand, just square off the end of the arm slightly to make it into a fist shape. Mark a few lines with a Dresden tool to make the fingers. Roll a pinch of skin tone SFP into a tiny oval with a pointed end and attach it across the top of the fist to make a thumb. Mark on the sleeve line as shown on the template and bend the arms at the wrist and elbow until they are almost at right angles. Leave to dry completely.

Head

8 Roll approximately 15g (½oz) of skin tone SFP into a thick cylinder shape, then press the top and sides with a cake smoother to square them off. Press down across the eye line to bring out the forehead and flatten the face at the same time. Cut the sides of the face at an angle with a sharp knife. Indent the eyes just below the forehead with the tip of a Dresden tool.

9 For the nose, roll a tiny pinch of skin tone SFP into a teardrop, pinch along the top to make a ridge and make it into a triangle shape. Cut the bottom straight and secure it to the middle of the face.

10 For the mouth, draw a straight line underneath the nose with the edge of a Dresden tool. Gently push the rounded edge of the Dresden tool beneath the mouth line to bring out the lower lip. Press in the sides of the face with the tip of your index fingers to accentuate the cheekbones. Cut the top straight with a sharp knife, then cut the bottom at a slight angle to define the jaw line. Leave to firm up.

Neck

11 Roll approximately 30g (1oz) of skin tone SFP into a sausage that is approximately the same width and thickness as the neck template, then use a knife to trim the top end straight and the base at a slight angle. Attach the neck to the torso with some softened skin tone SFP. Place a wedge of polystyrene underneath the neck to tilt it forward, then mark a V-shape on the front of the neck following the template. Stick the head onto the front of the neck.

Assembly

12 Stick the arms to either side of the torso with some softened skin tone SFP. If necessary, place a small piece of foam or polystyrene under the arms to hold them in place until completely dry.

13 Roll out a pinch of skin tone SFP to 5mm (¼") thick and use a 10mm (³⁄₈") round nozzle to cut out two small circles. Stick the ears to either side of the head with a little edible glue.

14 Roll two thin sausages and attach them over the shoulders with edible glue: the strips add to the design whilst strengthening the join between the arms and torso. Secure a strip around each forearm for the gloves, then secure another thin strip around the waist to make the the belt. Use the 10mm, no. 16 and no. 4 piping nozzles to emboss two or three circles into the front of the belt to make the buckle. Leave the whole piece to dry completely.

Hair

15 Insert the whole figurine into a spare polystyrene dummy.

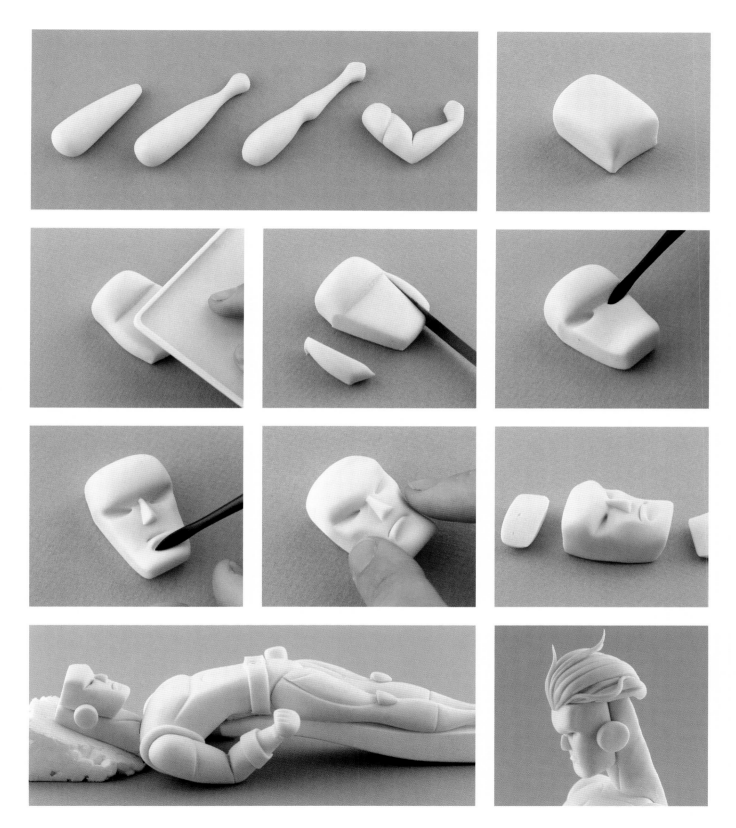

Roll 50g (1¾oz) of skin tone SFP into the shape of a lemon, then position the paste over the head so that one pointed end sits in the centre of the forehead. Mark several lines lengthways along the paste with the edge of a Dresden tool. Roll a few tiny sausages with pointed ends from skin tone SFP and arrange these loose strands of hair to give a flaming, fiery look. Position the hair over the head and leave to firm up. Do not glue in place as you will need to remove the hair to paint it separately.

COLOURING

TUTOR TIP

You can use an airbrush, a new toothbrush or a combination of both to produce vivid results with liquid food colours; see page 54 for more information about using these techniques. If you don't want some areas to be coloured, I recommend covering those areas with masking tape and removing the tape once the paint has dried completely. You should only use masking tape on the figurine and ensure that the tape doesn't touch any part of the cake that is going to be eaten.

16 Cover the whole pastillage support with masking tape, using little pieces of tape at a time and trying not to leave any part uncovered. Cover the lower half of the face, including the nose, in the same way.

17 Use the splashing technique to apply an initial layer of Sunflower liquid food colour over the chest, then gradually fading out over the rest of the body (see page 54). Use a soft paintbrush to paint the boots and gloves with a layer of Nasturtium liquid food colour.

18 Use an airbrush or the splashing technique to colour the ends of the limbs, sides of the chest, back, neck and top of head with the Nasturtium liquid food colour. Apply a layer of Poinsettia liquid food colour over the shoulders, neck and top of the head. Avoid painting the front of the chest as this is should be the bright focal point of the piece. Spray or flick a light layer of Bulrush liquid food colour over the ends of limbs, shoulders and top of the head. Be careful not to overdo this layer as you may make it too dark.

19 Airbrush the hair with an initial layer of Sunflower liquid food colour and then colour the front of the hair with Nasturtium liquid food colour, so it gradually fades out to resemble the colour of a flame. Leave the paint to dry completely.

20 Once the figure is dry, remove the masking tape from the face and the pastillage support. To make the eyes, roll out a small piece of Bridal White sugarpaste very thinly and cut out two long triangle shapes. Secure them into the eye sockets with edible glue.

TUTOR TIP

When you remove the masking tape, your may get paint on your fingertips. If you accidentally stain the white support, you can easily brush the colour away using a paintbrush dampened with clear alcohol.

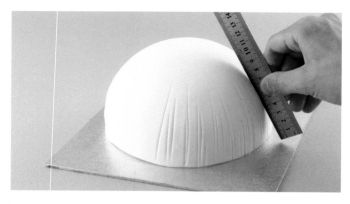

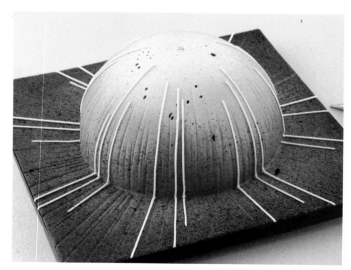

TUTOR TIP

It is not advisable to transport figurines on their bases as they may topple over; place the figurine in a cake box as explained on page 55 and assemble once you have arrived at the venue. Secure the pastillage support to the cake with some royal icing.

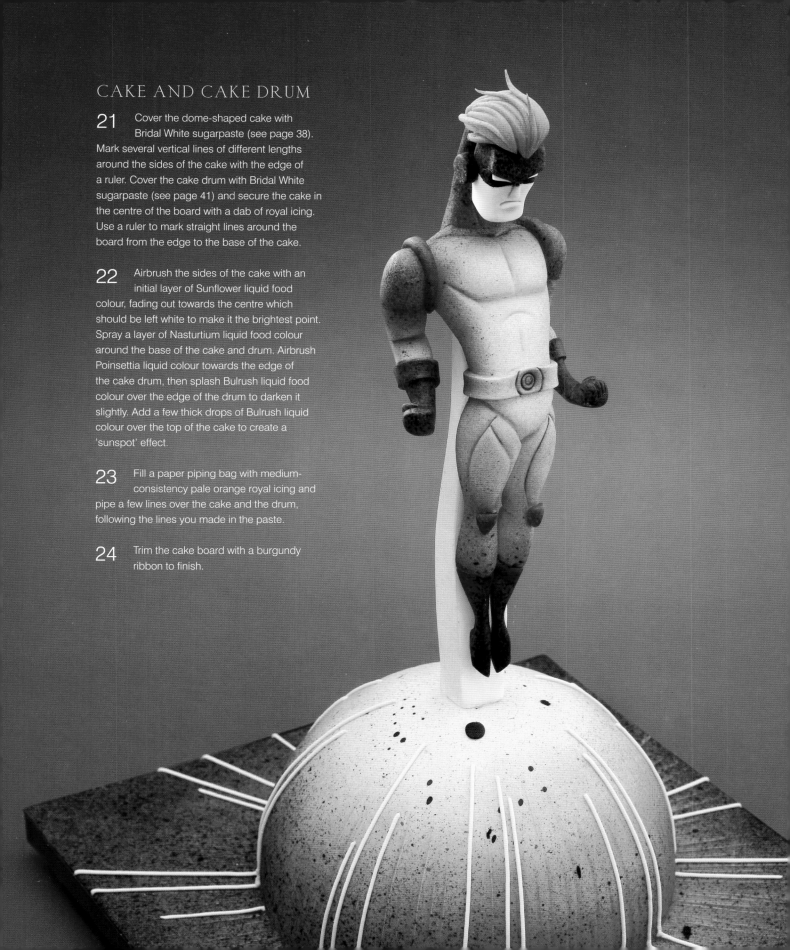

CAKE AND CAKE DRUM

21 Cover the dome-shaped cake with Bridal White sugarpaste (see page 38). Mark several vertical lines of different lengths around the sides of the cake with the edge of a ruler. Cover the cake drum with Bridal White sugarpaste (see page 41) and secure the cake in the centre of the board with a dab of royal icing. Use a ruler to mark straight lines around the board from the edge to the base of the cake.

22 Airbrush the sides of the cake with an initial layer of Sunflower liquid food colour, fading out towards the centre which should be left white to make it the brightest point. Spray a layer of Nasturtium liquid food colour around the base of the cake and drum. Airbrush Poinsettia liquid colour towards the edge of the cake drum, then splash Bulrush liquid food colour over the edge of the drum to darken it slightly. Add a few thick drops of Bulrush liquid colour over the top of the cake to create a 'sunspot' effect.

23 Fill a paper piping bag with medium-consistency pale orange royal icing and pipe a few lines over the cake and the drum, following the lines you made in the paste.

24 Trim the cake board with a burgundy ribbon to finish.

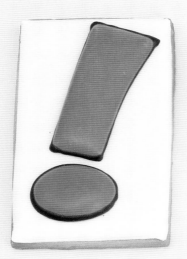

COMIC BOOK BISCUITS

Use the templates on page 249 to pipe the names and exclamation marks as run-outs on a sheet of cellophane (see page 30). Fit a piping bag with a no. 1 nozzle, fill with Black medium-consistency royal icing then pipe an outline around the name. Flood the letters with pale Berberis-coloured run-out icing and leave to dry. Repeat for the exclamation marks, but use Nasturtium-coloured icing to flood them instead.

Make the biscuit dough following the recipe on page 18, cut out 23 speech bubbles using the template provided or 23 7cm x 4cm (2¾" x 1½") rectangles, then bake as required.

Pipe an outline around the edge of the speech bubble biscuits with Berberis-coloured, medium-consistency icing and a no. 1 nozzle. Flood the biscuits with Berberis-coloured run-out icing and a no. 2 nozzle then leave to dry. Repeat for the rectangular biscuits but using white run-out icing instead.

Splash Poinsettia liquid food colour over the speech bubble biscuits using the method on page 54. Attach the names and the exclamation marks to the biscuits with royal icing.

STAR SUPREME

With her supreme style and elegance, this sugar starlet is sure to steal the show at any party! This timeless cake design would be perfect for a budding superstar or an aspiring diva – remember that you can change her outfit and features to make your very own personalised pop princess.

EDIBLES

15cm round x 12cm deep (6" x 4¾") cake, filled and crumb-coated (see page 34)

SK Sugarpaste (rolled fondant):

    700g (1lb 8¾oz) pale blue (Bridal White Sugarpaste + a touch of Hydrangea)

    400g (14oz) sky blue (Bridal White Sugarpaste + Hydrangea)

SK Sugar Florist Paste (SFP, gum paste):

    10g (¼oz) Black

    30g (1oz) pink (White SFP + Fuchsia)

    30g (1oz) poppy red (White SFP + Poppy)

    30g (1oz) ruby (Cyclamen SFP)

    250g (8¾oz) skin tone (White SFP + Warm Brown + Poppy)

    10g (¼oz) soft beige (White SFP + Chestnut)

    150g (5¼oz) White

SK Instant Mix Pastillage:

    100g (3½oz) palest blue (touch of Bluegrass)

SK Instant Mix Royal Icing:

    50g (1¾oz) black (Blackberry)

    50g (1¾oz) pale blue (touch of Hydrangea)

SK Professional Paste Food Colours: Bluegrass, Chestnut (soft beige), Edelweiss (white), Fuchsia, Hydrangea, Poppy

SK Quality Food Colour (QFC) Paste: Warm Brown

SK Professional Dust Food Colours: Cyclamen, Fuchsia, Poppy

SK Professional Liquid Food Colour: Poppy

SK Confectioners' Glaze

Edible glitter: silver

EQUIPMENT

Basic equipment (see pages 6 to 7)

25.5cm (10") square cake drum (board)

15cm (6") round cake card

Spare polystyrene dummy

Rubber cone tool (or a Dresden tool)

Round cutters: 1cm, 3cm ($^3/_8$", $1^1/_8$")

Round piping nozzle: no. 16

Stanley knife

Polystyrene balls: 3cm, 5cm ($1^1/_8$", 2")

Stephanotis cutter: small, from set of 3 (TT)

Six-petal blossom cutters: small and medium (TT)

30-gauge floral wires: white

Anemone leaf cutter: medium (TT)

Flower drying stand (SK), or similar

2m x 15mm width (79" x $^5/_8$") satin ribbon: white

Templates (see page 250)

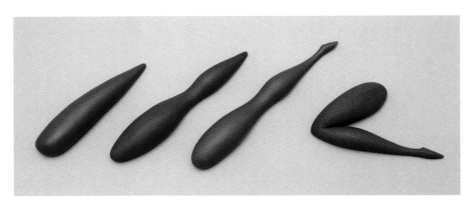

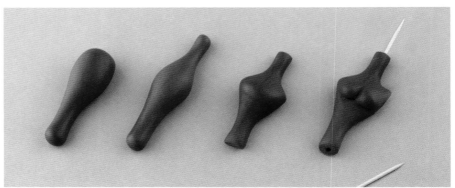
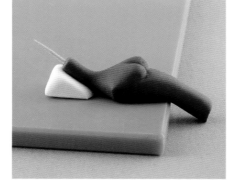

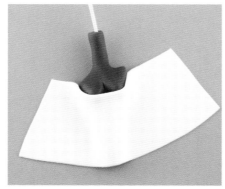

FIGURE

Left leg

1 Roll 45g–50g (1½oz–1¾oz) of skin tone SFP into a long cone shape and model the leg and foot following the instructions on page 51. Bend the leg at a 45° angle and pinch the bend of the knee to make it slightly pointed. Make the leg the same size as the template provided, position it so the inside leg is on the work surface and leave to dry.

Right leg

2 Roll 45g–50g (1½oz–1¾oz) of White SFP into another leg shape, then bend the knee to a 90° angle. You do not need to model the foot for this leg, as it will only be used to give shape and support to the skirt. Set the leg aside to dry.

Pelvis

3 Roll approximately 20g (¾oz) of White SFP into a teardrop shape for the pelvis. Position the paste on a spare polystyrene dummy and insert a piece of barbecue skewer down through the pelvis and into the polystyrene. Leave a piece of skewer protruding from the top for the torso.

4 Cut the sides at an angle to make the pelvis into a V-shape. Secure the top of the right leg to the pelvis with a little edible glue, then attach the left leg to the other side with softened White SFP. Place a piece of foam or polystyrene under the left foot to support the leg in position as it dries. Leave to dry completely.

Torso

5 Roll approximately 35g (1¼oz) of skin tone SFP into the shape of a bowling pin. Roll the thicker end with the side of your hand to narrow the paste and bring out the neck. Cut straight across the top of the neck and bottom of the torso to make it the same size as the template.

6 Pinch out the front of the torso to bring out the chest with your index finger and thumb, then pinch each side of the neck to bring out the shoulders. Use the sharp edge of a Dresden tool to mark a line down the middle of the chest and indent two curves to accentuate the bust.

7 Bring the paste of the left shoulder a little higher to break the symmetry and make the torso look more natural. Insert a cocktail stick into the top of the neck, then push another cocktail stick into the bottom of the torso and remove to make a hole. Mark a short line down the middle of the back with the sharp edge of a Dresden tool.

8 Position the torso over the edge of a non-stick board so the lower half hangs over the edge, in order to give the back a slight curve. Place a wedge of paste underneath the neck to tilt it slightly forward. Allow to dry overnight.

9 Roll out some White SFP into a thin sheet and cut it into a rectangle that is long enough and wide enough to wrap around the torso. Cut out a semicircle from the middle of one longer side of the rectangle using a 3cm (1¹⁄₈") round cutter.

10 Insert a cocktail stick into the base of the torso so you can hold it comfortably while attaching the top of the dress. Brush a little edible glue over the torso, excluding a V-shape on her back where you will need to trim away the paste. Wrap the paste around the torso, bringing the ends together at the back.

11 Use a pair of scissors to trim the excess paste at the join and the waist, then smooth out the join with your finger. Cut out a V-shape across the back with a sharp knife, then skewer the torso into a spare piece of polystyrene and leave to dry.

12 Once dry, push the torso onto the skewer protruding from the hips and secure with a dot of softened White SFP.

Arms

13 Roll 20g (¾oz) of skin tone SFP into a sausage and cut it in half. Model each piece into an arm (see page 50) and bend the hands backwards to a right angle.

14 Secure both arms to either side of the torso with a little edible glue: attach the left arm slightly higher than the right to prevent them looking too symmetrical. Position the left arm slightly closer to the hips than the right arm. Support the hands in place with a piece of foam or polystyrene if necessary.

TUTOR TIPS

When you are trying to create a more organic, natural figurine, it is important to avoid making the body look too symmetrical.

As this figurine is leaning back on her arms, the shoulders should be raised slightly to help give her a realistic posture.

tip of the tool. Holding the sides of the head, push the tip of a Dresden tool into the paste to open the mouth and give it depth. Place the Dresden tool under the top lip and push the paste upwards. To make the top lip look fuller, run the tip of a rubber cone tool (or Dresden tool) from one corner to the other and under the nose. For the lower lip, roll a pinch of skin tone SFP into a small sausage with pointed ends, bend it into a curve and attach it at the bottom of the mouth.

18 For the eyes, press the edge of a Dresden tool into the face on either side of the nose, just above the cheeks. Give shape to the eye sockets by pressing the rounded end of the Dresden tool into the paste. Roll two tiny, elongated ovals of White SFP and attach them into the bottom of each eye socket, then roll another sausage with pointed ends and secure it inside the mouth to make the teeth.

19 For the eyelids, roll two tiny ovals of skin tone SFP and flatten them down slightly with your finger. Trim one side with a 1cm (3/8") round cutter and secure them just above the whites of the eyes.

20 Roll two very small, pointed sausages from a piece of Black SFP and attach them at the base of the eyelids to make the lashes. Thinly roll out a small piece of soft beige SFP and cut out a tiny circle using a no. 16 round nozzle. Cut the circle in half and stick each half onto the white of the eye: position the irises so the figure is looking to the left. Use a Black food colour pen to draw pupils inside the irises, then paint dots of Edelweiss paste food colour on the edge of each pupil to highlight the eyes.

21 For the eyebrows, roll a pinch of Black SFP into two tiny sausages with pointed ends and glue

Head

15 Roll 25g–30g (¾oz–1oz) of skin tone SFP into a teardrop that is approximately the same size as the template provided. Make a groove across the middle line of the face using the side of your hand to bring out the cheeks and flatten the forehead. Raise the chin up by placing a dry wedge of paste under the face while you are working on the other details.

16 Pinch the paste in the centre of the face to bring out the nose and define the sides of it with the tip of a rubber cone tool (or Dresden tool). Open up the nostrils with the tip of a rubber cone tool or a barbecue skewer.

17 To make the mouth, draw a curved line underneath the nose with the edge of a Dresden tool and indent dimples into each corner with the

them in a curve over the eyelids. Paint the lips with Poppy liquid food colour and a fine paintbrush. Set the head aside until it firms up enough to handle.

Hair

22 Cut a 3cm (1⅛") diameter polystyrene ball in half with a Stanley knife and stick it to the back of the head with softened White SFP to fill out the head shape. Once firm, insert a cocktail stick into the base of the polystyrene to help you hold the head while you are piping the hair later.

23 Cut a 5cm (2") diameter polystyrene ball in half and cut out a semicircle from one side. Attach over the top of the polystyrene part of the head with softened White SFP: this will give the hair volume.

TUTOR TIP

If you prefer, you can use marshmallows instead of polystyrene to add volume to the hair.

24 Roll out some White SFP into a thin sheet and cut out a strip that is approximately 1.5cm (5/8") wide and long enough to wrap around the base of the head. Wrap the paste around the forehead and secure the ends at the base of the polystyrene ball.

25 Fill a paper piping bag with black firm-peak royal icing and snip off the very tip of the bag. Cover the polystyrene with curls of black piping: hold the head by the cocktail stick and turn it around in your hand while piping the curls. Make sure that you cover the whole area so no white parts are showing and leave to dry completely.

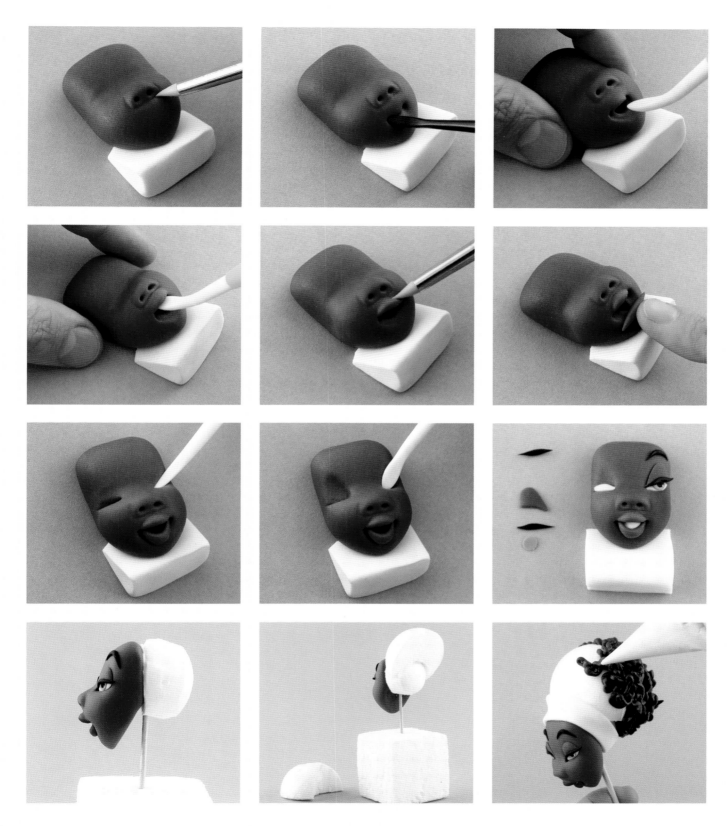

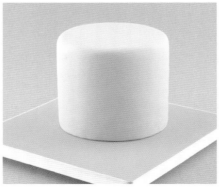

26 Remove the stick from the base of the head, then gently place the head on the cocktail stick protruding from the neck. Position the head so that she is looking over her left shoulder, then secure in place with a little softened skin tone SFP. Use a barbecue skewer to support the head until it is secure.

27 Roll two balls of skin tone SFP and make them into ears (see page 51). Add the ears on either side of the head, just below the headband. Roll two tiny balls of White SFP for the earrings and secure them to the ear lobes.

28 Roll out some White SFP into a thin sheet, cut out a strip with pointed ends and secure it across her chest. Cut out two thin strips of White SFP that are long enough to wrap around the arms, then secure the ends at the front and back of the shoulders so the straps hang loosely down each arm. Secure a strip of White SFP over the join at the top of the left leg to give it a neat finish.

29 At this stage brush the headband, dress, straps and right leg with some edible glue. Pick up some edible glitter on a dusting brush and sprinkle it over the white areas.

30 Use a small brush to paint some confectioners' glaze over the eyelids and lips for a glossy finish. Let the figurine dry completely.

SMALL FLOWERS

31 Roll out some ruby, poppy red and pink SFP into a thin sheet and cut out several small and medium flowers using the stephanotis and blossom flower cutters. Place the flowers on a foam pad and use a medium-sized ball tool to soften the edges. Pinch the back of some of the flowers and fold the petals in slightly. Dust the centre of each flower with either Poppy, Fuchsia or Cyclamen dust food colours.

BOUGAINVILLEA

32 Cut a few 30-gauge white floral wires into several pieces, dip the tip of each wire into some white run-out royal icing and leave them to dry hanging upside down from a flower drying stand or similar. Once dry, brush them with Fuchsia dust food colour, arrange them in groups of three and glue them together with a little non-toxic glue.

TUTOR TIP

If you are short on time, you can always use ready-made stamens instead of dipping floral wires into royal icing.

33 Roll out some poppy red SFP into a thin sheet and cut out several small petals using the anemone leaf cutter. Give each petal some movement and set aside to firm up. Glue three petals around each bunch of stamens with a little edible glue and leave to dry.

CAKE AND CAKE DRUM

34 Roll out 150g (5¼oz) of palest blue pastillage to 2mm (1/16") thick and cut out two sets of triangular panels using a craft knife and the templates provided. Leave to dry completely.

35 Cover the cake with pale blue sugarpaste (see page 34) and the cake drum with sky blue sugarpaste (see page 41). Position the cake slightly off-centre on the cake drum and secure it in place with a dab of royal icing. Trim both the cake and cake drum with white ribbon. Leave to firm up.

TUTOR TIP

It is important to leave the sugarpaste on both the cake and drum to firm up as you need the surface to dry before you sprinkle more glitter on the trail of the dress. It will be easy to remove any excess glitter if the sugarpaste surface is quite dry.

ASSEMBLY

36 Cut out a strip of White SFP that is approximately 27cm (10½") long and the same width as both thighs. Place one end of the strip on top of the cake and trail the paste down the side of the cake and onto the board. Secure it in place with edible glue.

TUTOR TIP

Make sure this strip is stuck firmly to the side of the cake and the drum so that it won't move out of place, especially if you want to transport the cake.

37 Transfer the figurine onto the cake so she is sitting on the top end of the white strip and insert the skewer protruding from the bottom of the hips into the cake. Secure with a dab of white royal icing. Trim the right side of the white strip to match the contour of the right leg for a neat finish.

38 Cut out another strip of White SFP to approximately 20cm (7¾") long and wide enough to wrap around the right leg. Position the paste over the top of the right knee and attach with edible glue: arrange the trail of the skirt so it is hanging over the first white strip, folding it gently to give some movement. Rub the paste at the knee with your fingers to blend the join so it looks seamless. Brush the trail of the dress with a little edible glue and sprinkle with some more edible glitter.

TUTOR TIP

The glitter will only stick to damp areas on the cake: simply remove any glitter that falls onto the cake drum with a dry brush.

39 Attach the triangular panels to the sides of the cake in a fan arrangement with enough royal icing to secure them in place. Secure four panels at the front and another four on the opposite side of the cake.

40 Arrange some flowers over the hair and attach with dabs of black royal icing. Secure some more flowers randomly over the cake and board with a dab of pale blue royal icing.

BLOSSOM BISCUITS

Bake 35 biscuits in the shape of five-petal blossoms following the recipe on page 18.

For the white flowers, fit a piping bag with a no. 1 nozzle, fill with medium-consistency uncoloured royal icing and pipe around the edge of the biscuits. Let down the icing to run-out consistency and flood inside the outline with a no. 2 nozzle (see page 30). Pick up some Ice White Fairy Sparkles on a dusting brush, then tap the brush with your finger to sprinkle the dust over the wet icing.

Make some small, pink flowers following the instructions on page 145 and secure them to the centre of the biscuits with edible glue. Pipe a dot of royal icing in the centre of the flowers and leave to dry.

To decorate the remaining biscuits, use the same method as for the white flowers but colour the icing with Fuchsia, Hydrangea and Poppy paste food colours to make the pink, blue and red flowers respectively. Decorate with Fairy Sparkles and top with a plunger cutter flower or piped petal design.

TO HAVE AND TO HOLD

A modelled bride and groom have been a favourite wedding cake topper for decades, so I wanted to give this design a contemporary twist by creating a pose where the figurines face each other. I have also stylised the figures by accentuating the square, masculine lines of the groom and the soft, flowing lines of the bride.

EDIBLES

20.5cm round x 8cm deep (8" x 3¹/₈") cake, filled and crumb-coated (see page 34)

SK Sugarpaste (rolled fondant):

  1.6kg (3lb 8½oz) Bridal White

SK Sugar Florist Paste (SFP, gum paste):

  150g (5¼oz) dark brown (White SFP + Bulrush)

  50g (1¾oz) reddish terracotta (White SFP + Terracotta + touch of Poppy)

  150g (5¼oz) skin tone (White SFP + touch of Teddy Bear Brown + touch of Pink)

  150g (5¼oz) terracotta (White SFP + Terracotta)

  300g (10½oz) White

SK Instant Mix Pastillage:

  200g (7oz) white (uncoloured)

SK Instant Mix Royal Icing:

  25g (just over ¾oz) light brown (Chestnut)

  50g (1¾oz) white (uncoloured)

SK Professional Paste Food Colours: Bulrush, Poppy, Teddy Bear Brown

SK Designer Paste Food Colour: Terracotta

SK Quality Food Colour (QFC) Paste Food Colour: Pink

SK Professional Dust Food Colour: Edelweiss (white)

SK Designer Pastel Dust Food Colour: Pastel Pink

SK Professional Liquid Food Colours: Bulrush, Chestnut

SK CMC Gum

EQUIPMENT

Basic equipment (see pages 6 to 7)

33cm (13") square cake drum (board)

Round cake cards: 12.5cm (5"), 20.5cm (8")

12cm round x 8cm deep (5" x 3¹/₈") polystyrene dummy

20.5cm round x 8cm deep (8" x 3¹/₈") spare polystyrene dummy

30-gauge floral wire: white

Primrose flower cutters: medium and small, from set of 3 (TT)

Foam pad

Floral tape: white

Flower drying stand (SK), or similar

Non-toxic craft glue

Cherry blossom stencil

Glass-headed pins

Small palette knife

Posy picks

1.35m x 15mm width (54" x ⁵/₈") satin ribbon: white

Templates (see page 250)

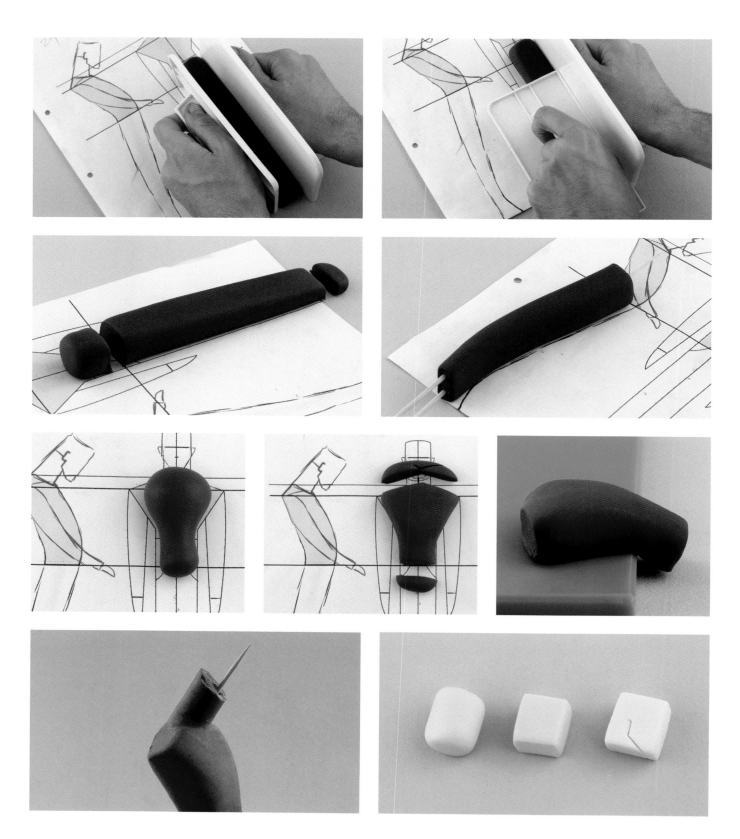

BASE

1 Glue a 12.5cm (5") cake card to the bottom of a 12.5cm (5") round polystyrene dummy, then cover with Bridal White sugarpaste (see pages 42 to 43) and allow to dry.

GROOM

Trousers

2 Roll 150g (5¼oz) of dark brown SFP into a long sausage that is the same width as the template of the groom's trousers. Press the sides and top with cake smoothers to square off the edges, then use them to narrow the paste slightly towards the bottom to make a wedge shape. Cut straight across the top and bottom of the trousers with a sharp knife to make the paste fit the template.

3 Turn the trousers on their side and bend the paste into shape following the groom's profile template. Insert two pieces of barbecue skewer into the bottom of the trousers, leaving a good length protruding from the base. Insert a cocktail stick into the top of the trousers where the jacket will be inserted and secured later on. Allow the paste to dry.

> ### TUTOR TIP
>
> To speed up the drying time, add an extra pinch of CMC gum to the paste before modelling the trousers.

Torso

4 Roll 100g (3½oz) of terracotta SFP into a pear shape. Press the thicker end with the side of your hand to bring out the chest and widen the

shoulder line, then flatten the other end slightly so it is the same thickness as the top of the trousers. Use a sharp knife to trim the bottom end straight, then follow the template to cut the top of the paste into the shape of the shoulder line. Position the torso over the edge of a non-stick board to give the back a slight curve and allow to firm up.

Neck

5 Roll a small piece of terracotta SFP into a sausage that is approximately the same length and width of the neck template, then use a knife to trim one end straight and cut the other at a slight angle. Insert a piece of barbecue skewer lengthways into the neck, so it protrudes from both ends. Skewer it into a spare block of polystyrene and leave to dry.

Assembly

6 Insert the trousers into a spare polystyrene dummy, then push the torso onto the cocktail stick protruding from the top of the trousers and secure with softened terracotta SFP. Remove any excess paste around the waist with your fingertip and smooth over the join.

7 Position the neck on the top of the torso so it is slightly tilted downwards and secure with softened terracotta paste. Fill in the gap at the join with softened paste for a neat finish, then leave to dry.

Head

8 Roll approximately 20g (¾oz) of skin tone SFP into a thick cylinder shape, then press the top and sides with cake smoothers to square off the edges. Use the front and profile templates to

ensure the head is the correct thickness, then cut the top and bottom ends straight with a sharp knife. Mark out the shape of the jaw line on either side of the head with a knife, following the template for reference. Leave to firm up.

9 Once the head is firm enough to handle, push it onto the skewer protruding from the neck, but do not secure it yet as you will need to remove it to finish the facial features.

Jacket

10 Roll out some terracotta SFP very thinly on a non-stick board, then cut out a semicircle shape using the groom template for reference. Attach to the middle of the back and bring the ends around the sides to finish the jacket. Gently run your fingers around the join to smooth out the paste and give a clean finish.

11 To make the cummerbund, paint a triangle shape at the base of the front of the jacket with Bulrush liquid food colour. Alternatively, roll out a small piece of Bulrush SFP, cut out a triangle shape following the template as reference and stick it in place. Roll a long, thin sausage of terracotta SFP and attach it around the torso to make the outline of the jacket, starting at the back and bringing the ends together at the front of the chest.

12 Fill a paper piping bag with light brown medium-consistency royal icing then snip off the very tip of the bag. Pipe a teardrop and scroll pattern all over the jacket to add detail and texture. Dampen a fine paintbrush with a little cooled, boiled water and brush through the teardrops to create a brush-embroidery effect.

BRIDE

Dress

13 Roll 250g (8¾oz) of White SFP into a long cone shape for the skirt, following the bride template as a guide. Run the palm of your hand over the paste to flatten it slightly, then cut the top and bottom straight using a sharp knife: the rounded side will form the back of the dress and the flatter side will make the front. Lightly grease a skewer with white vegetable fat and insert it almost ¾ of the way up the skirt, then remove. Lay the skirt flat and allow to firm up overnight.

TUTOR TIP

For the dress, you can use SFP or an equal mix of pastillage and SFP to speed up the drying time. Alternatively, you could add an extra pinch of CMC.

Torso

14 Roll 25g (just over ¾oz) of skin tone SFP into the shape of a bowling pin. Roll the thicker end between the sides of your hands to narrow the paste and bring out the neck. Lay the shape on a work surface and pinch out the wider top section of the torso to make the cleavage. Hold the sides of the torso and pinch the paste on either side of the neck between your thumb and index fingers: this will sharpen the shoulder line. Use a knife to cut the neck and bottom of the torso straight, making it fit the size of the template provided. Insert a piece of barbecue skewer into the top of the neck. Insert a cocktail stick into the bottom of the torso then remove to make a hole. Mark a short line down

the middle of the back with the sharp edge of a Dresden tool.

15 Position the torso over the edge of a non-stick board with the waist hanging down, in order to give the back a slight curve. Place a wedge of paste underneath the neck (as shown in the picture) to tilt the neck forward. Allow to dry overnight.

16 Fill a paper piping bag with a little medium-consistency white royal icing and snip off the very tip of the bag. Insert a cocktail stick into the base of the torso and hold it so you can pipe comfortably. Pipe a V-shape across the back and a curved line at the front to create the neckline of the dress. Let the icing dry for a couple of minutes.

17 Insert the torso into the top of the skirt and secure with a dot of softened White SFP. Dilute some Edelweiss dust food colour with a few drops of clear alcohol and use a small paintbrush to paint the bodice with the mixture. If necessary, apply a second layer once the first has fully dried.

Head

18 Roll 15g (½oz) of skin tone SFP into a teardrop that is the same size as the head template provided. Make a groove across the middle line of the face using the side of your little finger: this will bring out the cheeks and flatten the forehead. Pinch the paste in the centre of the face to bring out the nose. Lift the chin up by placing a wedge of paste under the jaw, then trim the top of the head straight with a sharp knife. Let the paste firm up.

19 Place the bride in front of the groom, so you can position

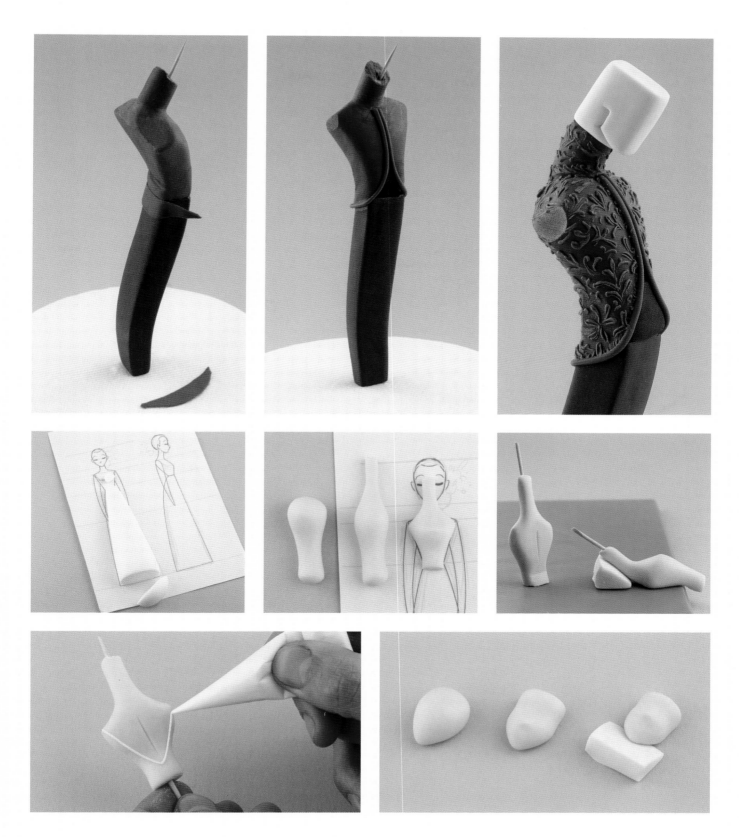

her head according to the angle of the groom's head. Push the bride's head onto the cocktail stick protruding from the neck so it is slightly tilted to one side and secure with softened skin tone SFP. Allow the head to dry completely.

20 Roll a small piece of reddish terracotta SFP into a teardrop large enough to cover the back of the head and attach with edible glue to fill out the head shape. Mark lines in the paste with a Dresden tool to make it look as if the hair is being pulled back. Roll a small ball of the same colour SFP for the bun and attach it to the nape of the neck with edible glue. Mark lines down the bun to give it texture.

21 For the eyelashes, roll two very small, pointed sausages from a piece of terracotta SFP and attach them along the middle line of the face following the diagram. Use a fine paintbrush and Chestnut liquid food colour to paint the eyebrows above each eye. Mix Pastel Pink dust food colour with a little cornflour and brush it over the cheeks using a soft paintbrush.

GROOM'S FACE

22 Remove the groom's head from the torso and insert a cocktail stick into the base so you can hold it comfortably. Following the diagram, paint on the hair and sideburns with Bulrush liquid food colour and a fine paintbrush. Paint two lines of Bulrush liquid colour across the middle of the face for the eyelashes. To make the eyebrows, roll out a pinch of dark brown SFP into a very thin sausage with pointed ends, cut it in half and attach above each eye.

23 For the nose, roll a tiny piece of skin tone SFP into a small wedge, cut out a trapezium shape and secure it to the middle of the face. Thinly roll out some skin tone SFP for the ears, cut out two tiny rectangles and attach them to either side of the head with edible glue. Dust the cheeks with Pale Pink dust food colour and a soft brush. Remove the cocktail stick and secure the head to the neck with softened skin tone SFP.

ARMS AND HANDS

24 Secure the bride and groom in position on the covered dummy: this will allow you to position the arms correctly. Insert a skewer into the hole in the bride's skirt and insert the bride into the covered dummy and secure with softened White SFP. Attach the groom to the dummy with softened dark brown SFP.

25 To make the groom's arms, roll some terracotta SFP into two sausages that slightly taper towards one end, making each of them the same length as the arm template. Press the top and sides of each arm with cake smoothers to square off the edges. Attach them to either side of the torso, securing the ends of the arms onto the skirt below the bride's waist.

26 For the groom's hands, roll two tiny teardrops of skin tone SFP and flatten them down. Cut a V-shape into one side to bring out the thumbs and attach to the sleeves and the dress with edible glue. Pipe over the sleeves in the same way as for the body of the jacket. Pipe a band at the join between the hands and the sleeves for a neat finish. Roll a thin sausage of terracotta SFP and attach it between the head and neck to cover the join.

27 For the bride's arms and hands, use skin tone SFP and follow

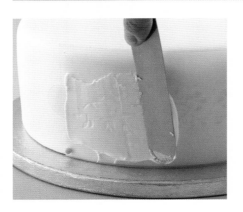

the instructions on page 48. Bend the left arm at a 45° angle, attach it to the side of the torso and secure the hand to the groom's chest. Bend the right arm slightly and secure it to the other side, attaching her right hand on top of the groom's left hand.

FLOWERS

28 Cut a few 30-gauge white floral wires into several pieces, dip the tip of each wire into white run-out royal icing and leave them to dry upside down from a flower-drying stand or similar.

29 Roll out some White SFP into a thin sheet and cut out several small and medium flowers using the primrose cutters. Place the flowers on a foam pad and use a medium ball tool to soften the edges. Pinch the back of the flower and fold the petals in slightly. Let the flower firm up then thread it onto a stamen, so it sits behind the royal iced tip. Secure with a dot of non-toxic glue and leave to dry.

TUTOR TIP

After you have cut out several flowers, keep them between food-grade acetate sheets that have been lightly greased with white vegetable fat to prevent them from drying out. Only take out a few at a time to soften the edges.

30 Arrange the flowers into three sprays of different sizes for each tier and tape together with white floral tape. Make a small flower arrangement and attach to the bride's hair with dots of white royal icing.

CAKE DRUM

31 Lightly dust a work surface with cornflour and roll out 200g (7oz) of white pastillage into a thin sheet. Set aside to dry for a few minutes until a skin forms over the paste.

32 Roll out 500g (1lb 1¾oz) of Bridal White sugarpaste to 1cm (³⁄₈") thick, brush the surface with cooled, boiled water and stick the pastillage sheet on top. Roll out the two pastes together to 4mm (³⁄₁₆") thick to create a cracked effect: roll the paste in every direction to make sure the cracks cover the whole surface for an uneven, natural look (see page 175).

33 Moisten the square board with a little edible glue and cover it with the cracked paste (see page 41). Trim the excess paste from around the base with a pizza wheel or sharp knife. Trim the board with white ribbon and allow to dry overnight.

CAKE

34 Cover the 20.5cm (8") cake with 600g (1lb 5¼oz) of Bridal White

sugarpaste (see page 34). Leave the paste to firm up overnight.

35 Secure the cake stencil to the side of the cake with a glass-headed pin in each corner, or hold in place. Spread some firm-peak white royal icing over the stencil using a palette knife, making sure to cover the whole design. Scrape off the excess royal icing, remove the pins and carefully lift the stencil away. Let the icing dry for a while before you continue around the rest of the cake. Decorate the covered cake dummy in the same way.

TUTOR TIP

If you are using pins, make sure you count how many you use so you can ensure that they have all been safely removed from the cake.

36 Position the cake slightly off-centre on the cake board and secure with a dab of royal icing. Dowel the cake (see page 42) then secure the couple on their polystyrene base on top of it with a dab of royal icing. Fill a paper piping bag with medium-consistency white royal icing and pipe beads around the base of each cake. Insert the sprays into posy picks and position them on each tier.

Important note: Make sure you remove the figurines, flowers and all the internal supports (dowels and skewers) before the cake is served.

BRIDE AND GROOM BISCUITS

Following the recipes on page 18 and a 6cm (2³/₈") round cutter, bake 30 vanilla biscuits for the bride and 30 chocolate biscuits for the groom.

For the bride biscuits, fit a paper piping bag with a no. 1 nozzle, fill with medium-consistency royal icing and pipe an outline around each biscuit. Let down some royal icing to run-out consistency and use a no. 2 nozzle to flood the biscuits with runny white icing (see page 30). Allow the icing to dry.

Pipe a running bead around the edge of each biscuit with medium-consistency white icing and a no. 1 nozzle, then leave to dry. Make flowers from White SFP following the instructions on page 159 for the main cake. Once they are dry, secure one flower to each biscuit slightly off-centre with a dot of white royal icing.

For the groom biscuits, outline and flood them in the same way as for the bride biscuits using dark Terracotta-coloured royal icing instead. Once the icing has dried, use Chestnut-coloured medium-consistency royal icing and a no. 1 nozzle to pipe the pattern from the groom's jacket over the biscuits.

GENTLE GIANT

Vikings are often portrayed as fierce and ruthless warriors, however, this gentle giant seems to be enjoying some peace and quiet on a solitary fishing trip. This cake design uses a variety of texturing techniques that really bring the Viking character to life.

EDIBLES

14cm round x 16.5cm deep (5½" x 6½") cake, layered and filled (see page 34)

SK Sugarpaste (rolled fondant):

600g (1lb 5¼oz) Bridal White

200g (7oz) chestnut brown (Bridal White + Bulrush + Nasturtium)

350g (12¼oz) light brown (Bridal White + Bulrush + Teddy Bear Brown)

100g (3½oz) terracotta (Bridal White + Terracotta)

100g (3½oz) Tuxedo Black

SK Sugar Florist Paste (SFP, gum paste):

10g (¼oz) Black

100g (3½oz) dark brown (White SFP + Bulrush)

100g (3½oz) orange (White SFP + Terracotta + Nasturtium)

400g (14oz) skin tone (White SFP + Nasturtium + touch of Teddy Bear Brown)

SK Instant Mix Pastillage:

300g (10½oz) pale brown (Teddy Bear Brown)

SK Instant Mix Royal Icing:

100g (3½oz) dark terracotta (Terracotta + touch of Bulrush)

20g (¾oz) pale blue (touch of Hydrangea)

SK Professional Paste Food Colours: Bulrush, Hydrangea, Nasturtium, Teddy Bear Brown

SK Designer Paste Food Colour: Terracotta

SK Designer Pastel Dust Food Colour: Pale Peach

SK Designer Metallic Lustre Dust Food Colours: Bronze, Dark Bronze

SK Professional Liquid Food Colour: Bulrush

EQUIPMENT

Basic equipment (see pages 6 to 7)

35.5cm (14") round cake drum (board)

Round cake cards: 8cm, 15cm (3⅛", 6")

Piece of thin card, e.g. from a cereal box or cake box

Large, serrated knife

New vegetable brush

Drinking straw

Round cutters: 1.5cm, 8cm, 9cm (⅝", 3⅛", 3½")

Large grass piping nozzle

18-gauge floral wires: white

1.15m x 15mm width (46" x ⅝") satin ribbon: black

Templates (see page 251)

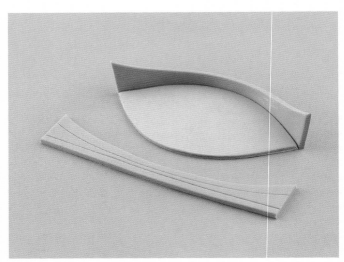
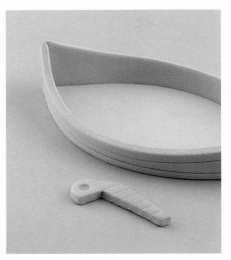

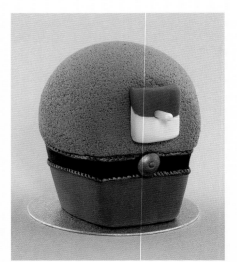

TEMPLATES

1   Trace all the templates onto a piece of thin card and cut them out with a pair of scissors or a craft knife.

CAKE DRUM

2   Divide 400g (14oz) of Bridal White sugarpaste into three pieces and use different amounts of Hydrangea paste food colour to make them three different shades of blue. Roll each shade of blue paste into sausages of different thicknesses. Roll out 200g (7oz) of Bridal White sugarpaste into a thin sheet then stick the sausages onto it, alternating the colours as you go. Roll over the paste to merge the colours, making it approximately the size of the cake drum. Cover the cake drum with the marbled paste (see page 41) and trim the board with black ribbon.

CANOE

3   Roll out 150g (5¼oz) of light brown pastillage to 6mm (just over ¼") thick and cut out the base of the canoe using the template provided. Roll out some more pastillage to the same thickness and cut out the sides of the canoe. Mark a straight and a curved line along the sides with the blade of a knife, making sure not to cut through the paste completely. Brush a little edible glue along the bottom of each side and secure around the base, bringing the ends together with a little edible glue.

4   Roll out some more pastillage to 6mm (just over ¼") thick and cut out the remaining parts of the canoe. Mark lines across each piece with the blade of a knife to make them look

wooden. Press a medium ball tool into the top of both sides of each piece. Once dry, secure them to the ends of the canoe with a little softened, light brown pastillage.

VIKING

Body

5   Place template A on the side of the cake and secure it in place with a barbecue skewer. Following the template, use a serrated knife to make a straight cut at the front and trim down the top and back of the cake. Remove the template once you are happy with the shape. Secure template B to the front and trim to shape again, following the template. Attach an 8cm (3⅛") cake card to the bottom of the cake with a dab of ganache or buttercream, then crumb-coat the cake (see page 34).

> ### TUTOR TIP
>
> The cake card will support the cake and help you lift it into the canoe.

Trousers

6   Roll out 150g (5¼oz) of chestnut brown sugarpaste to approximately 4mm (³⁄₁₆") thick and cut out a 4cm (1½") wide strip that is long enough to wrap around the base of the cake. Roll out some Tuxedo Black sugarpaste to the same thickness and cut out a 2cm (¾") wide strip. Stick the black strip along the top of the brown strip to make one piece of paste, then loosely roll it up from one end. Starting at the back, unroll the strip around the cake while pressing the paste down gently with the palm of your hand.

Bring the ends together at the back and trim the excess paste at the join. Smooth the paste with a cake smoother.

Shirt and belt

7   Roll out 350g (12¼oz) of light brown sugarpaste to 4mm (³⁄₁₆") thick and cover the top part of the cake (see page 34). Press the paste directly above the belt with the side of your hand, then trim away the excess with a sharp knife. Gently press the bristles of a new vegetable brush over the paste to texture it.

8   Roll very thin sausages of light brown sugarpaste and secure them around the top and bottom of the belt. Press the tip of a Dresden tool into the sausages and make indents all the way around them to add texture.

9   For the buckle, roll a small piece of light brown sugarpaste into a ball and flatten it down. Attach it centrally to the front of the belt and push the end of a drinking straw into it. Paint the buckle and the trim with Dark Bronze dust food colour diluted with a few drops of clear alcohol.

Neck

10   Roll a sausage of skin tone SFP and a sausage of orange SFP, stick them together and press down on the paste with a smoother to flatten them to approximately 1.5cm (⅝") thick. Cut out a square that is approximately 3.5cm x 3.5cm (1⅜" x 1⅜") using a sharp knife. Use edible glue to stick the paste to the top of the front of the body so that the orange piece is facing the top. Insert a long piece of plastic dowel down through the neck and into the body,

leaving a piece protruding to attach the head later.

Head

11 Roll 50g (1¾oz) of skin tone SFP into a pear shape, using the template provided as a size guide. Indent two curved lines on the upper half of the face using a 1.5cm (⅝") round cutter to make the closed eyes. Mark another two curved lines underneath the eyes for the eye bags, then run the rounded side of the Dresden tool gently under the marks to bring out the bags. Press the edge of a cutting tool into the top of each eye to mark out the brow. Trim the top of the head straight using a sharp knife: this will allow the helmet to sit comfortably on the head.

12 For the nose, roll 5g (just under ¼oz) of skin tone SFP into a sausage that is slightly narrower at one end. Press the top and sides of the nose to square off the bridge and help bring out the tip. Use a knife to make an indent on the top of the nose to define the tip. Push a small ball tool into the end of the nose to open the nostrils. Secure the nose between the eyes with a little edible glue. Trim the top straight with a sharp knife.

13 Dust the cheeks with Pale Peach dust food colour using a soft brush. Roll two tiny sausages with pointed ends from a piece of dark brown SFP and attach them along the lids to make the eyelashes. Leave the head to firm up.

14 Once the head has firmed up, shape approximately 40g (1½oz) of orange SFP into a rectangle. Cut out a semicircle from the upper half using a 9cm (3½") round cutter. Attach the beard to the lower half of the face, positioning it so the pointed ends make the sideburns. Use the edge of a Dresden tool to draw lines down the beard to add texture.

15 For the moustache, roll two sausages with pointed ends from some orange SFP and attach them underneath the nose so they are protruding from each nostril. Mark lines with the edge of the Dresden tool to give texture.

16 To make the ears, roll two teardrops of skin tone SFP and follow the instructions on page 51. Attach them to the sides of the head with a little edible glue.

Helmet

17 Roll 15g (½oz) of dark brown SFP into a dome shape that is the same diameter as the top of the head. Roll out some more dark brown SFP to 5mm (¼") thick and cut out a 1cm (⅜") wide strip and a long wedge shape. Secure the strip around the rim of the helmet and attach the wedge over the top. Make a few holes in the top section with the tip of a barbecue skewer.

18 For the horns, roll two pieces of dark brown SFP into 8cm (3⅛") long cone shapes. Halfway along each cone, make a mark with a Dresden tool and bend the paste to approximately a 90° angle. Bend the tips of the horns outwards, then mark lines along the horns with the edge of a Dresden tool. Push a piece of cocktail stick through the thicker ends and allow to firm up.

19 Insert the horns into either side of the helmet and secure with softened dark brown SFP. Paint the helmet with a layer of Dark Bronze dust food colour diluted with a few drops

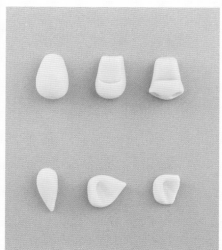

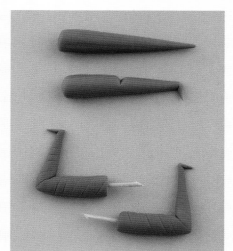
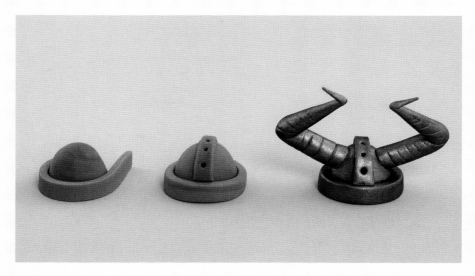

GENTLE GIANT

167

of clear alcohol. Apply a second layer of Bronze dust mixture to add some highlights. Push the head onto the piece of dowel protruding from the neck and secure with some softened skin tone SFP.

Arms

20 Roll 150g (5¼oz) of skin tone SFP into the shape of a chicken drumstick. Roll the paste at the middle of the drumstick with the side of your hand to separate the upper arm from the forearm. Make a mark at the elbow, moisten the inside of the elbow slightly and bend into a right angle. Attach the arm to the side of the body, then press lightly on the shoulder to help secure it and give shape at the same time. Support the arm and hand in position with a piece of foam until the arm has firmed up.

21 Make the left arm in the same way and secure it to the other side of the body so it sits on top of the right hand. Make marks for the fingers with the edge of a Dresden tool.

22 Roll out some chestnut brown sugarpaste into a thin sheet and press the bristles of a new vegetable brush over the paste to texture it, as before. Tear the edges of the paste with the vegetable brush. Cut out two semicircles using an 8cm (3¹/₈") round cutter and attach them over the shoulders.

Hair

23 Roll some orange SFP into a chicken drumstick shape, then flatten it slightly. Mark lines across the paste with a Dresden tool and snip into the smaller end with a pair of scissors to create loose strands.

24 Cut out two thin strips of chestnut brown sugarpaste and wrap them around the grooves in the hair for the hair bands. Attach a thin strip of orange SFP across the top of the head and mark parallel lines across it to add texture. Secure the pigtails to the sides of the head and onto the body with softened orange SFP.

Fur

25 Roll out 100g (3½oz) of terracotta sugarpaste and cut out a freehand leaf shape with one straight end. Secure over the top of the body with the straight end facing towards the neck.

26 Fit a large piping bag with a grass nozzle and fill with 100g (3½oz) of dark terracotta firm-peak royal icing. Cover the terracotta sugarpaste with short strands of royal icing. Attach the helmet to the top of the head with a dab of dark terracotta royal icing.

TUTOR TIP

When you want to achieve a deep colour, it is a good idea to colour the icing a few hours in advance to allow the colour to develop. Make sure to re-beat the icing before use.

FISHING ROD

27 Cut a 12.5cm (5") length of 18-gauge floral wire and moisten with edible glue. Push a ball of dark brown SFP onto the wire and roll the paste along it using your palms. Roll the paste into a narrow cone shape, leaving a piece of wire protruding from the thicker end. Allow to dry completely.

ASSEMBLY

28 Secure the canoe to the centre of the cake board with a dab of pale blue royal icing or softened paste. Place the figure in the canoe and secure in the same way. Insert the piece of wire protruding from the rod into the hands and glue with a dot of softened skin tone SFP.

29 Thinly roll out some Black SFP, cut out a very thin strip and leave it to dry on its side in a slightly curved position. Once dry, glue the line to the tip of the rod with a dot of softened dark brown SFP.

TUTOR TIP

As the fishing line is very thin, I recommend making a spare one in case it breaks as you are assembling it. Alternatively, you could use a thin strip of liquorice as it is more flexible and is less likely to break during transportation.

30 Fill a paper piping bag with pale blue run-out royal icing and snip off the very end. Pipe ripples around the canoe and where the line falls onto the board.

Important note: Make sure you remove all the internal supports (dowels and cocktail sticks) and the fishing rod before the cake is served.

TUTOR TIP

To make the fishing rod edible, you could use a Mikado biscuit instead.

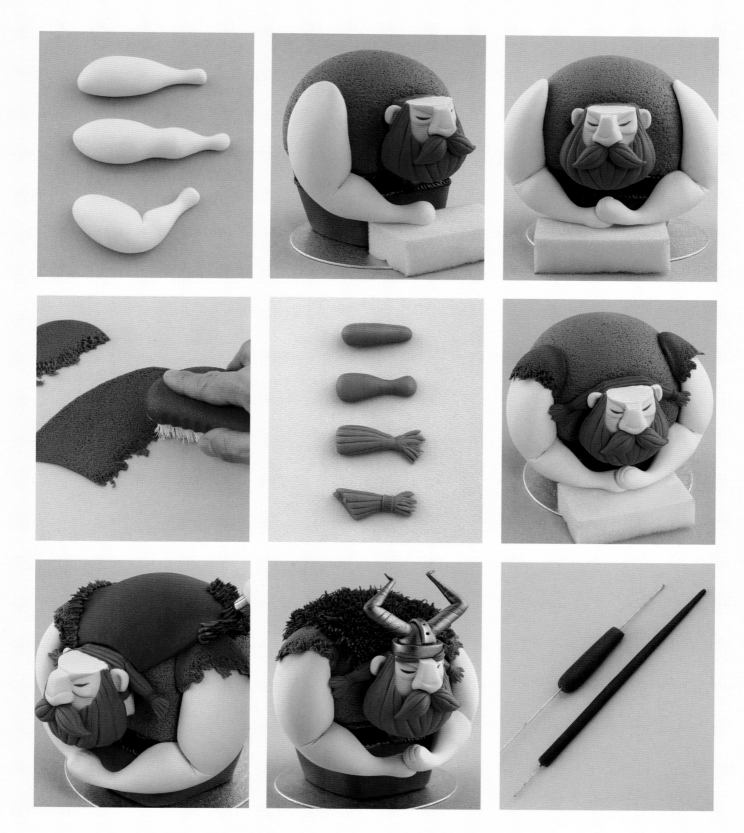

CATCH OF THE DAY BISCUITS

Use white royal icing and the fish eye templates to pipe the eyes onto a sheet of cellophane (see page 30). Leave to dry.

Make up the biscuit dough following the recipe on page 18, cut out 25 round or 35 semi-circle fish shapes using the template provided on page 251 and bake as required.

For the round fish, colour some medium-consistency royal icing with Teddy Bear Brown paste food colour. Fit a piping bag with a no. 1 nozzle, fill with brown icing then pipe an outline around the biscuits. Use a no. 2 nozzle and Teddy Bear Brown-coloured run-out icing to flood the biscuits (see page 30) then leave to dry.

Pipe wavy lines and dots for the scales using brown run-out icing and a no. 1 nozzle, then leave them to dry. Brush the surface of the biscuits with Silver, Antique Gold and Burnt Copper metallic lustre dust food colours diluted with clear alcohol to create an iridescent effect. Secure an eye to each biscuit with a dot of royal icing and paint a dot of Edelweiss paste food colour onto the pupil.

Decorate the semi-circle fish in the same way but use Poppy-coloured royal icing. Splash the biscuits with Gold and Burnt Copper metallic lustre dusts diluted with a few drops of alcohol.

IN THE DEAD OF NIGHT

Perfect for Halloween, this creepy cake would also make a spook-tacular birthday treat for fans of horror movies! The sophisticated use of colour and shading on this design creates areas of light and dark, making it appear as if the zombie figure is being struck by moonlight.

EDIBLES

15cm x 7cm deep (6" x 2¾") square cake, filled and crumb-coated (see page 34)

SK Sugarpaste (rolled fondant):

350g (12¼oz) dark blue (Bridal White sugarpaste + Wisteria)

1kg (2lb 3¼oz) light blue (Bridal White sugarpaste + touch of Gentian)

SK Sugar Florist Paste (SFP, gum paste):

50g (1¾oz) Black

20g (¾oz) forest green (White SFP + Dark Forest)

5g (just under ¼oz) ice blue (White SFP + Gentian)

100g (3½oz) palest blue-green (White SFP + touch of Bluegrass)

5g (just under ¼oz) pale yellow (White SFP + touch of Sunflower)

5g (just under ¼oz) poppy red (White SFP + Poppy)

5g (just under ¼oz) soft beige (White SFP + Chestnut)

55g (2oz) White

50g (1¾oz) yellow-green (Holly/Ivy SFP + touch of Sunflower)

SK Instant Mix Pastillage:

50g (1¾oz) forest green (Dark Forest)

300g (10½oz) light blue (touch of Gentian)

100g (3½oz) light green (touch of Sunny Lime)

50g (1¾oz) white (uncoloured)

SK Instant Mix Royal Icing:

100g (3½oz) light blue (touch of Gentian)

SK Professional Paste Food Colours: Bluegrass, Gentian, Poppy, Sunflower

SK Designer Paste Food Colours: Dark Forest, Jet Black, Sunny Lime

SK Professional Liquid Food Colours: Hydrangea, Wisteria

SK Professional Dust Food Colour: Bluegrass, Edelweiss (white)

SK Designer Pastel Dust Food Colour: Soft Green

SK Designer Dust Food Colour: Etruscan Brick

SK Professional Food Colour Pen: Black

SK CMC Gum

EQUIPMENT

Basic equipment (see pages 6 to 7)

10cm square x 5cm deep (4" x 2") polystyrene dummy

23cm (9") square cake drum (board)

15cm (6") square cake card

Pizza wheel

Spare polystyrene dummy

24-gauge floral wires: white

Flat, tapered modelling tool, from set of 12 (SK)

Round cutter: 1.5cm (⅝")

Small leaf cutter

Textured rolling pin, e.g. moire taffeta

60cm x 15mm width (24" x ⅝") satin ribbon: deep blue

Templates (see page 252)

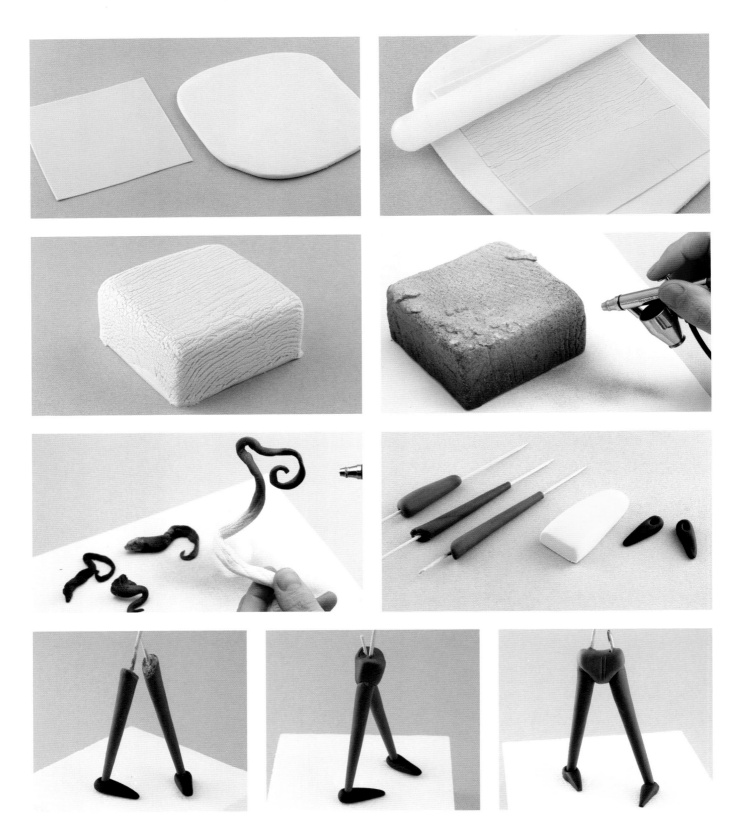

POLYSTYRENE BASE

1 Lightly dust the work surface with cornflour and thinly roll out 50g (1¾oz) of light blue pastillage. Set aside to dry for a few minutes until a skin forms over the paste.

2 Roll out 200g (7oz) of light blue sugarpaste to 1cm (³/₈") thick, brush the surface with cooled, boiled water and stick the pastillage sheet on top. Roll out the two pastes together to 4mm (³/₁₆") thick to create a cracked effect: roll the paste in every direction to make sure the cracks cover the surface for an uneven, natural look.

3 Moisten the square polystyrene base with a little edible glue and cover it with the cracked paste (see pages 42 to 43). Trim the excess paste from around the base with a pizza wheel. Using the trimmings, roll several small pieces of paste into small rock shapes and stick them around the edges of the base. Allow to dry for a couple of hours.

4 To colour the base, you can either use an airbrush or the splashing technique described on page 54. Evenly apply a thin layer of Hydrangea liquid food colour all over the base. Cover the bottom edge of the dummy with a thin layer of Wisteria liquid food colour, fading the colour as you move up the sides. Allow the base to dry.

TUTOR TIP

If you don't have an airbrush or are not confident using one, you can still achieve great results with the splashing technique. If desired, you can combine both splashing and airbrushing techniques to paint the base.

TREE ROOTS

5 Roll pieces of white pastillage into thick sausages and taper them at one end. Curl up the thinner end of each of the sausages to give the roots movement. Once the roots have dried, spray them with a thin layer of Wisteria liquid food colour using an airbrush or the splashing technique. Allow the paint to dry.

ZOMBIE

Legs

6 Roll 25g (just over ¾oz) of forest green pastillage into a thick sausage and split it in half. Moisten a barbecue skewer with edible glue and push it lengthways through one of the sausages. Roll the paste with your palm to extend it along the skewer, tapering the sausage at one end until it is the same length as the leg template. Cut the thicker end at an angle with a sharp knife. Repeat to make a second leg then insert the skewers into a spare piece of polystyrene to allow them to dry upright (so that the sides aren't flattened).

Torso

7 Roll 80g–85g (2¾oz) of light green pastillage into a thick sausage that narrows slightly at one end. Flatten the sausage slightly on one side by pressing it against the work surface and use a knife to cut the bottom edge straight. Allow to firm up overnight.

Shoes

8 Roll 10g (¼oz) of Black SFP into a sausage and split it in half. Roll each piece of paste into a long cone shape following the template, then flatten them slightly with a cake smoother or the heel of your hand. Push a barbecue skewer into the top of the thicker end of the shoes to make a hole for the legs. Allow to firm up.

9 Push each shoe onto the barbecue skewers protruding from the legs and secure with a dot of softened forest green pastillage. Brush away any excess paste for a neat finish. Insert both legs into a spare piece of polystyrene, positioning them so that the feet are wide apart. Turn the points of the shoes in towards each other.

Pelvis

10 Roll 15g (½oz) of forest green pastillage into the pelvis shape following the template, making sure it is the same thickness as the torso. Push the hips onto the skewers protruding from the top of the legs and secure in place with edible glue. Allow the hips to dry overnight or until they are completely dry.

TUTOR TIP

You might need to trim the skewer protruding from the left leg to make it easier to position the pelvis. However, ensure to keep a good length of skewer protruding from the right leg to support the torso.

11 Push the torso down onto the skewers protruding from the pelvis and secure with some softened forest green pastillage.

TUTOR TIP

As the torso has been left to dry overnight, it should be firm enough to handle but still soft enough inside to push the skewer through it comfortably.

Belt

12 Cut out a narrow strip of Black SFP and use edible glue to secure it around the waist where the torso joins the pelvis. To make the buckle, cut out a small, thin rectangle of Black SFP and an even smaller one from some soft beige SFP, then stick one on top of the other. Secure the buckle to the front of the belt with a little edible glue. Allow the whole structure to dry overnight.

Left arm

13 Cut a 24-gauge floral wire to 16.5cm (6½") in length and moisten it with edible glue. Roll 15g (½oz) of palest blue-green SFP into a sausage and push the wire through it lengthways. Roll the paste along the wire with your palm, tapering the sausage towards one end so that it extends over the end of the wire; it should be approximately the same length as the template provided. Make sure to leave a piece of unwired paste at the very end to create the hand: flatten the paste and cut a V-shape into one side to bring out the thumb. Use a knife to cut fingers into the rest of the hand.

14 Mark the wrist with a Dresden tool and bend the hand downwards so the thumb is facing up as shown in the picture. Mark and bend the fingers inwards at a 90° angle, then square off the arm using cake smoothers.

Important note: Due to this figurine's long, thin arms, it is necessary to use floral wires as internal supports. As the wire is inedible and poses a choking hazard, make sure that you remove the whole cake topper before the cake is served.

Right arm

15 Insert a 24-gauge floral wire into a sausage of palest blue-green SFP in the same way as for the left arm. Roll the paste along the wire, tapering the sausage towards the wrist and making sure to leave a piece of wire protruding from the end. Use your finger to narrow the paste a third of the way up from the wrist and create the elbow. Square off the edges of the arm with cake smoothers as before. Use a pair of scissors to grip the wire at the inner elbow and bend the forearm to a 45° angle using your other hand.

16 Pinch the paste at the elbow with your index fingers to smooth out any marks left by the scissors and leave the arm to dry on its side. Model the right hand from another piece of palest blue-green SFP in the same way as for the left hand and set aside to dry.

Head

17 Thinly roll out some pale yellow SFP, use a sharp knife to cut out three long tooth shapes in different sizes and leave to dry. They will be inserted into the lower jaw later.

18 Roll approximately 40g–45g (1½oz) of palest blue-green SFP into a pear shape. Flatten down the wider end slightly and press in the sides to create the shape of the head template.

19 To open the mouth, hold the sides of the head and push down on the lower half of the face with the tip of a flat, tapered modelling tool. This will give shape to the mouth and the lower jaw at the same time.

20 Press a small ball tool into the line across the centre of the face to make two eye sockets. Pinch the paste between the eye sockets and push the paste upwards with your other finger at the same time to create the nose. Push a small ball tool into the end of the nose to open up the nostrils. Run the rounded side of a Dresden tool gently around the nostrils to define the sides of the nose. Use a Dresden tool to mark lines on each side of the nose for the sunken cheeks, curved lines below the eyes for the bags, one horizontal line above the eyes and a couple of wrinkles on the upper lip. Allow the head to firm up.

21 Make two ears using the technique explained on page 51. Attach them to either side of the head with edible glue.

22 Fill the right eye socket with a small ball of palest blue-green SFP and indent a curved line across it with a 1.5cm (⅝") round cutter. Fill the left eye socket with a small ball of pale yellow SFP. To make the iris, roll a pinch of poppy red SFP into a small ball, attach to the eye and flatten down with

TUTOR TIP

Although I usually flatten the eyeballs down for other models, I think the zombie's eyes here should be bulgy to help exaggerate the gaunt look of the face.

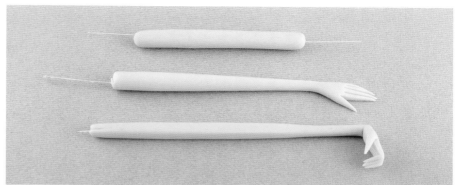

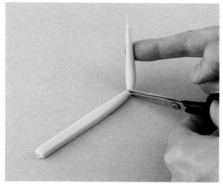

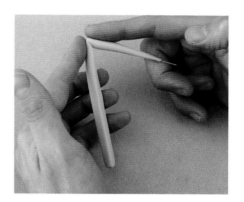

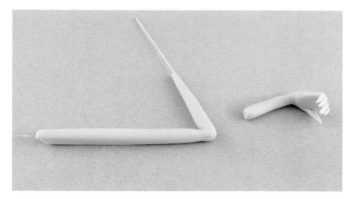

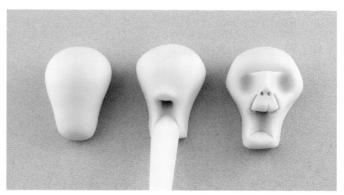

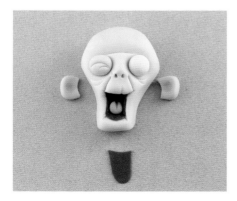

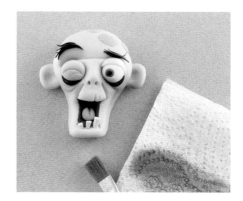

IN THE DEAD OF NIGHT

177

the tip of your finger. To make the pupil, roll a tiny ball of Black SFP, then secure to the middle of the iris and flatten.

23 To give depth to the mouth, knead a small amount of ice blue SFP with a tiny pinch of Black SFP to achieve a darker shade. Roll out the paste very thinly, cut out the shape of the mouth and secure inside the mouth. Roll a small piece of ice blue SFP into an oval shape, glue it inside the mouth and mark a line down the middle of the tongue with the edge of a Dresden tool.

24 For the left eyelid, thinly roll out a small piece of palest blue-green SFP, cut out a small leaf shape with a leaf cutter and secure it over the left eye. To accentuate the eye bags, roll two small pieces of Black SFP into sausages with pointed ends and secure them directly underneath the eyes.

25 Insert a row of three teeth into the bottom of the mouth and secure with edible glue.

26 For the spots on the forehead, roll three tiny balls in different sizes from yellow-green SFP, then flatten them down against the work surface. Stick over the top of the head on the left-hand side with edible glue.

27 Dust the cheeks, the inside of the ears and above the eyelids with Bluegrass dust food colour using a soft brush. Dust the forehead, tip of the nose, and the area below the nose with Soft Green dust food colour.

28 For the eyebrows, roll several pinches of Black SFP into very thin sausages with pointed ends. Secure the first sausages above the eyes so the right eyebrow is higher than the left, then layer the thin sausages on top to build up the brows.

29 Roll 15g (½oz) of palest blue-green SFP into a dome shape and stick it to the back of the head to fill out the head shape. Insert a skewer into the base of the head and leave it to dry upright in a spare piece of polystyrene to allow the back of the head to dry thoroughly.

Shirt

30 Roll out some yellow-green SFP into a thin sheet and cut out the shirt shape using the template. Drag the rounded side of a Dresden tool down the bottom end of the shirt to create a ripped effect. Cut out a hole from the shirt using a small leaf cutter or a sharp knife to enhance the effect.

31 Arrange the shirt over the torso and secure with edible glue. Gather the excess paste at the top and trim to cover the hunched back neatly. To make the neck roll 15g (½oz) of forest green SFP into a teardrop shape and attach it to the front of the top of the torso with edible glue. Position the neck below the shoulder line to accentuate the hunched back.

Sleeves

32 Roll out some yellow-green SFP very thinly and cut out a strip of paste that is wide enough to wrap around the arms. Tear the paste at the bottom with the rounded side of a Dresden tool. Wrap the paste around the top of the arms and secure with a little edible glue, making sure to hide the join on the inside of the arm.

33 Attach the arms to the sides of the body with softened yellow-green SFP and use a skewer to support the bent arm in place until it has completely dried. Place a piece of foam

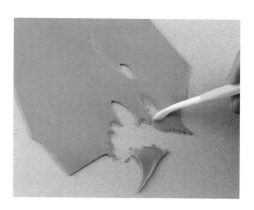

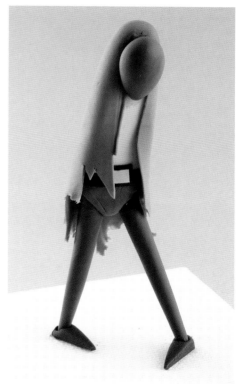

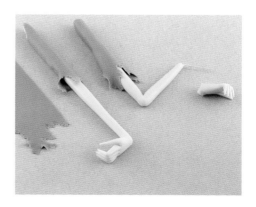

between the end of the skewer and the arm to add extra support.

34 Bend the piece of wire protruding from the right wrist downwards and carefully push the hand onto it. Secure the hand with softened pale blue-green SFP and brush away any excess paste around the wrist for a clean finish.

35 Push a cocktail stick through the neck and into the torso. Roll out a strip of forest green SFP that has pointed ends and glue it around the neck, securing it to the front of the shirt to create the collar. Push the head onto the cocktail stick and secure with softened forest green SFP. Support the head in position with two barbecue skewers until fully dry: place a small piece of dry paste between the end of the skewer and the chin to avoid marking the paste.

36 Dust the torn edges of the shirt and sleeves with Etruscan Brick dust food colour using a soft brush. Insert the figurine into the covered dummy and secure with dots of softened Black SFP under each shoe. If necessary, trim the barbecue skewers protruding from the shoes to the same height as the covered dummy base.

CROW

37 To make the main body, roll 15g (½oz) of Black SFP into a sausage with pointed ends and bend one end downwards to create a beak. Trim the top straight to define the back of the crow. Place the body onto a cocktail stick and stand it in a spare piece of polystyrene to work on the rest of the details. Open the nostrils and mark lines on each side of the beak with the tip of a Dresden tool.

38 For the wings, roll two small pieces of Black SFP into long teardrop shapes and flatten them down slightly. Use a Dresden tool to mark lines along one side to create feathers. Make a few more loose feathers by rolling pinches of Black SFP into long, flattened teardrop shapes, then leave them to dry. Attach a feather to the top of each wing and secure some more to the tail with edible glue.

39 To make the eyes, roll two tiny balls of White SFP and secure them above the beak. Draw a tiny pupil on each eye using a Black food colour pen. Roll two pinches of Black SFP into teardrop shapes and attach to the top of each eye with edible glue. Use a small pair of scissors to snip into the paste and give shape to the eyebrows. Secure the crow onto the zombie's hunched back with a dot of softened dark green SFP.

CAKE AND CAKE DRUM

40 Cover the cake drum with dark blue sugarpaste (see page 41) and emboss it with a fabric-effect textured rolling pin or mark parallel lines across it with the edge of a Dresden tool. Trim the board with a navy blue ribbon and set aside to dry.

41 Following the method on page 32, make sugar rocks from 100g (3½oz) of pastillage, ensuring to microwave it 20g (¾oz) at a time.

42 Cover the cake in the same way as for the polystyrene dummy using 100g (3½oz) of light blue pastillage and 700g (1lb 8¾oz) of pale blue sugarpaste. Mark crevices in the paste with the edge of a Dresden tool and airbrush the cake in the same way

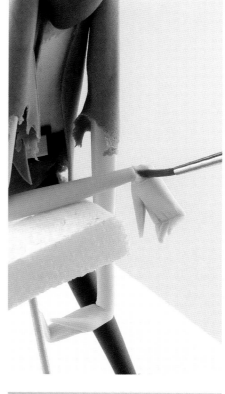
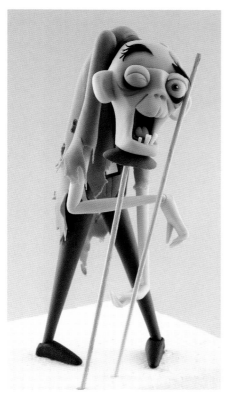

as the polystyrene base. Paint over the crevices with Wisteria liquid food colour and a fine paintbrush to give them depth.

43 Place the cake on the cake board at a 90° angle and secure with a dab of royal icing. Position the dummy base centrally on the cake and secure with a dab of royal icing.

44 Attach the pastillage rocks around the sides and on top of the cake with dots of pale blue coloured royal icing. Position a couple of tree roots at the back corner of the cake with dots of softened pale blue sugarpaste. Use a toothbrush to splash the cake and rocks with Wisteria liquid food colour and white dust food colour mixed with clear alcohol.

TUTOR TIP

The zombie figurine can be transported on its dummy base as explained on page 55 and assembled once you have arrived at the venue.

Important note: Please ensure that the recipient is aware that the figurine and its dummy should be removed before serving as they contain hidden inedible supports, such as floral wires and wooden skewers, which must not be eaten.

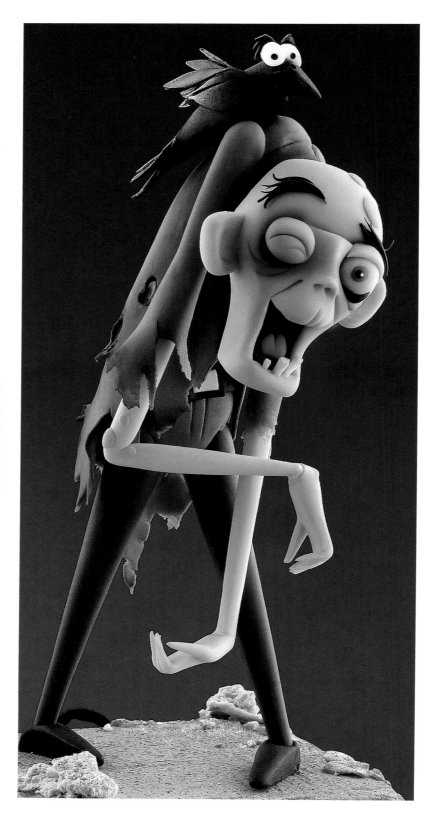

ZOMBIE BISCUITS

Colour some run-out royal icing with a touch of Daffodil paste food colour and prepare small amounts of Poinsettia- and Black-coloured run-out icing. Place the zombie eye templates under a sheet of cellophane and pipe run-outs for the eyes in pale yellow icing (see page 30). Drop a dot of Poinsettia-coloured icing into the run-out to make the iris, then a dot of Black icing for the pupil and leave to dry. Flick the eyes with Berberis liquid food colour using the method on page 54, and add a dot of Edelweiss paste food colour on the pupil. Allow to dry once more.

Make up the biscuit dough following the recipe on page 18 then cut out 25 zombie head biscuits using the template provided on page 252, and bake as required.

Colour some medium-consistency icing with Bluegrass paste food colour then use the icing with a no. 1 nozzle to pipe an outline around the biscuits. Flood the biscuits with Bluegrass-coloured run-out icing and a no. 2 nozzle (see page 30). While the icing is still wet, use Wisteria-coloured run-out icing to pipe the mouth shapes. Gently tap the biscuit to blend the two colours and smooth out the icing, then leave to dry.

Splash the biscuits with Wisteria liquid food colour diluted with a few drops of cooled, boiled water. Model the closed eyes following the instructions on page 176, then secure the open and closed eyes to the biscuits with royal icing. Pipe an inverted heart-shape for the nose with the same icing as for the mouth and a no. 1 nozzle. Draw the eyebrows and eye bags with a Black food colour pen. Pipe thin lines for the teeth with pale Berberis-coloured run-out icing and leave to dry.

TEA CEREMONY

Tea is enjoyed around the world in many different cultures; in Japan, the Tea Ceremony was introduced in the 9th century as a symbolic ritual of preparing and drinking tea. Why not celebrate this tradition with these characterful geisha figurines, which can be placed on top of any cake to finish the decoration.

EDIBLES

SK Sugarpaste (rolled fondant):

    200g (7oz) light turquoise (Bridal White + touch of Hydrangea)

SK Sugar Florist Paste (SFP, gum paste):

    150g (5¼oz) Black

    10g (¼oz) light blue (White SFP + touch of Bluegrass)

    10g (¼oz) light brown (White SFP + Teddy Bear Brown)

    200g (7oz) poppy red (White SFP + Poppy)

    50g (1¾oz) skin tone (White SFP + touch of Teddy Bear Brown + touch of Pink)

    10g (¼oz) terracotta (White SFP + Terracotta)

    100g (3½oz) White

    10g (¼oz) yellow (Marigold SFP)

SK Instant Mix Pastillage:

    50g (1¾oz) poppy red (Poppy)

    10g (¼oz) white (uncoloured)

SK Professional Paste Food Colours: Blackberry (black), Bluegrass, Edelweiss (white), Hydrangea, Poppy, Teddy Bear Brown

SK Designer Paste Food Colour: Terracotta

SK Quality Food Colour (QFC) Paste: Pink

SK Professional Liquid Food Colours: Blackberry (black), Poppy

SK Designer Pastel Dust Food Colour: Pastel Pink

SK Designer Metallic Lustre Dust Food Colour: Dark Bronze

SK Professional Food Colour Pens: Black (optional), Red

SK CMC Gum

EQUIPMENT

Basic equipment (see pages 6 to 7)

8cm round x 5cm deep (3¹/₈" x 2") polystyrene dummy

Spare polystyrene dummy

Food-grade foam pieces

Round cutters: 2cm, 7cm (¾", 2¾")

26cm x 5mm width (10" x ¼") satin ribbon: grey

Non-toxic glue

White seed-head stamens

Templates (see page 253)

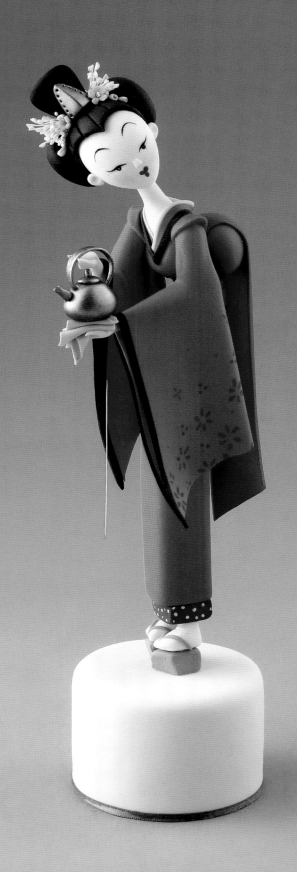

POLYSTYRENE BASE

1 Cover the round polystyrene base with light turquoise sugarpaste (see pages 42 to 43). Moisten the base with a little edible glue, secure a grey ribbon around it and allow to dry for a couple of days.

MAIN BODY

2 Knead 50g (1¾oz) of poppy red pastillage with 50g (1¾oz) of poppy red SFP and add a pinch of CMC to create a stronger modelling paste. Roll the paste into a long sausage, making it the same size as the template provided. Using the side of your hand, roll the paste ¾ of the way up the sausage to narrow the waist. Roll the top of the sausage thinner, pinch out the chest and cut a V-shape in the top to create the neckline. Use two cake smoothers to square off the top and sides of the skirt. Cut the bottom end straight with a sharp knife.

3 Lay the sausage on its side and bend it at the knees and the waist, following the template as a guide. Place a piece of foam under the waist to prevent it from flattening and losing its curved shape. Insert a barbecue skewer up to the knees and allow to dry for a couple of days. Once dry, skewer the main body into a spare piece of polystyrene.

TUTOR TIP

Even though the body has been left to dry for a couple of days, the paste inside may still be a little soft so it is advisable to pierce a hole in the polystyrene base before inserting the body into it.

FEET AND SHOES

4 Roll a small piece of White SFP into the shape of a bowling pin and create the foot as explained on page 51. Bend the foot at the ankle, use a Dresden tool to make an indent in the end of the foot to bring out the big toe and leave to dry upright. Repeat to make the second foot.

5 For the shoes, roll out some light brown SFP to 1cm (³⁄₈") thick. Place a foot on the paste and trim around it using straight cuts to make a rectangular shoe. Repeat to make the second shoe.

NECK

6 Roll some more White SFP into the shape of a bowling pin and flatten it down slightly. Cut the rounded end into a V-shape and secure on top of the chest with a little edible glue. Insert a cocktail stick through the neck and down to the waist. Leave to dry.

UNDERSKIRT AND OBI

7 Mix some poppy red SFP with a very small amount of Black SFP to achieve a darker shade of red. Roll out a small piece of paste to 5mm (¼") thick, cut out a square that is the same size as the base of the dress and round off the corners with your fingers. Push the square up the skewer and attach to the bottom of the main body with edible glue.

8 For the obi, roll some dark red SFP out into a thin sheet and cut out a long, narrow strip. Wrap around the waist up to the chest and secure in place with edible glue. Attach a thin strip of Black

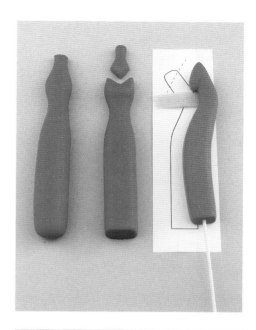

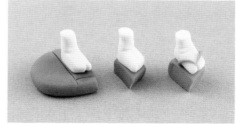

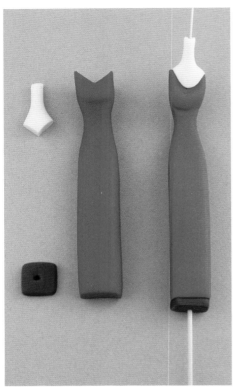

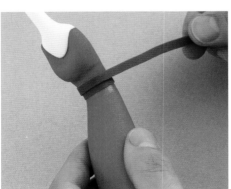

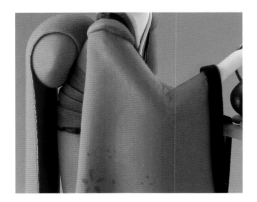

SFP around the base of the obi to finish. Insert the skewer back into a spare polystyrene dummy.

HEAD

9 Roll 20g (¾oz) of White SFP into a teardrop shape and flatten it slightly with your palm, making sure that the size of the head is the same as the template provided. Use the edge of a Dresden tool to mark on the eyelids just below the middle line of the face. Note that the eyes are positioned on the lower half of the head. Set aside to firm up.

10 To make the nose, roll some White SFP into a tiny teardrop and attach it in the middle of the face just below the eyes. Use the blade of a knife to flatten it into a wedge, then cut the sides and end straight to make a trapezium shape.

11 Paint on the eyelashes, eyebrows and pupils using Blackberry liquid food colour and a fine paintbrush. Use Poppy liquid food colour to paint a trefoil shape for the lips. Mix some Pastel Pink dust food colour with a little cornflour and dust over the cheeks with a soft brush.

12 Make the ears using White SFP as explained on page 51 and secure them to the sides of the head, so they fall just between the eyes and the nose. It is important to allow the head to

TUTOR TIP

If you are not confident enough to paint the facial details, you could use food colour pens to draw them on instead.

dry overnight before attaching the hair. The nose and mouth should sit centrally between the eyes, as shown in the diagram on page 253.

13 Roll out some Black SFP to 3mm (⅛") thick, cut out a circle using a 7cm (2¾") round cutter then cut it in half for the wig. Cut out two semicircles from the straight edge with a 2cm (¾") round cutter, leaving a pointed edge. Position the pointed edge centrally on the forehead and wrap the sides around the head. Trim any excess paste from the back of the head with a small pair of scissors. Mark several lines over the wig using the blade of a knife and leave the head to dry face-up.

14 Once the head is firm, roll a teardrop of Black SFP and secure to the back of the head to fill out the shape. Mark a few lines down the paste with the blade of a knife. Insert a skewer into the base of the head and leave to dry upright in a piece of polystyrene to avoid the hair becoming flat.

15 For the rest of the wig, roll two teardrops of Black SFP, flatten them slightly and secure to the sides of the head. Finish the hair with a small trapezium shape on top of the head to give some height. Allow to dry.

16 Make the kanzashi hair ornament by gluing several white stamens together with non-toxic glue. Make some tiny flowers from White and yellow SFP and model the headpiece from White SFP. Mark holes around the edge of the headpiece with a barbecue skewer, paint with Dark Bronze dust food colour diluted with a few drops of clear alcohol and secure to the front of the wig.

TEAPOT

17 Roll a small piece of skin tone SFP into an oval shape and gently press a small ball tool into the top to make a groove for the lid. Roll a pinch of skin tone SFP into a very small oval shape, flatten it down with your fingers and secure in the groove. Make a hole in the lid with a cocktail stick and secure a very small ball of SFP into it.

18 For the spout, roll a small piece of skin tone SFP into a bowling pin shape and flatten it down slightly. Attach to one end of the teapot and push the end of a paintbrush into the tip of the spout to open it up. Cut out a very narrow strip of paste and bend it into a C-shape for the handle. Once dry, secure the ends of the handle to the teapot with dabs of softened SFP. Once the teapot is completely dry, paint it with Dark Bronze lustre dust diluted with a few drops of clear alcohol.

ARMS

19 Using the skin tone SFP, make two arms as explained on page 48. Bend both of them at the elbow to a 90° angle. Leave the right arm to dry on its side with the hand bent over the edge of a non-stick board, making sure the thumb is facing upwards. Leave the left arm to dry flat with its hand straight and thumb facing upwards, as this arm will support the teapot.

LEFT SLEEVE

20 Roll out some poppy red SFP on a non-stick board and cut out the sleeve shape following the template provided. Position the top of the left arm at the top of the sleeve and secure it in place. Use a cutting wheel to trim the top of the paste to the shape of the arm and fold under the right-hand side of the sleeve.

TUTOR TIP

It is easier to make and attach the inner part of the sleeve first, then secure the outer part over the top once the first piece is completely dry.

21 Attach the left arm to the body with a piece of softened poppy red SFP and support it in position with a barbecue skewer. Secure the fold of the sleeve to the side of the legs with edible glue: this fold will help support the arm. Allow to dry completely before attaching the outer part of the sleeve.

22 Cut out another sleeve from the poppy red SFP and stick over the outside of the arm. Use a small knife to trim the excess paste from around the shoulder and along the arm where the sleeves join. Attach a very narrow, long strip of Black SFP around the hem of the sleeve to finish.

TUTOR TIP

For more advanced modellers, there is an alternative method for making the sleeves which will save you a little time. Simply roll out some poppy red SFP and cut out the alternative sleeve shape using the template provided. Secure the arm on top of the sleeve as shown in the picture opposite, then fold the paste over the arm. Attach to the torso and give the sleeves a little movement before allowing to dry.

COLLAR

23 Roll out some terracotta SFP and yellow SFP and use the template to cut out the shape of the collar from each colour. Position the terracotta piece on top of the yellow piece so that a small strip of yellow paste can still be seen. Wrap the collar around the neck and overlap the paste at the front, securing it to the chest. To finish, secure a narrow strip of Black SFP around the edge of the collar.

CLOTH

24 Roll out a thin sheet of light blue SFP and cut out a small rectangle. Fold it up loosely and attach it to the left hand with a little edible glue. Secure the teapot on top of the cloth immediately with a dab of softened SFP. Leave to dry completely.

TUTOR TIP

Before you create the right arm, the teapot needs to be in its final position as the right arm will be adjusted so it rests on the lid of the teapot. The lid will support both the hand and the arm.

RIGHT SLEEVE

25 Make the inner sleeve in the same way as for the left sleeve, position the right arm on it and secure it to the torso with a piece of softened paste. Make sure that the right hand is resting on the lid of the teapot and leave to dry. Make and attach the outer part of the sleeve, pleating it slightly to give it movement. Finish with a narrow strip of Black SFP around the hem.

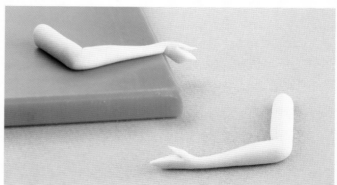
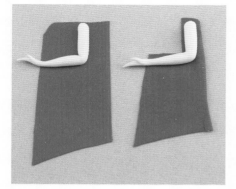
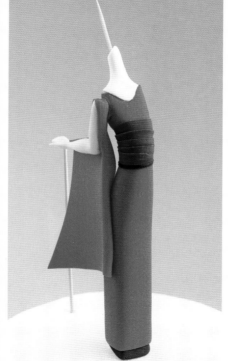
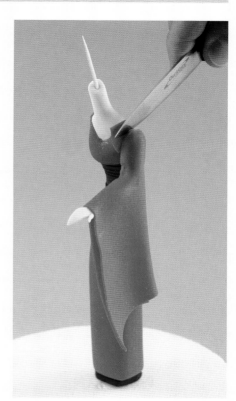
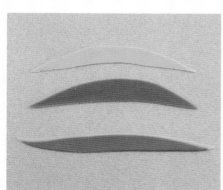

TUTOR TIP:
for advanced modellers

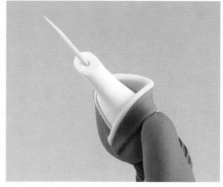
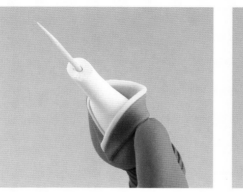

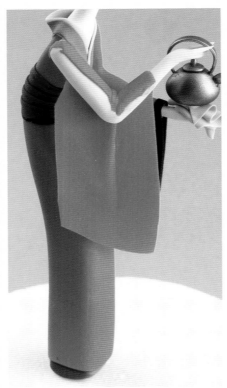

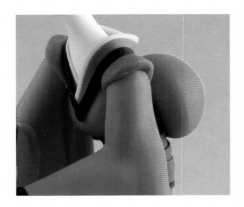
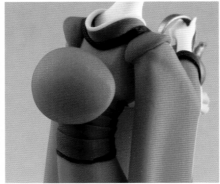
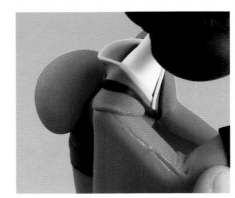

OBI AND SHOULDER PADS

26 To make the back of the obi, roll an oval of poppy red SFP and flatten it slightly on one side. Secure the flattened side to the back of the geisha with edible glue.

27 For the shoulder pads, use some dark red paste and roll it into a sausage with pointed ends. Flatten it down and cut it in half lengthways. Secure each piece over the top of the shoulders with the rounded side facing outwards: the pads cover the join between the arms and the torso and give a neat finish.

ASSEMBLY

28 Gently push the head down onto the cocktail stick protruding from the neck and secure in place with a little softened White SFP. Trim the base of the wig, if necessary, to make a clean line between the head and neck. Turn the head slightly so that she is looking down over her left shoulder. Support the head with barbecue skewers and leave to dry completely.

29 Roll a very thin sausage of poppy red SFP and stick it over the join between the inner and outer sleeves on the right arm. Rub over the paste to smooth out the join and give a neat finish.

30 Pierce the covered dummy with a skewer where you wish to insert the figurine. Spread a little softened white pastillage under the shoes and glue them on each side of the hole. Insert the skewer protruding from the base of the figurine into the covered dummy.

FINISHING TOUCHES

31 Roll out a thin sheet of dark red SFP and cut out the strip for the back of the kimono, following the template provided. Hang it over the back of the obi, secure in place and leave to dry.

32 Draw some basic flower shapes at the bottom of each sleeve using a Red food colour pen. Use the tip of a cocktail stick to paint dots of Edelweiss paste food colour over the underskirt. Secure the kanzashi to the front of the wig with a little piece of softened Black SFP.

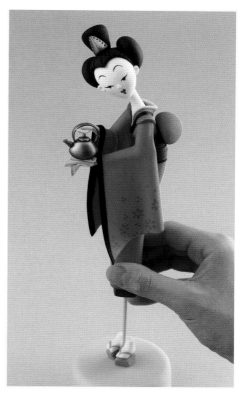

> ### TUTOR TIP
>
> For tall, slim figurines, like this geisha, it is advisable to transport them separately to the cake or dummy (see page 55 for more information about transporting figurines). Do not glue the underskirt to the shoes if you are planning to transport the figurine.

The soft, rounded features of this little geisha complement her tall, slender counterpart beautifully. Together, they complete the tea ceremony scene.

EDIBLES

SK Sugarpaste (rolled fondant):

    200g (7oz) olive green (Bridal White sugarpaste + touch of Olive)

SK Sugar Florist Paste (SFP, gum paste):

    100g (3½oz) Black

    30g (1oz) dark green (Holly/Ivy SFP)

    100g (3½oz) jade green (White SFP + Cactus)

    30g (1oz) moss green (White SFP + Dark Forest)

    30g (1oz) pale yellow (White SFP + touch of Marigold)

    250g (8¾oz) pea green (White SFP + Vine)

    50g (1¾oz) poppy red (White SFP + Poppy)

    50g (1¾oz) skin tone (White SFP + touch of Teddy Bear Brown + touch of Pink)

    100g (3½oz) White

50g (1¾oz) SK Instant Mix Pastillage

SK Professional Paste Food Colours: Blackberry (black), Cactus, Edelweiss (white), Hyacinth, Poppy, Marigold (tangerine), Teddy Bear Brown, Vine

SK Quality Food Colour (QFC) Paste: Pink

SK Designer Paste Food Colour: Dark Forest

SK Professional Liquid Food Colours: Blackberry (black), Poppy

SK Designer Pastel Dust Food Colour: Pastel Pink

SK Professional Dust Food Colours: Cactus, Nasturtium (peach)

SK Designer Metallic Lustre Dust Food Colour: Bronze

SK CMC Gum

EQUIPMENT

Basic equipment (see pages 6 to 7)

8cm round x 5cm deep (3¹/₈" x 2") polystyrene dummy

7cm (2¾") diameter polystyrene ball

Round cutter: 2cm (¾")

Spare polystyrene dummy

Foam pad

Sandpaper (new)

Lily of the valley cutter set (TT)

Textured rolling pin of your choice

White seed-head stamens

26cm x 5mm width (10" x ¼") satin ribbon: black

Templates (see page 253)

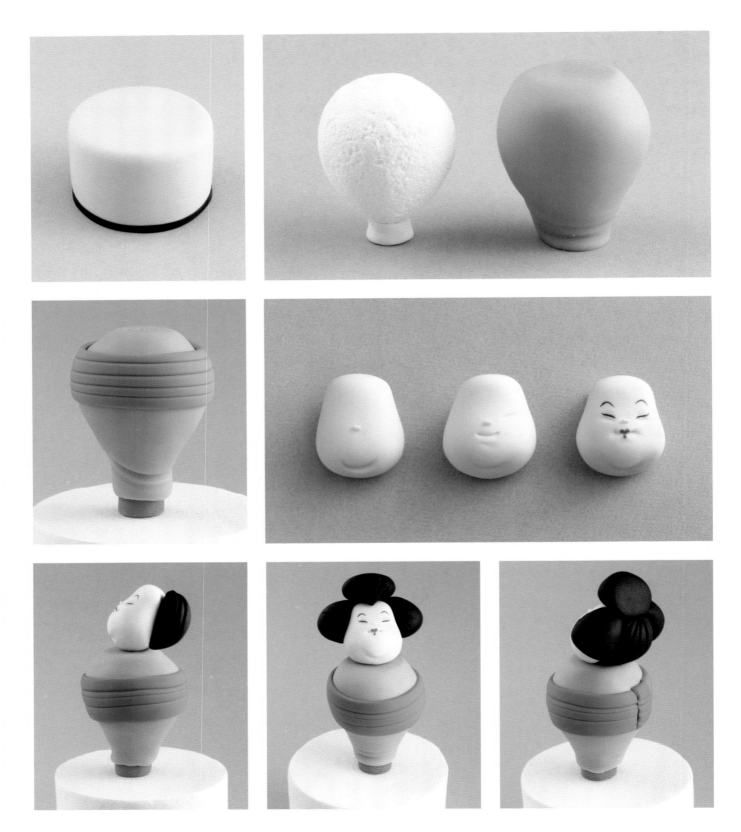

POLYSTYRENE BASE

1 Cover the round polystyrene base with olive green sugarpaste (see pages 42 to 43). Moisten the base with a little edible glue, secure a black ribbon around it and allow to dry for a couple of days.

MAIN BODY

2 Use a piece of sandpaper to file a 7cm (2¾") polystyrene ball into an egg shape: make sure that you do this away from any food preparation areas so particles of polystyrene cannot contaminate the cake. Roll a piece of pastillage into a small cylinder and attach it to the pointed end of the polystyrene with edible glue. Pierce a barbecue skewer up through the pastillage piece and allow to dry thoroughly.

3 Roll approximately 120g (4¼oz) of pea green SFP into a ball and cover the polystyrene body with the paste (see pages 42 to 43). Run the handle of a paintbrush around the narrower end to make pleats in the bottom of the kimono. Leave to dry until firm enough to handle.

4 For the underskirt, add a pinch of CMC to some poppy red SFP and roll out the paste to 1cm (⅜") thick. Cut out a small cylinder using a 2cm (¾") round cutter and attach to the base of the body with edible glue. Insert the skewer protruding from the main body into a spare polystyrene dummy.

BELT

5 Roll out some jade green SFP to 3mm (⅛") thick and cut out a strip that is as long as the diameter of the body and approximately 3cm (1⅛") wide. Mark several parallel lines along the paste with the edge of the Dresden tool and secure around the widest part of the body, with the join at the back. Trim off any excess paste with a small pair of scissors.

HEAD

6 Roll 50g (1¾oz) of White SFP into a pear shape, using the template provided as a size guide. Mark the chin using the blunt side of a 2cm (¾") round cutter. Gently run your finger under the indent to bring out the chin.

7 For the nose, roll a tiny piece of White SFP into a small oval and secure on the middle line of the face. Use the edge of a Dresden tool to mark the eyelids on either side of the nose, making them slant upwards slightly.

8 Use the edge of a Dresden tool to draw a curved line for the mouth, just below the nose. Press a small ball tool into the corners of the mouth to bring out the smile and cheeks. Rub your index finger over the corners of the mouth to smooth over any indent left behind by the ball tool. Draw a soft line just below the mouth with the rounded edge of a Dresden tool to define the lower lip.

9 Paint on the eyelashes and eyebrows with Blackberry liquid food colour and a fine paintbrush, then paint the eyelids with a mixture of Hyacinth and Edelweiss paste food colours. Paint a trefoil shape for the

lips using Poppy liquid food colour. Mix some Pastel Pink dust food colour with a little cornflour and brush over the cheeks with a soft brush. Leave to dry until firm enough to handle.

10 Roll approximately 20g (¾oz) of Black SFP into a teardrop and secure it to the back of the head to fill out the head shape. Mark a few vertical lines down the teardrop with the edge of a Dresden tool. Insert the head onto the skewer protruding from the main body, positioning it so that the head is tilted slightly backwards. Secure the head in place with a little edible glue.

11 Make two equally sized teardrops of Black SFP and attach them to the sides of the head with the pointed ends facing upwards. Mark several lines over the paste with a Dresden tool to resemble hair. Roll a third teardrop from Black SFP and pinch out the tip with your thumbs. Attach to the top of the head so the point sits in the middle of the forehead, then flatten down the back of the paste slightly.

COLLAR

12 Roll out some poppy red, jade green and pea green SFP and use the template to cut out the collar shape from each colour. Lay the pieces on top of each other so they overlap and stick them together, as shown in the

picture. Wrap the collar around the head so it sits just above the belt and overlap the ends. Trim to fit then pull on the back of the collar to loosen it slightly.

SLEEVES

13 Roll 35g (1¼oz) of pea green SFP into a long pear shape then gently widen the larger end with the heel of your hand to create the sleeve shape. Bend the smaller end of the pear shape upwards to make the bend in the elbow and bring out the shoulder. Trim the end of the sleeve straight using a sharp knife. Indent a few creases down the inside of the elbow with a Dresden tool and round off the sleeve with a cutting wheel.

14 Repeat step 13 to make another sleeve, then secure them either side of the body with edible glue. Set aside to firm up.

HANDS

15 Make two hands using skin tone SFP (see page 48), mark on the wrist and bend both hands backwards so the palms are facing upwards. Leave to dry until firm enough to handle. Once dry, trim off the excess paste above the wrist.

16 Secure the left hand to the end of the sleeve with a small piece of softened skin tone SFP. Put a little ball of paste on the end of a barbecue skewer then use this to support the hand as it dries: the ball of paste stops the skewer leaving a mark on the hand. Secure the right hand to the end of the right sleeve, positioning it on top of the left hand.

17 Roll out some dark green SFP, cut out a narrow strip and attach around the hem of each sleeve.

OBI

18 Roll approximately 30g (1oz) of pea green SFP into an oval, flatten one side slightly and attach it to the back of the geisha with edible glue.

FEET AND SHOES

19 Make the feet from White SFP and the shoes from moss green SFP as explained on page 189 for the first geisha.

KANZASHI

20 Roll out a small piece of White SFP and texture it with a textured rolling pin of your choice. Cut out the headpiece following the template and leave it to dry over a rolling pin to make it curved. Paint with Bronze dust food colour diluted with a few drops of clear alcohol.

21 Roll out a small piece of pale yellow SFP thinly and cut out several small flowers of different sizes using the lily of the valley cutters. Soften the edges with a ball tool on a foam pad and leave to dry. Thread the flowers onto a stamen and secure in place with a dot of non-toxic glue. Once completely dry, dust the centres with Nasturtium dust food colour.

22 Paint two cocktail sticks with Edelweiss paste food colour and leave to dry.

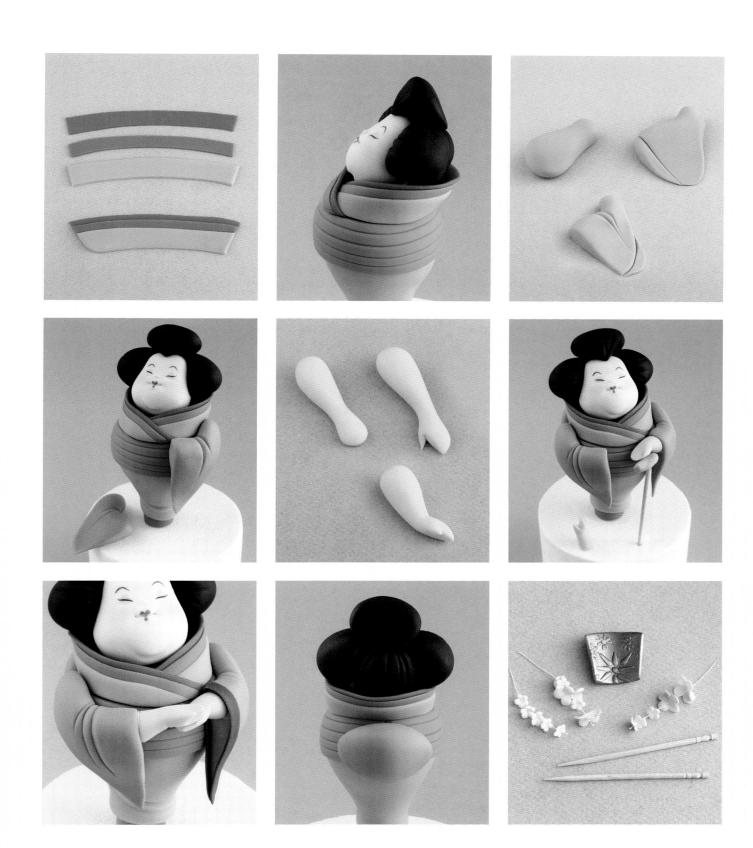

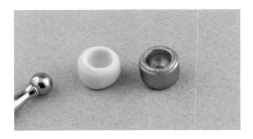

CUP

23 Roll a small pinch of skin tone SFP into a cylinder then push a small ball tool into the top. Once dry, paint with the Bronze food colour mixture.

FINISHING TOUCHES

24 Secure the bronze headpiece and the white sticks to the back of the wig with a small sausage of softened Black SFP. Paint white dots over the underskirt using a cocktail stick and Edelweiss paste food colour.

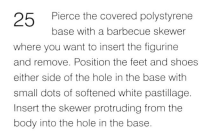

25 Pierce the covered polystyrene base with a barbecue skewer where you want to insert the figurine and remove. Position the feet and shoes either side of the hole in the base with small dots of softened white pastillage. Insert the skewer protruding from the body into the hole in the base.

26 Roll out a thin sheet of dark green SFP and cut out a strip for the back of the obi, following the template provided. Hang over the back of the obi, secure in place and leave to dry.

27 To finish, attach the flowers to the wig with softened Black SFP and dust the bottom of the sleeves with Cactus dust food colour.

TUTOR TIP

It is not advisable to transport figurines on their bases as they may topple over; place the figurine in a cake box as explained on page 55 and assemble once you have arrived at the venue.

If you can't decide which geisha is your favourite, then try creating both figures and arrange them on this beautiful cake to create a complete tea ceremony scene.

EDIBLES

23cm round x 7cm deep (9"x 2¾") cake, filled and crumb-coated (see page 34)

SK Sugarpaste (rolled fondant):

  1kg (2lb 3¼oz) pale blue (Bridal White + a touch of Hydrangea)

  300g (10½oz) palest blue (Bridal White + a very small touch of Hydrangea)

SK Sugar Florist Paste (SFP, gum paste):

  100g (3½oz) White

SK Instant Mix Royal Icing:

  100g (3½oz) palest blue (very small touch of Hydrangea)

EQUIPMENT

Basic equipment (see pages 6 to 7)

30.5cm (12") round cake drum (board)

15cm round x 5cm deep (6"x 2") polystyrene base

Small primrose flower cutter (TT)

Medium lily of the valley flower cutter (TT)

30-gauge floral wire: white

Black stamens (or white stamens painted with black liquid food colour)

Non-toxic craft glue

Floral tape: white

Foam pad

Piping nozzle: no. 3

Cherry blossom stencil

Posy picks

1.95m x 15mm width (77" x ⅝") satin ribbon: white

POLYSTYRENE BASE

1 Roll out 300g (10½oz) of pale blue sugarpaste and cover the dummy base (see pages 42 to 43). Leave the sugarpaste to dry.

CAKE DRUM

2 Roll out 300g (10½oz) of palest blue sugarpaste and cover the cake drum (see page 41). Trim the board with white ribbon and allow to dry.

FLOWER SPRAYS

3 For the stamens, cut several 30-gauge wires into small sections. Brush the tip of each wire with non-toxic craft glue and attach two black stamens to the end. Set aside to dry.

4 Roll out some White SFP very thinly on a non-stick board, cut out several flowers using the small primrose cutter and shape them as explained on page 200. Leave to firm up.

5 Once dry, thread the wires with black stamens through the centre of the primrose flowers, then secure with a dot of non-toxic glue. Leave them to dry.

6 Roll out some more White SFP very thinly on a non-stick board and cut out several flowers using the lily of the valley cutter. Soften the edges on a foam pad with a medium ball tool to cup them. Allow them to firm up.

7 Pierce the centre of the flower with a scribing tool to create a hole. Thread five to seven lily of the valley flowers onto pieces of 30-gauge wire to make several stems. Secure the flowers to the wire with a dot of non-toxic glue and leave to dry.

8 To make a small flower bud, roll tiny pieces of White SFP into teardrop shapes. Moisten the end of a piece of 30-gauge wire with edible glue and insert into the pointed end of the bud. Insert the wires into a spare piece of polystyrene and allow them to dry.

9 Take several buds, lily of the valley flowers and primroses and tape together with white floral tape to make a

spray. Repeat to make a second spray of the same size.

CAKE

10 Roll out 700g (1lb 8¾oz) of pale blue sugarpaste and cover the cake (see page 34). Allow the paste to dry overnight.

11 Decorate the sides of the cake and the polystyrene base using some palest blue royal icing and the flower stencil, as explained on page 159.

ASSEMBLY

12 Secure the cake centrally on the cake board with a dab of royal icing, then dowel the cake (see page 42). Centre and glue the covered polystyrene base onto the cake with a dab of royal icing.

13 Fit a paper piping bag with a no. 3 nozzle, then fill the bag with medium-consistency palest blue royal icing and pipe a running bead border around the bottom of each tier.

14 Insert the flower arrangements into posy picks and place on the cake.

Important note: The flower arrangements contain inedible glue, wires and stamens so must be safely removed from the cake before serving.

CHERRY BLOSSOM BISCUITS

Bake 30 6cm (2³/₈") round biscuits following the recipe
provided on page 18.

Colour some medium-consistency royal icing with a touch
of Hydrangea paste food colour, fit a piping bag with a
no. 1 nozzle and fill the bag with the pale blue icing. Pipe
an outline around each biscuit, then let down the remaining
icing to make it run-out consistency. Fit a piping bag with a
no. 2 nozzle, fill it with the runny icing and flood inside the
outline (see page 30). Leave to dry.

Decorate the biscuits using a cherry blossom stencil and
firm-peak white royal icing, following the instructions for the
main cake. Pipe a dot of medium-consistency black royal
icing in the centre of each of the flowers and leave to dry.

THE ILLUSIONIST

The dismayed illusionist outwitted by his mischievous rabbits would make a magical scene for a party cake and delight both young and old alike. This amusing design demonstrates just how easy it is to tell a story through the medium of sugar. You can make the illusionist look angry, surprised or confused by simply adjusting the shape of his mouth and the position of his eyebrows.

EDIBLES

12.5cm x 6cm (5" x 2³/₈") round cake, filled and crumb-coated (see page 34)

SK Sugarpaste (rolled fondant):

    350g (12¼oz) mauve (Bridal White sugarpaste + touch of Plum)

    150g (5¼oz) deep plum (Bridal White sugarpaste + Plum + Cyclamen)

SK Sugar Florist Paste (SFP, gum paste):

    200g (7oz) Black

    30g (1oz) Cyclamen

    30g (1oz) light grey (White SFP + touch of Blackberry)

    10g (¼oz) pale pink (White + touch of Cyclamen)

    5g (just under ¼oz) purple (White SFP + Violet)

    100g (3½oz) skin tone (White SFP + touch of Nasturtium + touch of Teddy Bear Brown)

    5g (just under ¼oz) terracotta (White SFP + Terracotta)

    200g (7oz) White

SK Instant Mix Pastillage:

    100g (3½oz) light grey (white + touch of Blackberry)

SK Professional Paste Food Colours: Blackberry (black), Cyclamen (ruby), Edelweiss (white), Nasturtium (peach), Teddy Bear Brown, Terracotta, Violet (purple)

SK Designer Paste Food Colour: Plum

SK Professional Liquid Food Colour: Blackberry (black)

SK Professional Dust Food Colour: Fuchsia

SK Designer Pastel Dust Food Colour: Pastel Pink

SK Designer Metallic Lustre Dust Food Colour: Silver

SK Professional Food Colour Pen: Black

SK CMC Gum (optional)

EQUIPMENT

Basic equipment (see pages 6 to 7)

20.5cm (8") cake drum (board)

Spare polystyrene dummy

Round cutters: 1cm, 2.5cm, 4.5cm, 6cm, 7cm (³/₈", 1", 1³/₄", 2³/₈", 2³/₄")

24-gauge floral wire: white

1.05m x 15mm width (41½" x ⁵/₈") satin ribbon: black

Small lily of the valley cutter (TT)

Templates (see page 254)

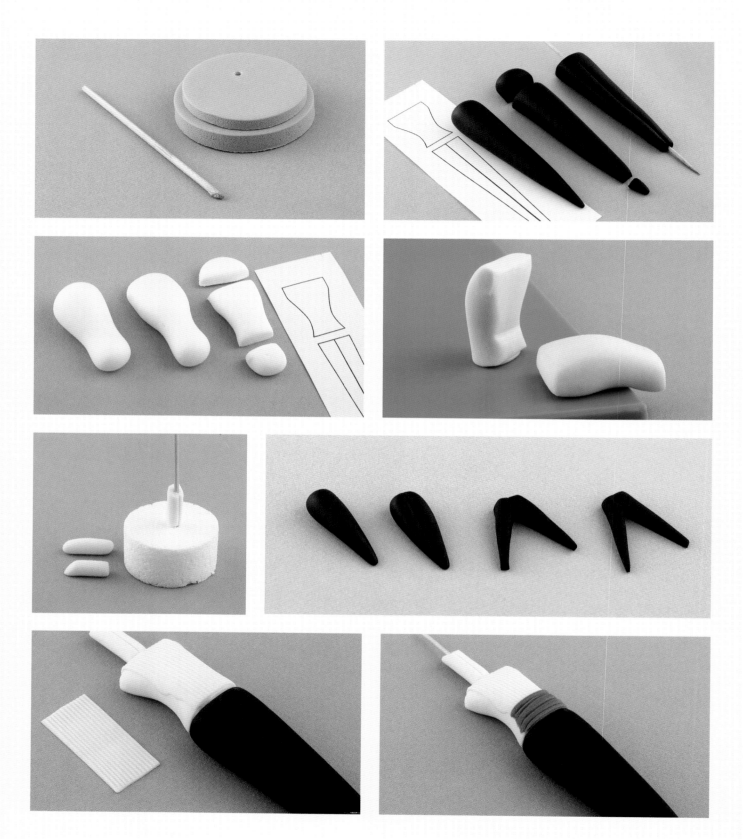

PASTILLAGE BASE

1 Roll out the light grey pastillage to a 1cm (3/8") thickness and cut out a 7cm (2¾") circle with a round cutter. Gather the trimmings, roll them out to a thickness of 5mm (¼") then cut out a 6cm (2³/8") circle. Secure the smaller circle centrally on top of the larger circle with a little edible glue. Use a barbecue skewer to pierce a hole through the base that is slightly off-centre: this is where you will insert the figurine later. Leave to dry completely.

ILLUSIONIST

Trousers

2 Roll 100g (3½oz) of Black SFP into a long cone shape that is the same width as the template provided. Run the palm of your hand along the paste to flatten it slightly. Press the sides with cake smoothers to square off the edges and make the paste fit the shape of the template. Cut straight across the top and bottom with a sharp knife, then use a blade tool to draw a line down the front and back to separate the legs. Insert a skewer into the bottom of the trousers until a small piece protrudes from the top. Leave to dry on a flat surface overnight.

TUTOR TIP

To speed up the drying time, add an extra pinch of CMC gum to the paste before modelling the trousers.

Torso

3 Roll 50g (1¾oz) of White SFP into a pear shape. Press the thicker end with the heel of your hand to bring out the chest and shoulder line, then flatten the other end slightly so it is the same thickness as the waist of the trousers. Trim both ends straight with a sharp knife, making the torso the same length as the template provided. Push a skewer up through the base of the torso to make a hole, then remove it. Position the torso over the edge of a non-stick board to give the back a slight curve. Allow to firm up.

Neck

4 Roll a small piece of White SFP into a sausage, then use a knife to trim one end straight and cut the other end at a slight angle. Insert a piece of barbecue skewer lengthways into the neck, so it protrudes from both ends. Indent a vertical line down the neck, insert it into a spare piece of polystyrene and leave to dry.

Shoes

5 Roll a small piece of Black SFP into a thin cone, then flatten it slightly with a cake smoother to make a wedge shape. Cut in half lengthways with a sharp knife then stick the wider ends together with a little edible glue to make a V-shape. Make a hole through the join with a skewer and secure to the pastillage base, making sure that the hole in the shoes lines up with the hole in the base.

Shirt and cummerbund

6 Roll out some White SFP into a very thin sheet and mark several parallel lines down it with the edge of a ruler. Cut out a rectangle measuring approximately 6cm long x 2.5cm wide (2³/8" x 1") and secure to the front of the torso with a little edible glue.

7 At this stage, carefully push the torso onto the skewer protruding from the legs and secure with a little softened White SFP. Push the skewer from the neck into the torso, secure with softened White SFP and wipe away any excess paste from around the neck and waist for a clean finish.

8 Roll out some light grey SFP very thinly and cut out a rectangle that is approximately 2cm long x 1.5cm wide (³/4" x ⁵/8") in size. Mark a few parallel lines across the paste with the edge of a Dresden tool and stick over the bottom of the shirt: there's no need to wrap the sash the whole way around the waist as it will distort the shape of the jacket once it is in place. Run your fingertip over the edge of the paste to blend the sash with the torso. Leave the body to dry flat overnight.

Head

9 Roll approximately 30g (1oz) of skin tone SFP into a teardrop shape, following the size of the head diagram for reference. Push your fingertips into the middle line along the face to create the eye sockets and bring out the bridge of the nose simultaneously. Hold the bridge of the nose between your thumb and index finger and push the paste upwards with your other finger to make the tip of the nose. Run your finger around the sides of the nose to smooth out the paste and give it more definition.

10 Push a ball tool into the eye sockets to hollow out the eyes. Gently rub your fingertips over the marks

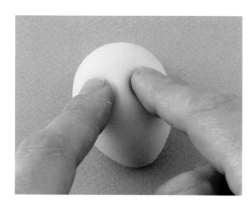

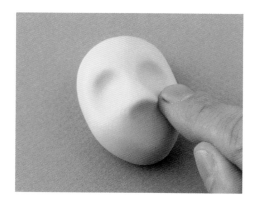

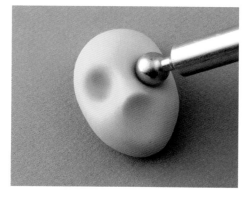

left by the ball tool to give a smooth finish to the eye area and re-define the bridge of the nose, if necessary. Push a small ball tool into the end of the nose to open up the nostrils. Run the rounded side of a Dresden tool gently around the nostrils to give them more definition.

11 Push the rounded end of a Dresden tool into the paste just below the nose to open up the mouth, then push the tip of the tool upwards underneath the mouth to bring out the lower lip. Mark lines down the sides of the mouth and under the eyes with the rounded edge of the Dresden tool.

12 Lay the head on a flat surface and position a wedge of spare paste under the chin so it dries sticking out at an angle: this will create a more realistic profile.

13 Roll two small balls of White SFP and secure them in the eye sockets with edible glue. Flatten them down slightly with your fingers so they do not bulge out.

14 For the moustache, roll a pinch of Black SFP into a tiny sausage with pointed ends and secure below the nose with a little edible glue. Roll another very small Black SFP sausage with pointed ends, turn up the ends and attach to the chin. Push the paste up in the middle of the goatee beard with the tip of a Dresden tool.

15 Roll two tiny teardrops of terracotta SFP for the eyelashes and secure them over the top of the eyeballs with the pointed ends on the outside. For the eyebrows, roll two small teardrops of Black SFP and position them above the eyes at different angles to give the face a puzzled expression. Use a soft brush

to dust the cheeks with a little Pastel Pink dust food colour. Roll two very small pinches of Black SFP into tiny balls and attach them to the eyes so they sit slightly off-centre to make the pupils.

16 Make the ears as explained on page 51 and attach them to the sides of the head. Allow the head to firm up before adding the hair.

17 Roll approximately 20g (¾oz) of Black SFP into a teardrop shape and flatten one side slightly. Attach the flattened side to the back of the head to fill out the head shape and mark a few lines down the paste with the handle of a paintbrush. Insert the head into a spare polystyrene dummy so you can work on the rest of the hair comfortably.

18 To make the hairline, roll a piece of Black SFP into a sausage with pointed ends and flatten it down with your fingers. Attach this piece around the head and secure the ends in front of the ears to create sideburns and fill in the hairline at the same time. Push the edge of a Dresden tool repeatedly over the paste to resemble hair. Allow it to firm up.

Jacket

19 Insert the skewer protruding from the body into a spare polystyrene dummy. Roll out some Black SFP into a thin sheet and cut out the jacket shape following the template. Attach to the back first so the jacket overhangs the waist and shoulders then secure around the sides of the torso with a little edible glue, leaving the front of the jacket open. Bring the paste at the top together and trim the excess with a small pair of scissors to make a neat join at the shoulder line.

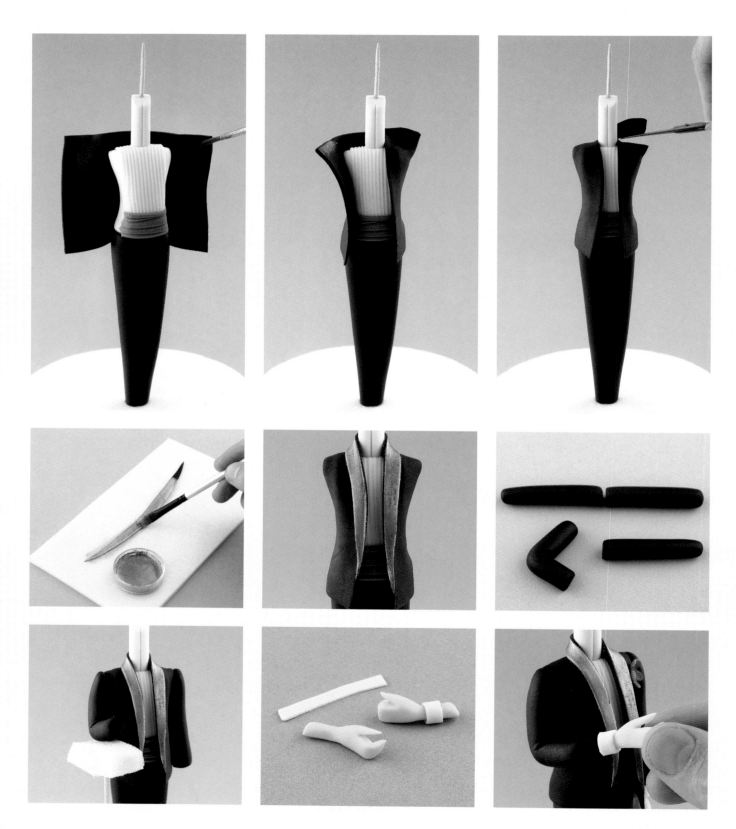

20 For the lapels, thinly roll out some Black SFP and cut out a strip following the template. Paint the lapels with Silver metallic dust food colour diluted with a few drops of clear alcohol. Secure around the neck and to the front of the jacket with a little edible glue. Use a lily of the valley cutter and some purple SFP to make a small flower and attach to the lapel.

Arms

21 Roll approximately 20g (¾oz) of Black SFP into a sausage and cut it in half. Leave one of the sausages straight and bend the other to a 90° angle at the elbow. Attach the arms to either side of the body and use a skewer to support the bent arm in place until it has dried fully. Place a piece of foam between the end of the skewer and the arm to avoid marking the paste. Attach two tiny balls of Black SFP to the outside of each sleeve to make buttons. Set aside to firm up.

Hands and cuffs

22 Make two hands from skin tone SFP as explained on page 48, but you do not need to indent the fingers. Bend the fingers into shape so one hand is closed and the other hand is ready to hold the wand. Leave them to firm up.

23 Once the hands are firm enough to handle, roll out some White SFP thinly, cut out two narrow strips and wrap them around the wrists to create the cuffs. Once the hands and cuffs are completely dry, use a sharp knife to cut the excess paste flush with the cuff. Spread some softened White SFP over the ends of the wrists and attach to the arms.

HAT

24 Roll 30g (1oz) of Black SFP into a thick sausage then press both ends against a non-stick board to flatten them and make the edges straight.

25 Roll out some Black SFP thinly, cut out a 1cm (³⁄₈") wide strip of Black SFP then paint it with Silver dust food colour diluted with a few drops of clear alcohol. Secure it around one end of the sausage, use a pair of scissors to trim the ends at the join and leave to dry.

26 For the brim, roll out some Black SFP and cut out a 4.5cm (1¾") circle. Roll it out slightly in one direction to make an oval shape, then cut out the centre with a 2.5cm (1") round cutter. Turn the hat upside down and attach the brim to the base of the hat with edible glue. Leave to dry.

WAND

27 Moisten a 6cm (2³⁄₈") piece of 24-gauge floral wire with a little edible glue and thread a small ball of Black SFP onto it. Roll the paste between your fingers until you have completely covered the wire. Remove any excess from the ends and allow it to dry. Finish the tip of the wand with a very small strip of White SFP.

RABBITS

Head

28 Roll approximately 10g (¼oz) of White SFP into a rounded teardrop and insert a cocktail stick into the wider end so you can keep the head upright and avoid flattening the sides.

29 Press a 1cm (³/₈") round cutter into the lower half of the face to create a curved line. Open up the mouth underneath the line by pushing the paste down with the rounded tip of a Dresden tool. Push a small ball tool into each corner of the mouth to make dimples, then gently rub your fingertip over the marks to smooth out the paste. To give the mouth depth, roll out some Cyclamen SFP very thinly and cut out the shape of the mouth using a cutting wheel. Secure in the mouth with a little edible glue.

30 To make the muzzle, roll a small pinch of White SFP into an oval and secure it above the mouth. Press the blade of a craft knife down the middle to divide the muzzle into two sections. Roll a tiny ball of pale pink SFP then flatten it slightly into an oval and attach to the top of the muzzle. Use a soft brush to dust the cheeks with Pastel Pink dust food colour.

31 For the tongue, mix a tiny piece of Cyclamen SFP with a pinch of White SFP to make a slightly paler shade. Roll the paste into a tiny oval shape and stick it into the bottom of the mouth. Flatten it down slightly and mark a line down the middle of the tongue with the edge of a Dresden tool.

32 Draw two tiny ovals just above the muzzle with a Black food colour pen. Paint a curved line above each eye using a fine paintbrush and Blackberry liquid food colour for the eyebrows.

33 Roll a tiny teardrop of White SFP for the teeth and attach it under the muzzle with a little edible glue. Once secure, use a small pair of scissors to trim the bottom of the paste straight and make a snip in the teeth to separate them. Make two holes in the top of the head with the tip of a cocktail stick where the ears will be inserted.

Ears

34 For the ears, roll two long teardrops of White SFP and insert a piece of white floral wire into the narrower end of each one, leaving a short length sticking out. Flatten the teardrops down slightly with your finger and push a medium-sized ball tool into the middle to give them shape. Bend the ears into the desired position and allow to dry completely. Once dry, insert the wires into the holes in the rabbit's head and secure them with a little edible glue.

Important note: It is not usually advisable to use wire inside sugar models, however here it is needed because the ears have to be bent into shape. Make sure the rabbits and the illusionist's wand are safely removed from the cake before it is served.

35 Repeat steps 28 to 34 to make three more rabbit heads. Change the shape of the mouth, eyes and the position of the eyebrows to create different facial expressions. Leave to dry completely before securing the heads onto the bodies later.

Body, legs and tail

36 Roll 10g (¼oz) of White SFP into a small pear shape and split the narrower end in two with a craft knife to separate the front legs. Twist the front legs inwards slightly so any marks left by the knife are hidden. Use a Dresden tool to make an indent on either side of the body to bring out the back legs and make two marks on the rounded end of each front leg to create the paws. Roll a tiny ball of White SFP for the tail and attach it to the back of the body with a little edible glue. Roll two tiny teardrops of White SFP, attach them to the sides of the body under the back legs then make two marks on the rounded ends to make the back paws. Insert a cocktail stick into the top of the front legs where the head will sit.

ASSEMBLY

37 Secure the rabbit's body to the top of the illusionist's head with a little edible glue while it is still soft. Insert a cocktail stick through the rabbit's neck and into the illusionist's head and allow to firm up. Roll a few thin sausages of Black SFP and position them in between the rabbit's paws to make it look like the rabbit is sinking into his quiff.

38 Insert the skewer protruding from the base of the illusionist's body into the hole through the feet, pastillage base and polystyrene base. Stick the trousers to the shoes with a little softened Black SFP. Gently push the illusionist's head onto the cocktail stick that is protruding from the neck and secure in place with a little softened White SFP. Paint tiny dots of Edelweiss paste food colour on the illusionist's pupils to highlight the eyes.

39 Push the rabbit's head onto the cocktail stick protruding from its body and secure with a dot of softened White SFP. Position the wand in the illusionist's right hand and secure with some softened skin tone SFP.

40 Repeat step 36 to create a second rabbit's body. Position the second rabbit onto the pastillage base so it is standing upright behind the illusionist's trousers and make sure to secure it to both the base and the trousers for extra support. Insert a cocktail stick into the neck and allow the body firm to up. Place one of the rabbit heads onto the cocktail stick at a slight angle and allow the whole figurine to dry completely.

CAKE AND CAKE DRUM

41 Cover the cake with mauve sugarpaste (see page 34) and the cake drum with deep plum sugarpaste (see page 41). Position the cake slightly off-centre on the cake drum and secure it in place. Trim both the cake and cake drum with black satin ribbon.

42 To make the handkerchief, roll out some Cyclamen SFP into a thin sheet and dust the surface with Fuchsia dust food colour. Fold up the paste loosely and attach to the cake drum with a little edible glue. Secure the hat onto the handkerchief and attach another rabbit's head to the top of the

hat. Make two little paws as for the other rabbits and attach them to the brim of the hat.

43 Make another rabbit's body following step 36 and secure it over the edge of the cake to make it look as if it is trying to climb up the side. Insert a cocktail stick into the rabbit's body and push the remaining rabbit head onto it once the body has firmed up.

44 When you are ready to present the cake, place the figurine onto the cake and secure in place with softened pastillage or royal icing. There's no need to dowel the cake as the pastillage base will prevent the figurine from sinking into the cake and the skewer will provide extra support.

TUTOR TIP

It is not advisable to transport figurines on their bases as they may topple over; place the figurine in a cake box as explained on page 55 and assemble once you have arrived at the venue.

Important note: Please ensure that the recipient is aware that the figurine and rabbits should be removed before serving as they contain inedible supports that must not be eaten.

BUNNY BISCUITS

Make up the biscuit dough following the recipe on page 18, cut out 25 bunny heads using the template provided on page 255, and bake as required.

Fit a piping bag with a no. 1 nozzle, fill with medium-consistency uncoloured royal icing, then pipe an outline around each biscuit. Flood the biscuits with uncoloured run-out icing using a no. 2 nozzle (see page 30). While the icing is still wet, colour some run-out icing with Fuchsia and a touch of Daffodil paste food colours, then pipe long teardrops inside the ears and dots on the cheeks. Pipe the open mouths with Cyclamen-coloured run-out icing and use a dot of paler Cyclamen icing to make the tongue. Drop a dot of white run-out icing into the mouth for the front teeth and leave to dry.

Use some Cyclamen-coloured run-out icing and a no. 1 nozzle to pipe the nose in the middle of the biscuit, then use the tip of a cocktail stick to pull it into a triangle shape. For the closed mouths, pipe a dot, dash or curved line with the same Cyclamen-coloured icing. Pipe ovals for the eyes with Black run-out icing and use a tiny drop of white run-out icing to highlight them. Paint on the eyebrows and closed eyes with a fine paintbrush and Black liquid food colour, then paint a thin line for the muzzle using Fuchsia liquid colour.

TRICK OR TREAT?

TRICK OR TREAT?

Children can really have fun at Halloween, going out trick or treating in their favourite fancy dress. This little girl in her witch costume would be the perfect way to finish off a celebration cake for the occasion.

EDIBLES

SK Sugar Florist Paste (SFP, gum paste):

150g (5¼oz) Black

10g (¼oz) dark brown (Bulrush SFP)

30g (1oz) pale lilac (White SFP + touch of Wisteria)

30g (1oz) poppy red (White SFP + Poppy)

200g (7oz) purple (Violet SFP)

100g (3½oz) skin tone (White SFP + touch of Teddy Bear Brown + touch of Pink)

10g (¼oz) turquoise (White SFP + Gentian)

50g (1¾oz) White

50g (1¾oz) yellow (Marigold SFP)

SK Instant Mix Pastillage:

50g (1¾oz) pale brown (White + Teddy Bear Brown)

100g (3½oz) white (uncoloured)

SK Instant Mix Royal Icing:

20g (¾oz) black (Blackberry)

50g (1¾oz) pale pink (Rose)

50g (1¾oz) deep pink (Cyclamen)

SK Professional Paste Food Colours: Blackberry (black), Cyclamen (ruby), Edelweiss (white), Gentian (ice blue), Marigold (tangerine), Poppy, Rose, Teddy Bear Brown, Wisteria

SK Designer Pastel Dust Food Colour: Pale Pink

SK Professional Liquid Food Colours: Blackberry (black), Chestnut (soft beige)

SK CMC Gum

SK Professional Food Colour Pen: Black

EQUIPMENT

Basic equipment (see pages 6 to 7)

3cm (1⅛") diameter polystyrene hemisphere

Spare polystyrene dummy

Round cutter: 3.5cm or 4cm (1⅜" or 1½")

Cotton pad

Small piece of thin card, e.g. from a cereal box or cake box

Piping nozzles: 2 x no. 3, no. 7

Cellophane sheets

Templates (see page 255)

BODY

1   Roll out 100g (3½oz) of white pastillage to 5mm (¼") thick on a non-stick board and cut out the body shape using the template provided. Bend the paste into a cone shape, overlapping the ends, and leave to dry overnight standing up on the wider end.

TUTOR TIP

If you don't have enough time to allow the pastillage to dry overnight, you can use a wafer ice cream cone and wrap it in a thin layer of pastillage instead to help it hold the shape. Allow the pastillage to dry for a short while to firm up slightly then continue to build the rest of the character.

WITCH'S HAT

2   To make the brim of the hat, add a pinch of CMC to 50g (1¾oz) of Black SFP, roll it out to 3mm (⅛") thick and cut out a circle using an 8.5cm (3⅜") round cutter. Roll it out further in one direction to make an oval shape. Leave to dry on a flat surface with a tiny piece of a cotton pad under one of the sides to give a wavy shape.

3   For the top of the hat, add a pinch of CMC to 30g (1oz) of Black SFP and roll it into a long cone that is the size of the template provided. Make three marks along the cone with the edge of a Dresden tool and bend the paste at these marks to make a hooked shape, as shown on the template. Leave to dry.

4   Attach the top of the hat to the brim with a tiny piece of Black SFP softened with cooled, boiled water.

5   For the hatband, roll out 20g (¾oz) of purple SFP and cut out a 2cm (¾") wide rectangle. Attach the paste around the base of the cone with edible glue. Trim the excess paste at the join with a small pair of scissors.

6   For the buckle, roll out a piece of pale lilac SFP and cut out the buckle shape using the template provided. Secure to the front of the hat with a little edible glue.

BASKET

7   Roll out 30g (1oz) of pale brown pastillage and press the edge of a ruler into the paste to mark hatched lines. Place over a 3cm (1⅛") diameter polystyrene hemisphere and trim the excess pastillage using a 3.5cm or 4cm (1⅜" or 1½") round cutter. Leave to dry.

NECK

8   Roll a small piece of skin tone SFP into a cone shape that is approximately the size of the template provided. Insert a skewer through the neck and leave to dry.

COSTUME

9   For the underskirt, roll out a small piece of Black SFP on a non-stick board and cut into a triangle shape that is approximately the length of the pastillage body. Use the edge of a ruler to mark several lines lengthways for the pleats. Secure to the front of the pastillage cone with a little edible glue.

10   Thinly roll out 150g (5¼oz) of purple SFP on a non-stick board and cut out the shape of the outfit using the template. Fold the sides under a little

to create a hem, pleat gently and attach around the cone, leaving the underskirt at the front uncovered. Arrange the trail of the skirt in gentle folds. Trim the excess paste from the top of the cone neatly with a pair of scissors.

11 Secure the neck to the top of the outfit with a little softened skin tone SFP. Roll out some purple SFP and cut out the collar using the template provided. Secure around the neck with the narrower side at the base. Roll out some more Black SFP, cut out a strip that is 1.5cm ($^5/_8$") wide and glue it underneath the collar. Trim the excess paste at the back with a small pair of scissors.

HEAD

12 Add a touch of CMC to 35g–40g (1¼oz–1½oz) of skin tone SFP and roll it into a rounded teardrop shape (see template for size). Press a medium ball tool halfway up the face along the eye line to create the sockets where the eyes will be placed later on.

13 For the mouth, make an indent in the lower half of the face with a small piece of card and pull down to make an open mouth (see page 115).

14 For the nose, roll a tiny piece of skin tone SFP into a rounded triangle shape and glue it between the eyes. Open up the nostrils using the handle of a paintbrush.

15 For the eyes, roll two small ovals of White SFP and glue them in the eye sockets with a little edible glue. Flatten them softly with your fingertip to prevent them from bulging out. Push a small ball tool into the lower half of the eyes, where the irises will be placed. Roll two tiny pieces of turquoise SFP into balls and glue them into the eyeballs with

a little edible glue. Flatten them gently with your fingertip so the irises are level with the eyeball. Draw a small pupil on the iris using a Black food colour pen. Use a fine paintbrush to add a dot of Edelweiss paste food colour to highlight the eyes.

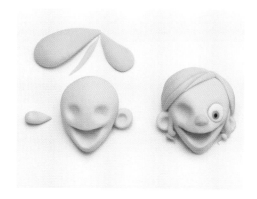

> **TUTOR TIP**
>
> When you have finished making the eyes, it is important to flatten down the eyeballs, irises and pupils to prevent the character's eyes from bulging out.

16 For the eyelashes, roll two tiny sausages of Black SFP which are pointed at both ends then glue them over the top of the eyes following the eye contour. Paint single eyelashes coming out of the paste with a fine paintbrush and Blackberry liquid food colour. Use Chestnut liquid food colour and a fine paintbrush to paint the eyebrows above each eye.

17 Mix some Pale Pink dust food colour with a little cornflour and dust it over the cheeks and inside the mouth.

18 For the tongue, roll a tiny ball of poppy red SFP, glue it in the lower half of the mouth and flatten it down.

19 For the teeth, roll a tiny pinch of White SFP into a sausage with pointed ends, flatten it slightly and attach across the upper part of the mouth with edible glue. Open up the middle of the sausage with a small knife to create a gap in the front teeth.

20 Use the tip of a cocktail stick and Chestnut liquid food colour to paint freckles over the cheeks and nose.

21 Make and attach the ears as explained on page 51.

22 Roll out some yellow SFP into two teardrop shapes, making one slightly bigger than the other. Press down on each teardrop shape to flatten them slightly. Dab a little edible glue over the forehead and attach the teardrops in place to make her fringe, pressing the paste gently around the back of the ears. Make a few marks with the edge of a Dresden tool to texture the hair and add a few loose strands to her fringe and down the sides of her face. Set aside to dry.

23 Once the hair has dried out and the whole piece is easy to handle, push the head down into the skewer protruding from the top of the neck and secure in place with softened SFP.

TUTOR TIP

The figure's head doesn't have to be in an upright position; you can tilt it slightly to one side to give it natural movement.

---

24 Attach the hat to the top of head and the basket at the front right below the belt with softened Black SFP. Hold them in the right position using a few skewers as support. Leave to dry overnight.

ARMS

25 Roll some purple SFP into a sausage that tapers slightly at each end and divide it into two pieces, each about 6cm (2³⁄₈") long. Bend each piece halfway along and set aside.

26 Roll out some purple SFP on a non-stick board and cut out the sleeves using the templates provided. Attach each arm to the sleeves while still fresh and give some movement to each sleeve. Secure both arms and sleeves to the torso and under the basket with a little edible glue. Leave to dry.

27 Make and attach the hands as explained on page 48.

WIG

28 Place 50g (1¾oz) pale pink and 50g (1¾oz) deep pink firm-peak royal icing in small plastic piping bags fitted with no. 3 nozzles. Place a sheet of cellophane on a flat surface and pipe several curly lines using pale pink and deep pink royal icing. Leave to dry overnight.

TUTOR TIP

You need to apply a lot of pressure to the piping bag in order to make the strands of icing curly.

---

29 Roll two sausages of purple SFP and attach one of them to the collar to fill the gap under the hat, and the other to the top of the back. These sausages will not only help support the curls, but also will give the wig more volume.

30 Once the royal icing curls are completely dry, stick the first row of curls across the very bottom of the sausages with some royal icing. Attach another row of curls on top of the previous one and continue to layer the rows from bottom to top to create the overall shape of the wig. Cover the sausages first, then continue around the sides and front of the head, filling all the gaps with curls.

BROOM

31 For the broom handle, roll some pale brown pastillage into a thin sausage that is approximately 11.5cm (4½") in length and cut one of the ends straight.

32 For the head of the broom, roll out some yellow SFP and cut out a strip that is 11.5cm long x 5cm wide (4½" x 2"). Make several cuts along the width of the strip, making sure not to cut all the way across, and roll up. Glue to the straight end of the broomstick with a little edible glue. Roll a thin sausage of dark brown SFP and glue between the head and the handle.

SWEETS

33 Roll out some poppy red SFP on a non-stick board and cut out several small cubes. Once firm enough to handle, pile the sweets inside the basket and stick them in place as you go.

CAT

34 For the body, roll 10g (¼oz) of Black SFP into a bottle shape and flatten on one side to make it completely straight. Insert a cocktail stick into the neck and leave to dry for a couple of hours before adding the head.

35 Roll 10g (¼oz) of Black SFP into an oval shape for the head and push it down onto the cocktail stick. Make two tiny holes in the centre of the

head using the tip of a cocktail stick. Model two pinches of Black SFP into flattened teardrop shapes for the ears, then press a bulbous cone tool into the ears to shape them. Secure to the top of the head. Make a small oval for the muzzle and mark a line down the front with a Dresden tool. Attach the muzzle just below the eyes and finish with a tiny ball of poppy red SFP for the nose.

36 For the tail, roll a small piece of Black SFP into a thin, tapered sausage and secure to the back of the cat. Roll two tiny balls and secure at the front for the feet.

FINISHING TOUCHES

37 For the patches, roll out some pale lilac SFP and cut out a few squares of different sizes. Press the edge of the Dresden tool into the edges of the squares to tear them slightly and glue them randomly over the costume.

38 Use a small pinch of pale lilac paste to create a brooch and attach it to the front of the dress. Model a small amount of the same paste into a button shape and attach to the front of the collar.

39 Cut out a long strip of Black SFP to make the trim for the sleeves. Cut out semicircles from one side of the strip using the tip of a no. 7 nozzle and attach to the edge of the sleeves. Pipe a few dots of black royal icing to finish off the hem of the outfit.

40 Roll a very thin sausage of Black SFP and secure it around the neck to create a necklace. Finish it off with a tiny ball of Black SFP in the centre.

WITCH'S CAT BISCUITS

Use the templates on page 255 to pipe the cats' eyes as off-pieces on a sheet of cellophane (see page 30). Use Black run-out icing to pipe a curve over the top of each eye, then pipe white run-out icing below the black line and use a cocktail stick to draw the icing to the corners. Pipe on the black pupils while the icing is still wet, then drop a tiny dot of white royal icing onto the pupils to highlight them. Leave to dry.

Make up the biscuit dough following the recipe on page 18, cut out 25 cat head shapes using the template provided on page 255 and bake as required.

Fit a piping bag with a no. 1 nozzle, fill with Thrift-coloured medium-consistency royal icing and pipe an outline around the edge of the biscuits and the inner ears. Flood inside the ears with pale Thrift-coloured run-out icing, then flood the rest of the biscuit with darker Thrift-coloured run-out icing (see page 30). Gently tap the biscuit a few times on the work surface to smooth out the icing. Pipe the open mouths with Cyclamen-coloured run-out icing. While the icing is still wet, pipe a tongue inside the mouth with pale Cyclamen run-out icing. Allow to dry.

Pipe a dot of Poppy-coloured run-out icing for the nose and use a cocktail stick to draw the shape while the icing is still wet. Pipe the whiskers using a no. 1 nozzle and medium-consistency Black royal icing. Draw the hair in the ears, the muzzle and the closed mouths with a Black food colour pen.

SANTA'S LITTLE HELPERS

These cheerful elves are getting Santa's sleigh ready to deliver presents on Christmas Eve. This project offers you a great opportunity to play with facial expressions using one simple head shape. You can also make each elf distinct by adding sideburns, a goatee beard, or a fringe, so use your imagination and don't be afraid to experiment!

EDIBLES

15cm square x 5cm deep (6" x 2") cake, layered and filled (see page 34)

SK Sugarpaste (rolled fondant):

500g (1lb 1¾oz) Bridal White

50g (1¾oz) dark brown (Bridal White + Bulrush)

400g (14oz) pale olive (Bridal White + small touch of Olive)

50g (1¾oz) soft beige (Bridal White + Chestnut)

SK Sugar Florist Paste (SFP, gum paste):

5g (just under ¼oz) Black

50g (1¾oz) bright green (White SFP + Leaf Green)

150g (5¼oz) dark green (White SFP + Holly/Ivy)

20g (¾oz) olive green (White SFP + touch of Olive)

50g (1¾oz) orange (White SFP + Berberis)

5g (just under ¼oz) poppy red (White SFP + Poppy)

100g (3½oz) skin tone (White SFP + touch of Nasturtium + touch of Teddy Bear Brown)

5g (just under ¼oz) terracotta (White SFP + Terracotta)

100g (3½oz) White

SK Instant Mix Royal Icing:

5g (just under ¼oz) black (Jet Black)

20g (¾oz) white (uncoloured)

SK Instant Mix Pastillage:

300g (10½oz) white (uncoloured)

SK Professional Paste Food Colours: Berberis, Bulrush, Chestnut (soft beige), Edelweiss (white), Holly/Ivy (dark green), Leaf Green, Poppy, Nasturtium (peach), Teddy Bear Brown

SK Designer Paste Food Colours: Jet Black, Olive, Terracotta

SK Professional Dust Food Colours: Edelweiss (white), Nasturtium (peach)

SK Professional Liquid Food Colours: Chestnut (soft beige), Holly/Ivy (dark green)

EQUIPMENT

Basic equipment (see pages 6 to 7)

28cm (11") square cake drum (board)

5cm, 6cm and 8cm (2", 2³/₈" and 3¹/₈") square cake cards (or a 15cm (6") square cake card cut into 5cm, 6cm and 8cm (2", 2³/₈" and 3¹/₈") squares)

Spare polystyrene dummy

Piece of thin card, e.g. from a cereal box or cake box

Craft knife

5mm (¼") round cutter

Piping nozzle: no. 2

Large stephanotis cutter, from set of three (TT)

Cellophane sheet

1.15m x 15mm width (45½" x ⁵/₈") satin ribbon: ivory

Templates (see page 254)

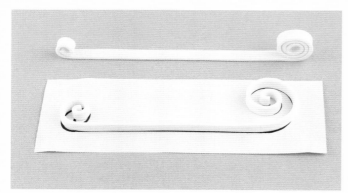

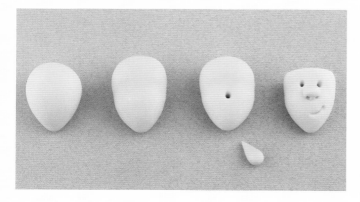

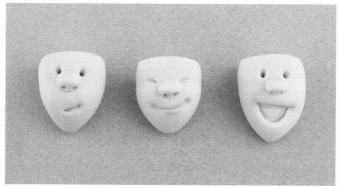

SLEIGH

1 Trace the sleigh template onto a thin piece of card and cut it out with a pair of scissors.

2 Mix together 50g (1¾oz) of dark brown sugarpaste and 50g (1¾oz) of soft beige sugarpaste to create an ivory colour. Mix a small piece of ivory sugarpaste into 200g (7oz) of white pastillage to make an off-white shade. Roll out the pastillage to a 4mm (³/₁₆") thickness and cut out the sides of the sleigh using a craft knife and the template. Leave the pieces to dry.

TUTOR TIP

As pastillage dries very quickly once exposed to the air, it is advisable to make one side at a time to prevent the paste from drying out before you cut it into shape.

3 For the rim, roll 30g (1oz) of White SFP into a sausage, cut it in half then roll each half into a 32cm (12½") long sausage. Curl up both ends of the sausages and stick them along the top of each side of the sleigh with a little edible glue.

4 To make the snowflake design, roll out a small piece of White SFP and cut out 16 small diamond shapes with a plain-bladed knife or a small cutter if you have one. Attach them to the sides of the sleigh in pairs, following the picture for reference. Snip the tip off a paper piping bag filled with medium-consistency white royal icing and finish the design with piped lines, dots and teardrops.

5 For the blades, knead 50g (1¾oz) of White SFP with 50g (1¾oz) of pastillage. Roll out 50g (1¾oz) of the paste to 4mm (³/₁₆") thick and cut out a 42cm long x 1cm wide (16½" x ³/₈") strip. Place it on its side and shape the paste following the blade template. Repeat to make a second blade and let them both dry.

TUTOR TIPS

As these blades are quite fragile, I suggest making spares in case of breakages.

By mixing SFP and pastillage together, it slows the drying time of the paste and allows you more time to work with it than if you just used pastillage alone.

ELVES

Heads and facial expressions

6 Roll 10g–15g (¼oz–½oz) of skin tone SFP into a teardrop shape. Roll your finger across the middle of the teardrop to bring out the cheeks. Roll a small piece of skin tone SFP into a teardrop shape for the nose. Open a hole in the middle of the face with the tip of a cocktail stick, insert the narrower end of the paste and secure with a little edible glue. Open the nostrils with the tip of a cocktail stick. Repeat to make two more heads.

7 To make a smile, draw a curved line underneath the nose with the edge of a Dresden tool. Indent dimples into each corner of the mouth with a small ball tool and run your finger over the paste to soften the marks. Gently run the rounded edge of a Dresden tool beneath the mouth line to bring out the lower lip. Push the tip of a Dresden tool into the mouth to open it slightly, if desired.

8 For an open mouth, press a small piece of cardboard into the lower half of the face as explained on page 115. Push a small ball tool into the corners of the mouth to make dimples, then smooth them over with your finger. Roll out a pinch of terracotta SFP very thinly, cut out a piece the same shape as the mouth and secure it inside. To make the top teeth, roll a pinch of White SFP into a sausage with pointed ends and flatten it down on the work surface. Make an indent down the middle of the teeth with the edge of a cutting tool and secure it in the top of the mouth.

9 To make open eyes, push the tip of a cocktail stick into the paste above the nose. Fill a paper piping bag with a small amount of black run-out royal icing then snip off the very tip of the bag. Fill the eye sockets with the black icing, but do not overfill them or they could look like they are bulging out. Once the icing has dried, paint a white dot on each eye with Edelweiss paste food colour and a fine paintbrush.

TUTOR TIP

If you are less confident, you can always draw the eyes on with a Black food colour pen, then paint a white dot to highlight them.

10 For closed eyes, use a Dresden tool to indent two small, slanted lines on either side of the top of the nose. For the eyelashes, paint curved lines inside the eyes with Bulrush liquid food colour and a fine paintbrush.

11 Trim the top of the heads straight with a craft knife so that the hats will sit comfortably on them. Leave the heads to firm up overnight.

Necks

12 Roll a small pinch of skin tone SFP into a ball and push it onto a cocktail stick moistened with a little edible glue. Roll the paste along the cocktail stick, making the neck longer than necessary, then trim to the length required to support the head. Leave some cocktail stick protruding from both ends, skewer into a piece of polystyrene and leave to dry.

Ears

13 Roll two small pinches of skin tone SFP into sausages with pointed ends, then flatten them down slightly with your finger. Press a bulbous cone tool lengthways into the ears to shape them, then allow them to firm up.

Hats

14 Skewer the heads into a polystyrene base to allow you to work comfortably on the rest of details.

15 Roll 15g–20g (½oz–¾oz) of dark green SFP into a cone shape with a flat base. Secure it to the top of the head with a little edible glue and bend the top slightly to one side. Press a cocktail stick across the front of the hat to create a fabric effect.

16 To make the ear flaps, roll a piece of dark green SFP into a long, oval shape and flatten it down. Cut it in half and attach a flap to either side of the head so the straight ends meet the brim of the hat. Make a hole in the each ear flap with the tip of a barbecue skewer, following the eye line as a guide. Insert the ears into the holes and secure with a little softened skin tone SFP.

17 Knead some White SFP with a pinch of bright green SFP to make a paler shade of green. Roll the paste into a small ball then attach to the tip of the hat with edible glue.

Hair and eyebrows

18 To make a fringe, goatee beard or sideburns, roll tiny pieces of orange SFP into teardrops and attach them to the face with edible glue. Texture the paste with the edge of a Dresden tool. Roll two very small teardrops of Black SFP for the eyebrows and secure them to the bottom of the hat: change the angle to create different expressions. Fill in the back of the head with a flattened teardrop of orange SFP and texture the paste with the sharp edge of a Dresden tool. Allow the hair to firm up.

19 Mix some Nasturtium dust food colour with a little cornflour and dust it over the cheeks, nose and tip of the ears. Paint freckles over the cheeks with Chestnut liquid food colour and a fine paintbrush.

Legs

20 Roll 10g (¼oz) of dark green SFP into a sausage, cut it in half and model a pair of legs following the instructions on page 51. Narrow the toe to a point, then curl up the very end. Use a Dresden tool to mark the legs behind the knee then bend them to the required angle. Leave one pair of legs straight for the elf sitting on the board. For the elf sitting on the presents, bend the legs to 90° and pinch the bend to bring out the knees. Position them over the edge of a spare piece of polystyrene and leave to dry. For the cross-legged elf, bend both legs to a 45° angle, pinch the

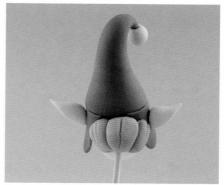
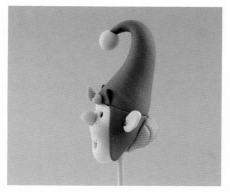

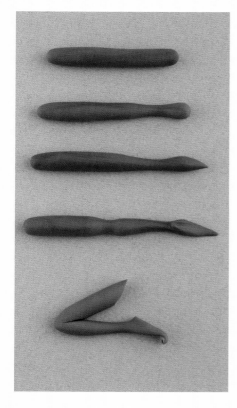

bend to bring out the knees and leave to dry flat. Once dry, stick the tops of the thighs together with softened dark green SFP, support the legs with a piece of paste under each knee and leave to dry completely.

21 Once the legs are dry, roll some tiny balls of bright green SFP and attach them to the elves' knees.

Torsos

22 Roll 10g (¼oz) of bright green SFP into a cone shape and secure it onto the legs with a little edible glue. Roll out some dark green SFP into a thin sheet and cut out a 1cm (³/₈") wide strip. Attach the strip around the middle of the torso, bringing the ends to the back, and trim any excess for a neat join. Roll a sausage of pale green SFP and secure around the bottom of the body to make the jacket trim. Use a 5mm (¼") round cutter (or a piping nozzle) to cut out a buckle from a thin sheet of bright green SFP. Attach it to the centre of the belt and finish with a tiny disc of poppy red SFP.

Arms

23 Roll 5g (just under ¼oz) of bright green SFP into a sausage and cut it in half. Cut the arms to size

TUTOR TIPS

When you are attaching the arms, make sure that they are resting in a natural position.

I make the hands once the elves are positioned on the final cake so they will sit naturally in the required position.

following the template as a guide, then secure to the body in the required position.

Collar

24 To make the collar, roll out a thin sheet of olive green SFP and cut out a flower using a large stephanotis cutter. Secure to the top of the body and insert the neck through the collar and into the body. Secure with a little edible glue and let dry.

25 Leave the bodies to dry completely.

CAKE DRUM

26 Roll out 400g (14oz) of pale olive sugarpaste and cover the square cake drum (see page 41). Dilute some Holly/Ivy liquid food colour and Edelweiss dust food colour with a few drops of cooled, boiled water and splash the colours over the paste using a toothbrush (see page 54). Trim the board with ivory ribbon and set aside to dry.

TUTOR TIP

I prefer to use white dust food colour diluted with a few drops of cooled, boiled water rather than white paste food colour for this technique, as it tends to dry quicker.

CAKES

27 Cut out 5cm, 6cm and 8cm (2", 2³/₈" and 3¹/₈") squares from the 15cm (6") square cake. Secure a cake card of the corresponding size underneath each cake with a dab of filling. Crumb-coat and chill in the fridge.

TUTOR TIP

If you don't have or can't find cake cards of the correct size, cut a 15cm (6") square cake card into the sizes required.

28 Divide 500g (1lb 1¾oz) of Bridal White sugarpaste into 200g (7oz) for the larger cake and 150g (5¼oz) for each of the smaller cakes. Mix them with different amounts of ivory sugarpaste to make three different ivory shades. Cover each of the cakes with a different shade of sugarpaste (see page 34).

29 Cut out several dots of white sugarpaste using a 5mm (¼") round cutter and a no. 2 piping nozzle, then stick them all over the smallest cake. Fill a paper piping bag with medium-consistency white royal icing. Snip off the very tip of the bag and pipe a white line down the sides of the cake to create the parcel ribbon.

30 Attach 1cm (³/₈") wide strips of pale ivory sugarpaste around the medium-sized cake to make the ribbon. For the bow, fill a paper piping bag with white run-out royal icing, snip the tip off the bag and pipe loops onto a cellophane sheet. Allow them to dry.

31 Once the loops have dried, release them from the cellophane and secure to the front of the cake with dots of royal icing.

ASSEMBLY

32 Position the largest cake towards the back of the cake drum and secure with a dot of firm-peak royal icing. Secure the blades to the cake board on either side of the cake

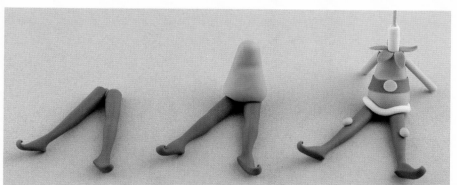

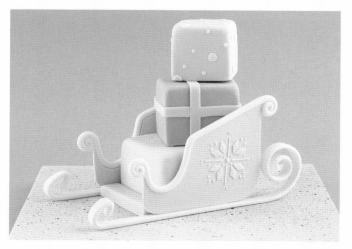

with dots of white royal icing. Attach the sleigh pieces to the sides of the cake and onto the blades with white royal icing. Scrape off the excess icing with the tip of a cutting tool if necessary.

33 Roll out some pale ivory sugarpaste to 1cm (³/₈") thick, cut out a 1.5cm (⁵/₈") wide strip that is the length of the side of the base cake and secure it to the front of the sleigh. Stack the presents on top of the cake and secure with royal icing.

34 Remove the elf heads from the spare polystyrene, take out the cocktail stick and push them onto the necks, tilting them slightly to one side. Position the cross-legged elf on top of the cakes, the seated elf on top of the base cake and the lying elf on the cake drum. Secure in place with a touch of royal icing.

35 For the hands, roll a pinch of skin tone SFP into a teardrop and flatten it down. Cut a V-shape into one side to bring out the thumb. Repeat to make a second hand in the same way, making sure the thumb is on the opposite side. Attach the hands to the elves' sleeves with a little edible glue and position as required on the cake.

36 To finish, roll tiny balls of poppy red SFP and scatter them over the board, securing them in place with edible glue.

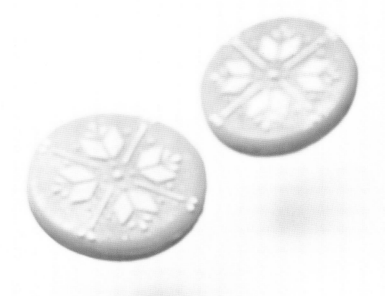

SNOWFLAKE BISCUITS

Bake 30 6cm (2³/₈") round biscuits following the recipe provided on page 18.

Make up some medium-consistency royal icing and colour with a small touch of Olive paste food colour. Fit a piping bag with a no. 1 nozzle, fill with the icing and pipe around the outline of the biscuit. Let down the very pale olive icing to run-out consistency. Fit a piping bag with a no. 2 nozzle, fill with the icing and flood inside the outline (see page 30). While the icing is still wet, sprinkle Ice White Fairy Sparkles over the biscuits and leave to dry.

Cut out a snowflake design (as used on the sleigh in the main project) from Bridal White sugarpaste and secure onto each biscuit with a little edible glue. Over-pipe lines, dots and teardrops with medium-consistency white royal icing and a no. 1 nozzle to make the snowflake pattern. Sprinkle the pattern with some more Fairy Sparkles and leave to dry.

TEMPLATES

All the templates in this book are at half of the actual size. Enlarge the templates to 200% for the correct size.

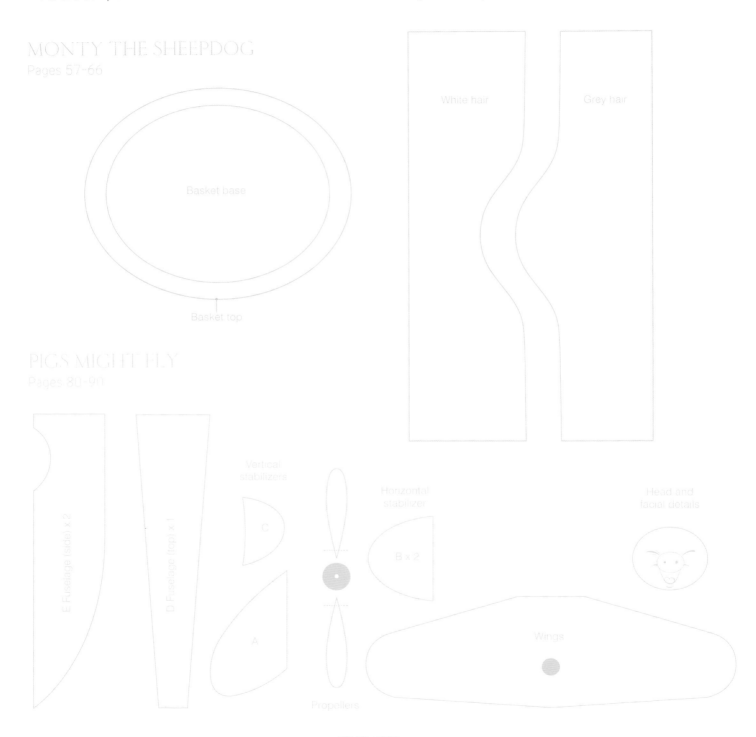

MONTY THE SHEEPDOG
Pages 57-66

Basket base

Basket top

White hair

Grey hair

PIGS MIGHT FLY
Pages 80-91

E Fuselage (side) x 2

D Fuselage (top) x 1

Vertical stabilizers

C

A

Propellers

Horizontal stabilizer

B x 2

Wings

Head and facial details

Clouds

BUON APPETITO!
Pages 68-78

Head and facial features

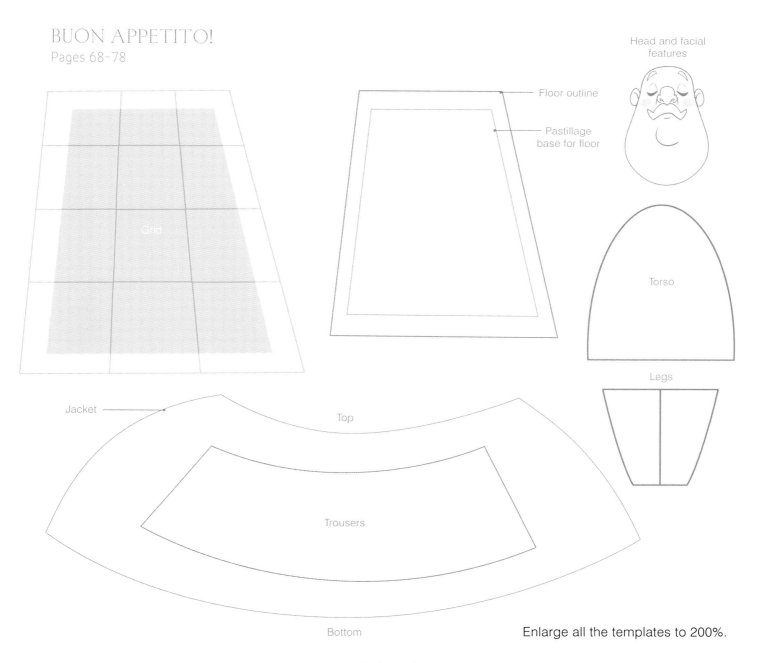

Grid

Floor outline

Pastillage base for floor

Torso

Legs

Jacket

Top

Trousers

Bottom

Enlarge all the templates to 200%.

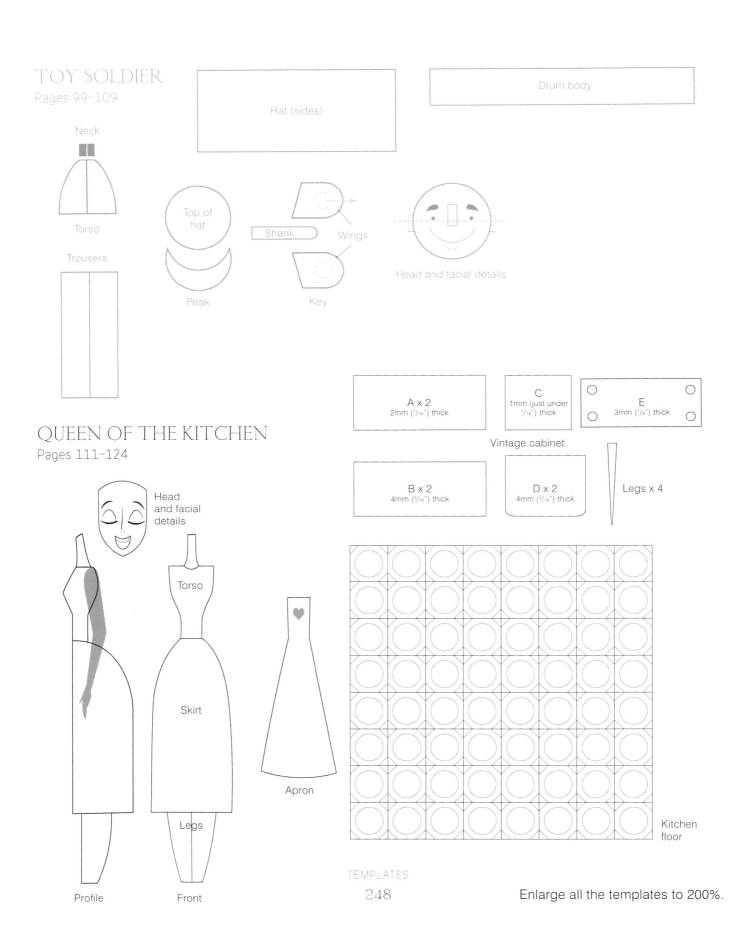

TOY SOLDIER
Pages 99-109

Neck

Torso

Trousers

Hat (sides)

Drum body

Top of
hat

Peak

Shank

Wings

Key

Head and facial details

QUEEN OF THE KITCHEN
Pages 111-124

Head
and facial
details

Torso

Skirt

Apron

Legs

Profile

Front

A x 2
2mm (¹/₁₆") thick

C
1mm (just under
¹/₁₆") thick

E
3mm (¹/₈") thick

Vintage cabinet

B x 2
4mm (³/₁₆") thick

D x 2
4mm (³/₁₆") thick

Legs x 4

Kitchen
floor

Enlarge all the templates to 200%.

SOLAR SUPERHERO

Pages 125–136

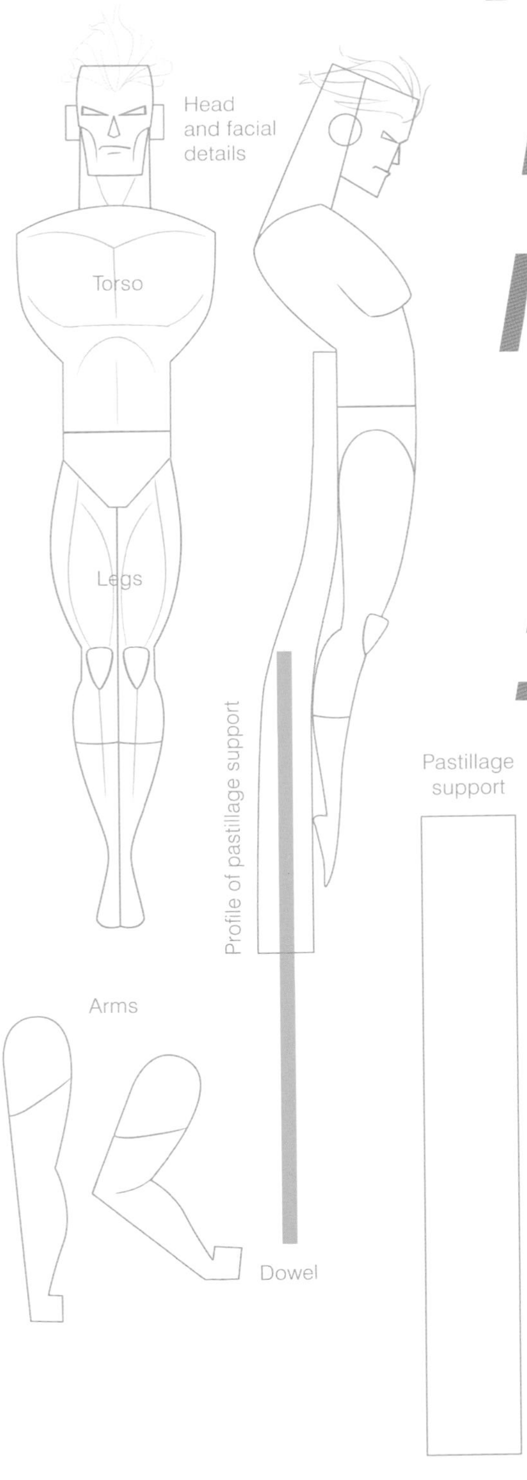
Front
Profile
Head
and facial
details
Torso
Legs
Profile of pastillage support
Pastillage
support
Arms
Dowel

Letters and numbers for biscuits

A B C D E F G

H I J K L M N

Ñ O P Q R S T

U V W X Y Z

1 2 3 4 5 6 7

8 9 0

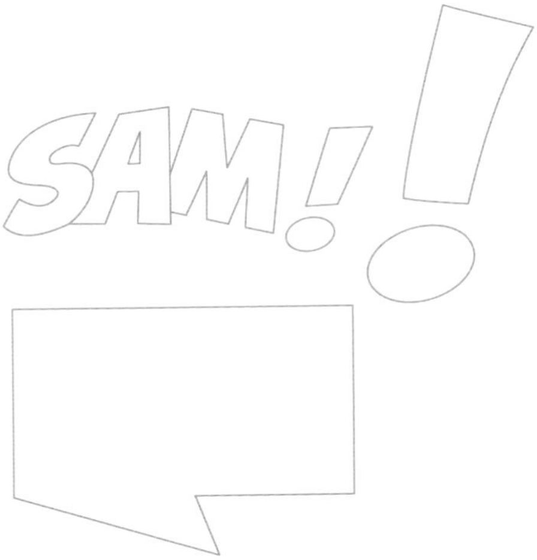
SAM!

Biscuit shape

Enlarge all the templates to 200%.

STAR SUPREME
Pages 137-148

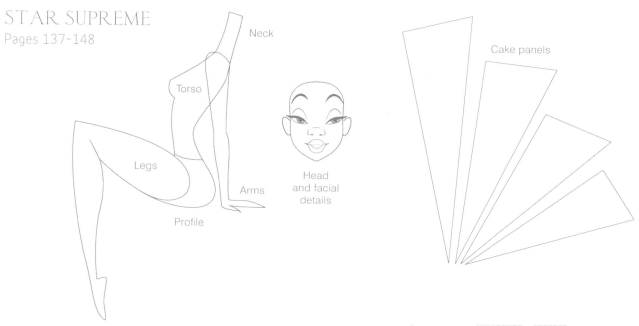

Neck

Torso

Legs

Arms

Profile

Head and facial details

Cake panels

TO HAVE AND TO HOLD
Pages 149-160

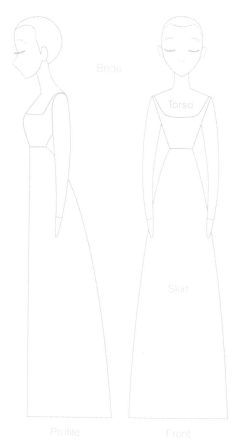

Bride

Torso

Skirt

Profile

Front

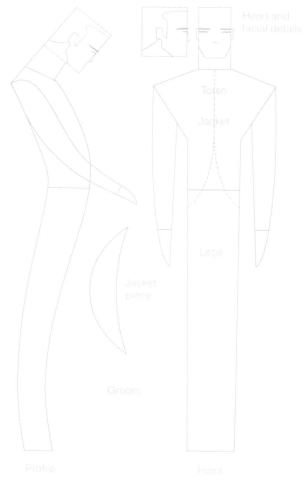

Head and facial details

Torso

Jacket

Legs

Jacket piece

Groom

Profile

Front

Enlarge all the templates to 200%.

GENTLE GIANT
Pages 161-170

Canoe

Side x 2

Body

Ornaments x 2

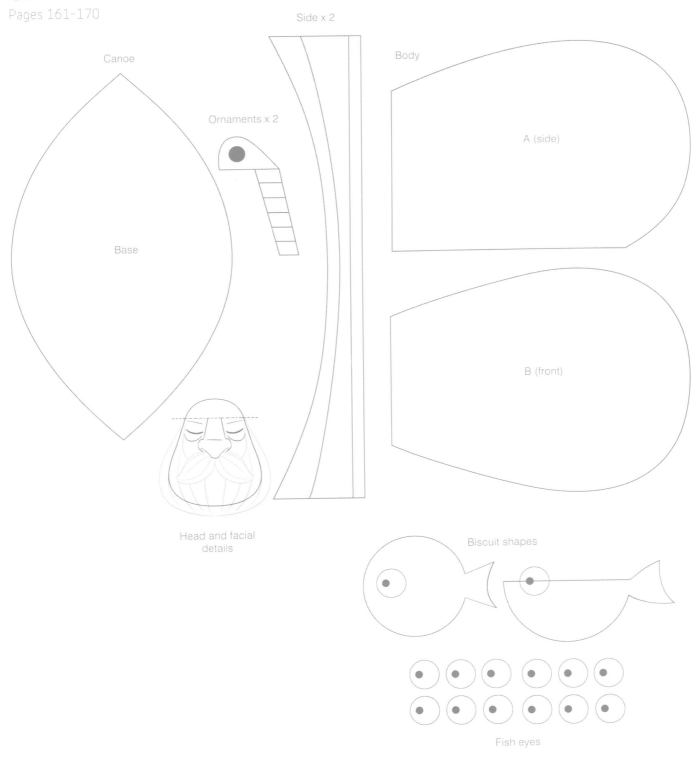

Base

A (side)

B (front)

Head and facial
details

Biscuit shapes

Fish eyes

Enlarge all the templates to 200%.

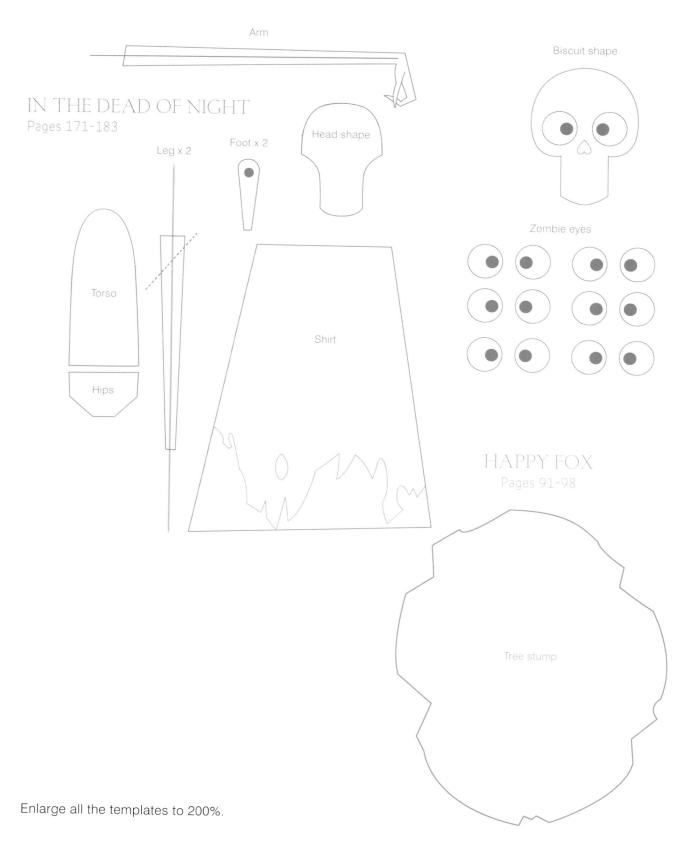

Arm

IN THE DEAD OF NIGHT
Pages 171-183

Leg x 2

Foot x 2

Head shape

Torso

Hips

Shirt

Biscuit shape

Zombie eyes

HAPPY FOX
Pages 91-98

Tree stump

Enlarge all the templates to 200%.

Head and
facial details

Hair

Body

The top of the
sleeve follows
the angle of
the arm

Sleeve (inner
and outer)

Back of
obi

Alternative
sleeve shape

Collar

Headpiece

TEA CEREMONY: PART 2
Pages 196–203

Head and
facial details

Sleeve

Back of obi

Collar

Enlarge all the templates to 200%.

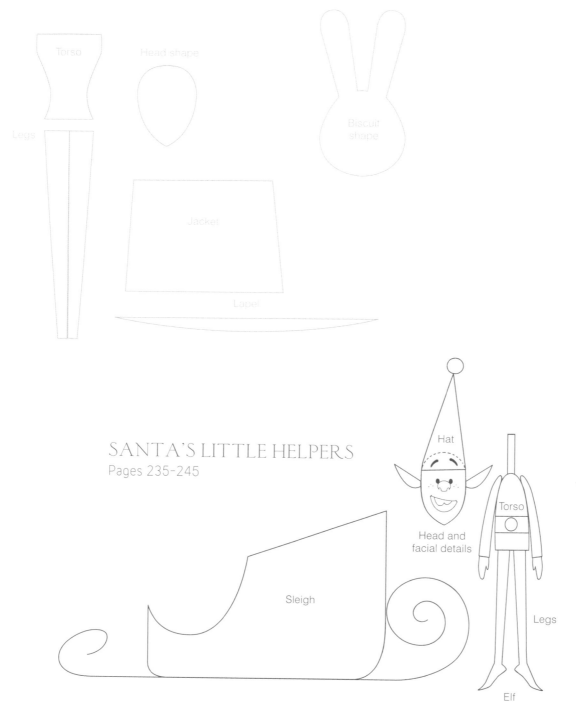

Torso

Head shape

Biscuit shape

Legs

Jacket

Lapel

SANTA'S LITTLE HELPERS
Pages 235-245

Hat

Head and facial details

Torso

Legs

Sleigh

Elf

Enlarge all the templates to 200%.

TRICK OR TREAT

Pages 223-233

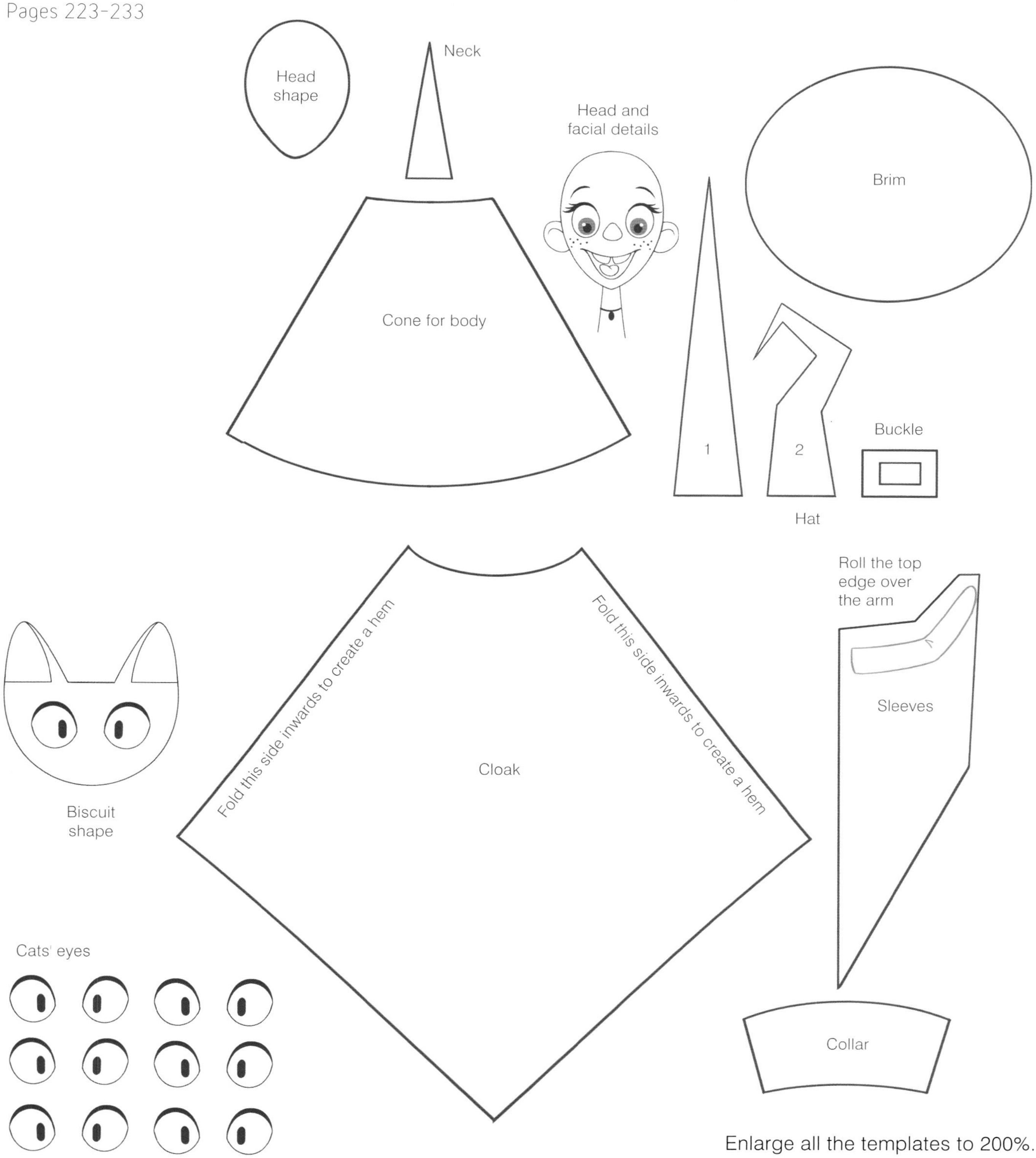

Head shape

Neck

Head and facial details

Brim

Cone for body

Hat

1

2

Buckle

Roll the top edge over the arm

Fold this side inwards to create a hem

Fold this side inwards to create a hem

Cloak

Sleeves

Biscuit shape

Cats' eyes

Collar

Enlarge all the templates to 200%.

SUPPLIERS

Squires Kitchen, UK
3 Waverley Lane
Farnham
Surrey
GU9 8BB
0845 61 71 810
+44 (0) 1252 260 260
www.squires-shop.com

Squires Kitchen International School, UK
The Grange
Hones Yard
Farnham
Surrey
GU9 8BB
0845 61 71 810
+44 (0) 1252 260 260
www.squires-school.co.uk

Distributors

UK

Culpitt Ltd.
Northumberland
www.culpitt.com

Guy, Paul & Co. Ltd.
Buckinghamshire
www.guypaul.co.uk

Squires Kitchen
Surrey
www.squires-shop.com

For your nearest sugarcraft supplier, please contact your local distributor.

Europe

Cake Supplies
Netherlands
www.cakesupplies.nl

Dom Konditera LLC
Belarus/Russia
www.domkonditera.com

Sugar World – Aliprantis Ltd.
Greece
www.sugarworld.gr

Tårtdecor
Sweden
www.tartdecor.se

Carlos Lischetti's first book, *Animation in Sugar*, is available in English, Spanish, Italian and Dutch from all good cake decorating suppliers and bookshops.

 B. Dutton Publishing is an award-winning publisher of cake decorating titles. To find out more about our books, follow us at **www.facebook.com/bduttonpublishing**.